Bomber Command's War Against Germany

Publisher's Note

This official history is reproduced as close as possible to the form in which it was originally written. Aside from correcting obvious spelling mistakes or typographical errors, we have striven to keep the edits and alterations to the absolute minimum.

Bomber Command's War Against Germany

Planning the RAF's Bombing Offensive in WWII and its Contribution to the Allied Victory

An Official History
by Noble Frankland, D.F.C., M.A., D.Phil

BOMBER COMMAND'S WAR AGAINST GERMANY
Planning the RAF's Bombing Offensive in WWII and its Contribution to the Allied Victory

This edition published in 2020 by Air World Books,
an imprint of Pen & Sword Books Ltd,
47 Church Street, Barnsley, S. Yorkshire, S70 2AS.

This book is based on file reference AIR 41/57, from a series of records from the Air Ministry, which is held at The National Archives, Kew, and is licensed under the Open Government Licence v3.0.

Text alterations and additions © Air World Books

ISBN: 978 1 52679 087 3

All rights reserved. No part of this publication may be reproduced, stored in or introduced into a retrieval system, or transmitted, in any form, or by any means (electronic, mechanical, photocopying, recording or otherwise) without the prior written permission of the publisher. Any person who does any unauthorized act in relation to this publication may be liable to criminal prosecution and civil claims for damages. CIP data records for this title are available from the British Library

Typeset by Mac Style
Printed and bound in the UK by TJ Books Limited,
Padstow, Cornwall.

Pen & Sword Books Ltd incorporates the imprints of Air World Books, Pen & Sword Archaeology, Atlas, Aviation, Battleground, Discovery, Family History, History, Maritime, Military, Naval, Politics, Social History, Transport, True Crime, Claymore Press, Frontline Books, Praetorian Press, Seaforth Publishing and White Owl

For a complete list of Pen & Sword titles please contact:

PEN & SWORD BOOKS LTD
47 Church Street, Barnsley, South Yorkshire, S70 2AS, UK.
E-mail: enquiries@pen-and-sword.co.uk
Website: www.pen-and-sword.co.uk

Or

PEN AND SWORD BOOKS,
1950 Lawrence Road, Havertown, PA 19083, USA
E-mail: Uspen-and-sword@casematepublishers.com
Website: www.penandswordbooks.com

Contents

List of Abbreviations   vii
List of Code Names   xi
Introduction: The Background to the Bombing Offensive   xii

Part I
The First Bombing Offensive, 1939–1941

Chapter 1   The Collapse of the 'Knock Out Blow' Theory and the Origins of Attritional Bombing   3

Chapter 2   The Failure of the First Bombing Offensive: An Analysis of the Principal Assumptions on Which Hopes of Success Rested   15

Part II
The First Lessons of Experience: A New Design for the Bombing Offensive, 1941

Chapter 3   The Transition from Precision Attack to Area Bombing   31

Chapter 4   The Weapon More Accurately Measured and the Origins of Strategic Misconception   48

Part III
The Crisis for Bomber Command, 1942

Chapter 5   The Attack on German Morale   65

Chapter 6   The First Effects of Strategic Bombing   92

Part IV
The Climax of Area Bombing and the Return to Selective Bombing, 1943–1944

Chapter 7	The Year of Conflict, 1943	109
Chapter 8	The Effects of R.A.F. Destruction and the Promise of American Strategy	131

Part V
Air Superiority and the Final Offensive, 1944–1945

Chapter 9	The Problem of How to Use Air Power in Triphibious War	149
Chapter 10	The Vindication of Strategic Bombing and the Collapse of Germany	171

Appendix I: Note on Statistical Methods of Measuring Bombing Effect	191
Appendix II: Letter by Air Commodore Slessor, Director of Plans, 13 April 1940	199
Appendix III: Letter by Air Vice-Marshal Bottomley, Deputy Chief of the Air Staff, 14 February 1942	202
Appendix IV: Letter by Air Vice-Marshal Bottomley, Assistant Chief of the Air Staff, 10 June 1943	206
Appendix V: Letter by General H.H. Arnold, Commanding General, US Army Air Forces	210
Appendix VI: Report by Air Chief Marshal A.T. Harris, Commanding-In-Chief, Bomber Command, 3 November 1943	212
Appendix VII: Letter by Air Marshal Bottomley, Deputy Chief of the Air Staff, 1 November 1944	216
Appendix VIII: Directive No.2 for the Strategic Air Forces in Europe	218
Notes	220

List of Abbreviations

A.A.	Anti-Aircraft
A.A.S.F.	Advanced Air Striking Force (in France)
A.C.A.S. (I)	Assistant Chief of the Air Staff (Intelligence)
A.C.A.S. (Ops.)	Assistant Chief of the Air Staff (Operations)
A.C.A.S. (Plans)	Assistant Chief of the Air Staff (Plans)
A.D.I.	Assistant Directorate of Intelligence, Air Ministry
A.E.A.F.	Allied Expeditionary Air Force
A.F.C.	Anglo-French Staff Conversations
A.H.B.	Air Historical Branch, Foreign Section
A.M.	Air Ministry
A.O.	Chiefs of Staff Committee, Technical Sub-Committee on Axis Oil
A.O.C.	Air Officer Commanding
A.O.C.-in-C.	Air Officer Commanding-in-Chief
A.S.V.	Air to Surface Vessel (Radar device for detecting submarines)
A.V.M.	Air Vice Marshal, R.A.F
B.A.F.F.	British Air Forces in France
B.B.S.U.	British Bombing Survey Unit
B.C.	Bomber Command or Bombing Committee
B.C./S.	Bomber Command Secret File
B. Ops.	Bomber Operations, Air Ministry
B.O.T.	Board of Trade
CAB.	Cabinet Resolution
C.A.S.	Chief of the Air Staff
C.C.S.	Anglo-American Combined Chiefs of Staff Committee
C.D.	Confidential Document or Civil Defence
C.G.	Commanding General (American)

C.I.D.	Committee of Imperial Defence
C.I.G.S.	Chief of the Imperial General Staff
C-in-C.	Commander-in-Chief
C.I.O.S.	Combined Intelligence Objectives Sub-Committee
C.I.U.	Central Interpretation Unit
C.O.S.	War Cabinet, Chiefs of Staff Committee
C.O.S. (O).	Chiefs of Staff Committee (Operations)
D.B. Ops.	Director of Bomber Operation's, Air Ministry
D.C.A.S.	Deputy Chief of the Air Staff
D. C-in-C.	Deputy Commander-in-Chief
D.D.B. Ops.	Deputy Director of Bomber Operations
D.D.I.	Deputy Director of Intelligence, Air Ministry
D.D. Photos.	Deputy Director of Photography, Air Ministry
D.D. Plans.	Deputy Director of Plans, Air Ministry
D.H.	De Havilland
Do.	Dornier
D.O.	War Cabinet, Defence Committee (Operations) or demi-official
D. of O and I.	Director of Operations and Intelligence, Air Ministry
D. of Plans.	Director of Plans
D./S.A.C. or D.A.C.	Deputy Supreme Commander, Allied Expeditionary Force
D.S.A.S.O.	Deputy Senior Air Staff Officer
E.O.U.	Economic Objectives Unit, U.S. Embassy
E.T.O.U.S.A.	European Theatre of Operations, United States Army
F.C.I. (A.T.) Industrial	Committee of Imperial Defence, Sub-Committee on Intelligence in Foreign Countries, (Air Targets Sub-Committee)
F.D.	Foreign Documents Library, Heddon House
G.P.	General Purpose Bomb
G.R.	General Reconnaissance
H.C. Deb.	House of Commons Debates (*Hansard*)
He.	Heinkel
H.E.	High Explosive Bomb

I.E.	Initial Equipment
I.I.C.	Industrial Intelligence Centre
J.I.C.	War Cabinet, Joint Intelligence Sub-Committee of the Chiefs of Staff Committee
J.P.	War Cabinet, Joint Planning Staff
J.P.C.	Committee of Imperial Defence, Joint Planning Sub-Committee
Ju.	Junkers
Me.	Messerschmitt
M.E.W.	Ministry of Economic Warfare
M.H.S.	Ministry of Home Security
Min.	Minute
M.T.	Motor Transport
Mtg.	Meeting
O.R.B.	Operations Record Book
O.R.S. (B.C.)	Operational Research Section (Bomber Command)
O.T.U.	Operational Training Unit
P.F.F.	Path Finder Force
Plans (Ops.)	Plans (Operations) Air Ministry
P.M.	Prime Minister
P.O.G.	War Cabinet, Lord Hankey's Committee on Preventing Oil from reaching Germany
P.O.G. (L)	War Cabinet, Lloyd Committee on the German Oil Position
P.R.U.	Photographic Reconnaissance Unit
R.E.8.	Research and Experiment Department of the Ministry of Home Security and later the Air Ministry
R.F.C.	Royal Flying Corps
R.N.A.S.	Royal Naval Air Service
S.A.S.O.	Senior Air Staff Officer
S.H.A.E.F.	Supreme Headquarters, Allied Expeditionary Force
S.O.E.	Special Operations Executive
S. of S.	Secretary of State
S.W.C.	Supreme War Council
U.S.A.A.F.	United States Army Air Force

U.S.S.B.S.	United States Strategic Bombing Survey
U.S. St. A.F.	United States Strategic Air Forces in Europe
U.S.S.T.A.F.	*ditto*
U.S.S.T.A.F.E.	*ditto*
V.C.A.S.	Vice Chief of the Air Staff
W.A.	Western Air Plan
W/C.	Wing Commander
W.M.	War Cabinet Minute
W.P.	War Cabinet Paper

List of Code Names

Gee or T.R.1335	Radar aid to navigation
H2S	Radar aid to navigation and blind bombing device
Oboe	Radar aid to navigation and blind bombing device
Gee-H.	Radar aid to navigation and blind bombing device
Window	Metallised paper dropped by bombers to confuse enemy radar defences
Arcadia	Washington War Conference, December 1941 to January 1942
Symbol	Casablanca Conference, January 1943
Trident	Washington Conference, May 1943
Quadrant	Quebec–Washington Conference, August to September 1943
Sextant	Cairo-Tehran Conference, November to December 1943
Octogen	Quebec Conference, Sept. 1944
Overlord	The invasion of France in 1944
Pointblank	The attack of the German Air Force and its supporting industry

Introduction

The Background to the Bombing Offensive

The history of war often suggests that the past can teach little about the future. To the superficial mind invention neutralises experience. The invention of gunpowder, of the steam turbine, the submarine and the conquest of the air have each cast doubt upon the value to the man of action of the study of history. Each, in its day, apparently presaged a revolution in the art of war. To the superficial mind there was nothing which the Admirals of 1914 could learn from Hannibal's campaigns, when the galley had given way to the dreadnought. There was little which Joffre and French could learn from Marlborough and Prince Eugen when already the tank was supplanting the horse on the battlefield. Above all what lesson in air power could there be in history, which before 1903 had known no aeroplane?

These arguments have derived much strength from the habit of preparing for the last war. Certainly, the military methods of 1870 cost France the flower of her armies in 1914, while the lessons of 1914 seemed to cost France the war in 1940. In truth it is, however, as Jomini reminds us, the methods of war and not its principles which are revolutionised by invention. History should charge the mind with the principles of conduct and not with the details of action. It is not history which has misled the generals but the generals who have mis-read history.

The conquest of the air, more than any previous invention, suggested a consultation with prophets rather than historians. Here was not only a new weapon, but a new medium of warfare. Yet even in this tremendous possibility there was more to be learnt in history than crystal gazing. In particular, there was more to be learnt from Mahan's exposition of the principles of sea power than from Giulio Douhet's speculations about air power.

Mahan had pointed out that the exercise of naval power depended for its success upon command of the sea.[1] To his mind the first principle of naval policy was the destruction or neutralisation of the opposing fleet. With the evidence of many wars as his witness, he had suggested that there was no variant to this principle. In general, he had pointed out, it was the British who had acted upon this premise and their enemies who had sought the variants. The most common form of attack upon the British was by what the French called the 'guerre de course'. The wide oceans seemed to offer a vast area of escape and it should be possible for light naval forces to prey upon British commerce while evading her fleets of war. Since Britain depended for her life upon this commerce and since her battle fleets were generally of great strength, this idea had an irresistible appeal to the weaker naval powers.

Thus, in the war of Spanish Succession, feeling unable to challenge British command of the sea in a naval battle, Louis XIV withdrew his main fleets from the oceans and "increased the number of cruisers upon the more frequented seas."[2] According to the French account these cruisers inflicted heavy blows upon British commerce and "served advantageously the cause of the two peoples". (The French and the Spanish.) The English account, on the other hand, while admitting privations suffered, constantly refers to the increasing prosperity of the nation as a whole.[3]

The invention of the submarine offered immeasurably better prospects of success in the 'guerre de course'. This was a weapon admirably suited to the need for evasion of the opposing naval forces and well fitted to strike directly at the commerce of its enemy. In the submarine the Germans believed that they had found a weapon with which they could render British command of the sea ineffective and with which they could destroy the arteries leading to the heart. In two world wars the German submarine waged this 'guerre de course' against Britain and, though on both occasions it proved to be a serious threat, it was twice defeated. History upheld the principles which Mahan had enunciated from history and Germany starved in 1918 as surely as the grass had grown in the streets of Amsterdam in 1652.

If Mahan's doctrine of sea power, or for that matter Clausewitz's of land war, had been applied to air power, then clearly the first object of war in the air would have been the destruction or neutralisation of the opposing air force. Appearances were, however, against such an acceptance. If the area of escape offered by the oceans was large, that offered by the air was larger. If the submarine's prospects in the 'guerre de course' were good, those of the bomber aircraft were better. It must suffice at this stage to say that appearances triumphed, and that for four years the British bombers, like the French cruisers and German submarines before them, sought their strategic object directly.

Locally their attacks were devastating and on the whole, they succeeded in evading the opposing air force, but until 1944 the German war economy continued to expand just as British commerce had flourished throughout the war of Spanish Succession. Eventually, however, Mahan's doctrine of sea power was translated into a doctrine of air power and, with command of the air, or, as it is more generally called, air superiority, strategic bombers did, in the last year of the war, inflict blows upon Germany which were yet more decisive than those delivered by British sea power against Holland in 1652 or Germany in 1918.

To enlarge upon this thesis is to anticipate the whole experience of the six years war in the air from 1939–1945 with which this volume is concerned, but merely to recognise it is to grasp the basic point at which history might have served the new doctrine of air power which had its origins in the First World War. The suggestion is therefore that the conquest of the air did not revolutionise the principles of war, but only its methods or tactics. The first Air Staffs could have learnt more from Mahan and Clausewitz than from all the prophetic imaginations of H.G. Wells and Giulio Douhet.

To suggest that those who controlled the first air forces in history ignored the precepts of history would be to exaggerate, but equally to claim that these precepts were correctly grasped would be optimistic, even to-day after nearly half a century of aviation and two world wars. The doctrine of sea power has developed over countless thousands of years. Experiences as old as civilisation itself and as modern as the atomic bomb all contribute to the trend of naval thought. In the case of aviation these developments by comparison have been telescoped into a second of time. To realise the speed of developments in military aviation it is necessary to visualise the Battle of Jutland as an event taking place not much more than forty years after man first floated precariously upon the most primitive of rafts.[4]

The aeroplane was born into an age of scientific and mechanical advance which had already changed the face of the earth, and it was therefore possible to pass from the Wright brothers' biplane to the Lancaster bomber in forty years. This was almost miraculous and it would indeed have been equally remarkable if the doctrine of air power had been grasped with similar speed. In the way that man's material powers seem to have outstripped his spiritual capacity, so in the case of aviation mechanical developments tended to outpace the doctrines they should have served.

It may have been this very speed at which the aeroplane was developed from the 'raft' to the 'dreadnought' stage that impressed its wondering masters with the illusion of a revolution at hand. Here was a machine which knew no frontiers of land or sea, which could pass swiftly over all the cumbrous vehicles and vessels of land and water. Its possible application to the art of war was obviously intensely exciting. Whether as an adjunct to armies and navies or as a force of independent potential, air forces could scarcely fail to stimulate new theories of war.

Especially was this so during the early military development of air forces. For years the Grand Fleet of the British Empire glared at the High Seas Fleet of the German Empire, and for years the two could not come to grips. For years millions of soldiers, sunk miserably in trenches, were locked in mortal but indecisive conflict on the Western Front. Hundreds of yards of insignificant territory were bought with hundreds of thousands of priceless lives. The military deadlock in which millions perished was the greatest tragedy which history records. Flanks could not be turned and frontal assaults could make no headway. Defence had defeated attack. War had descended to the level of butchery. The 'front' became the impenetrable barrier beyond which lay the nation. Only the mass slaughter of men at the 'front' could damage the nation. The military strategy of 1914–1918 was to kill Germans, but, as Mr. Churchill had pointed out, the victory left the victors scarcely to be distinguished from the vanquished.[5]

Many devices were tried to break the deadlock, among them the tank, gas and the aeroplane, but the aeroplane was clearly something more than simply a means of intensifying the war at the front. It could also carry the war behind the front and strike directly at the heart of the enemy. As soon as this was realised, the conception of strategic bombing began to unfold. The race for air supremacy began.

The same influences of temperament, geography and environment which had made Britain a great maritime power might also make her a great air power, but curiously it was Germany which launched the first strategic bombing offensive. These raids had been carried out by Zeppelins and in 42 attacks made in 1915 and 1916, 501 people had been killed, 1,224 injured and £1,410,409 worth of damage had been done. The possibility of these attacks had been foreseen in London and at the Admiralty, where responsibility for air defence lay, there had been something approaching a panic. The First Sea Lord, Lord Fisher, had gone so far as to suggest that German prisoners of war should be executed in retaliation.

Mr. Churchill's cooler judgement of the situation, which was presently to be vindicated, caused Lord Fisher to threaten resignation with more than customary vehemence. If, however, Lord Fisher had misjudged the capabilities of airships against which he believed there was no defence, the possibility that bombing carried out by aeroplane might prove yet more serious still existed. Gigantic gas bags moving slowly through the air towards London proved to be a simple proposition for the much faster 'fighter' aeroplanes of the R.N.A.S. and the R.F.C. which defended England, but it might be a different matter with bomber aeroplanes which could fly much faster than airships, and which would in all probability discontinue the Zeppelins' convenient habit of wire-lessing the time of their departure. Clearly the aeroplane was a defence against the Zeppelin, but whether the aeroplane could be a defence against the aeroplane was another question.

Major General Trenchard thought not. "The aeroplane is not a defence against the aeroplane", he said in September 1916. The area of escape was practically unlimited. The doctrine that the bomber would always get through was thus pronounced. The only way to deal with bombing attacks was to mount a counter bombing offensive. This would throw the enemy on to the defence in the air and eventually the bombers could reach out to vital industrial and military targets well behind the lines.

The first attacks of the Englandgeschwader, armed with twin engine Gotha bombers capable of 80 m.p.h. and an altitude of 15,000 feet, seemed to demonstrate the truth of this doctrine. In their first attack on London, carried out in daylight on 13 June 1917, a mere fifteen or sixteen of these machines killed 162 people, injured 432 and secured direct hits on Liverpool Street Station. Armed with machine guns and flying in strict formation, the Gothas were but slightly disturbed by the British fighters and all returned home safely.

That the re-organised British defences presently began to take a heavy toll of German bombers and drove them to seek greater security in night attack was suggestive, but not conclusive. If the means of air defence could be improved, so could the means of air attack. Major General Trenchard's doctrine of the offensive was not seriously shaken by the eventual failure of the Gothas.

This doctrine of the offensive suggested a role for air power, which as yet was far in advance of the design of the air forces in being and of the organisations created for their control. The aeroplane had originally been thought of as a means of increasing the efficiency of warfare on land and sea. As a means of reconnaissance, it offered both armies and navies an incomparably more efficient service than had ever existed before. As a means of 'spotting' for artillery or naval guns it was much preferable to the almost stationary and highly vulnerable balloon. Obviously, however, it would be attacked as soon as it began to perform valuable services. The 'fighter' aircraft was thus an inevitable development from an early stage. A second possibility also existed. Could not the aeroplane also destroy what it could see and instead of 'spotting' for artillery, drop its own shells, or bombs?

This was the origin of the bomber aircraft. Thus, for the R.N.A.S. and the R.F.C. bombers and fighters became equally indispensable parts and a war in the air became certain. Still a third possibility existed. If bombers could destroy military equipment when it had reached the front, would it not be even more effective to prevent that equipment ever getting there by destroying the factories which produced, or cutting the lines of communication which carried it? Here was the origin of strategic bombing.

Now if strategic and independent bombing was to be the primary role of air power, then clearly air forces would be more akin to navies than to armies. The idea of destroying war potential by bombing was not inherently different to the idea of starving a war economy by blockade. Just as naval power was a means of waging an "independent" offensive so air power might also be. If the aeroplane used at the front in support of the army in the field was, like the tank, a means of increasing the efficiency of land fighting, the aeroplane used in the strategic sphere was a potential means of rendering military and naval operations "secondary and subordinate". So, at any rate General Smuts believed in 1917. "As far as at present can be foreseen", he reported "there is absolutely no limit to the scale of its future independent war use." If this was so, the core of air power would be the long-range bomber and aircraft, like ships, would form an independent fighting service.

This emphasis upon the strategic and independent role of air power in 1917 was the more striking because at the time the battle on land along the Western Front absorbed the attention of nearly all minds. Few were willing to believe there could be any other decisive theatre of operations. Fewer still would believe that there could be any other decisive medium of operations.

Yet General Smuts believed that even in 1918 "continuous and intense pressure against the chief industrial centres of the enemy as well as on his lines of communication may form an important factor in bringing about peace". After all, the deadlock of the trenches, which focussed so much attention on the means of breaking through the enemy lines, could also stimulate ideas on how to circumvent trench warfare altogether.

Thus, by the time the R.A.F. came into being on 1 April 1918 it was clear that the new fighting service would have two principal and, to a certain extent, competing roles. The first and in the eyes of those who had created the Service, the most important, would be the strategic offensive against "the chief industrial centres of the enemy". The second and at the time still the most powerfully backed, was the continued support of the Army and the Navy. To discharge these two functions, the one independent and the other auxiliary, the R.A.F. would need fighters and bombers, fighters to engage the enemy air force and bombers to destroy enemy naval, military and economic targets. For the independent offensive, however, not only bombers, but long-range bombers, would be needed. "Continuous and intense pressure" could not be applied by a force incapable of reaching even the Ruhr.

A limited experience of strategic bombing was already to hand from the activities of the R.N.A.S. Luxeuil Wing in 1916 and from the 'Independent Force' commanded by Major General Trenchard in 1918. The Luxeuil Wing had carried out some attacks upon iron works and factories in the Saar Valley some sixty miles behind the lines. Formations of from nine to fifteen bombers with fighter escort attacked by day and single aircraft attacked by night, but the results were practically unknown and the consuming needs of army support voiced by Sir Douglas Haig brought the experiment to an end before anything but a fragmentary experience of the problems of strategic bombing could be gained.

The Independent Force under Major General Trenchard went a little further but even this force, which never exceeded about 125 bombers, got little beyond the fringe of the problem. These small and, by later standards, primitive bombers, D.H.4s and 9s, F.E.2Bs and twin engined Handley Pages, could only fly for relatively short distances. Even the best machines could not go beyond 150 miles from their bases and they were always at the mercy of the weather and not infrequent engine failures. There were no fighters to escort these bombers. It was obvious that such a force could achieve very little material damage and it was only to be hoped that it might create a disturbing effect upon the Germans. Indeed, Major General Trenchard believed at the time that the moral effect of bombing stood to the material in the proportion of 20 to 1. This was significant, but perhaps what was even more significant was the fact that it was found necessary to attack German aerodromes because of the losses which the German fighters inflicted on the British bombers. Of the 543 tons of bombs dropped by the Independent Force between 6 June and 11 November 1918, 220 tons were aimed at German aerodromes.

Thus, at this early stage the fundamental principle of war in the air was indicated. If they were to be effective, bombers must enjoy a mastery of the air. Command of the sea was enjoyed by the navy which had destroyed or neutralised the enemy fleet. Command of the air would be enjoyed by the air force which could destroy or neutralise the enemy air force. How this air superiority was to be gained was, however, a problem which it took many years and many bloody encounters to solve. All the same it already appeared that there were three ways in which the enemy air force might be defeated or neutralised. The enemy fighters might be destroyed in the air either by guns carried in the bombers or by fighter escorts. It might be destroyed at its bases by attacks on aerodromes, or in production by attacks on its factories.[6] It might be neutralised by evasion, and for evasion the bombers would need superior speed or else the cover of darkness.

The solution of these problems would suggest whether bombers should be large and slow or fast and small; whether they should fly by day or night; whether they should fly in company with fighters or unescorted; whether they should carry their own defences or only bombs. To a certain extent it would also suggest the kind of targets they should attack.

Beyond this lay many other problems as yet hardly recognised and certainly not capable of solution on the evidence available. There was the problem of how to find the target, especially if the flight was carried out at night and having found it, how to hit it, especially again, at night. There was the immense problem of which would be the most profitable targets and what kinds and weights of bombs would be effective against them.

Obviously, all these problems had to await the arrival of a long-range bomber for their solution. The experiment was to be carried out by the four engine V.1500 Handley Page night bomber, capable of carrying thirty 250lb bombs from England to Berlin. A home base force, No. 27 Group, began to form in September 1918, but at the time of the Armistice only three of the new bombers had been delivered and what the strategic bombing offensive of 1919 might have achieved remained the great enigma of the twenty years before Bomber Command went into action in the Second World War.

When therefore the Allies were delivered from Armageddon by victory, the strategic bombing offensive was no more than a theory untested in practice. It was nevertheless a theory which suggested that independent air power would be a principal and perhaps the decisive element in any war of the future. The air had become a medium of operations upon which the future of nations and perhaps even of civilisations might depend. It was also obvious that strategic bombing could not be accomplished simply by building aeroplanes, manufacturing bombs and training pilots.

On the contrary, war in the air was clearly a highly scientific business which would call not only for clear thinking to determine what was needed, but also the genius of invention to supply it. If Britain was to enter a second world war with a supremacy in the air comparable to that which she had enjoyed in 1914 on the sea, then there were many problems connected with the capabilities of bombers which would have to be resolved. This would mean constant and vigorous experiments and as Mr. Churchill had suggested in 1917, "the hitting of objectives from great heights by day or night is worthy of as intense a volume of scientific study as, for instance, is brought to bear upon perfecting the gunnery of the fleet".[7] Whether this work was well or badly done would appear if war came again.

The British public believed that war would not come again. The sigh of relief which people not unnaturally breathed in 1918 practically caused the nation's armed forces to expire. More discreetly and behind closed doors the government told the departments from time to time that there would be no war for ten years.[8] As a result very little money was forthcoming to rebuild Britain's fighting services which always fall into decay as soon as a war is won. Following hard upon the confidence that there would be no more war came the great economic crisis of the late twenties and early thirties. The Service estimates had to be cut again and again. The passing of the years saw Britain's military preparedness declining to impossible levels and yet those very forces which caused the Treasury to adopt an ever more parsimonious attitude to the Services also gave birth to the forces which were in time to engulf Britain in a second world war.

Immediately Hitler had been carried to power, Germany once again began to assume the menacing aspect which Europe had known in the years before 1914. A new armaments race began, but this time air power seemed to be the crux of the situation. In the race for naval supremacy before 1914 Britain had always kept several jumps ahead of Germany, but in the race for air supremacy before 1939 she not only cast away a commanding lead, but fell several jumps behind. Each new German expansion caused consternation in London, but each time, at least as far as the offensive arm of the R.A.F. was concerned, it was a case of too little and too late.

The R.A.F. went to war in 1939 under the crushing disadvantage of inferiority to the enemy. The doctrine of the offensive was almost, but not quite, forgotten, its policy was distorted and its prospects were grim indeed. For this disaster, successive British Governments, the organs of public opinion and ultimately the British people must bear the prime responsibility. To successive British Air Staffs is due the credit not only for keeping alive the doctrine of the offensive ultimately to be vindicated, but also for providing the means of defence against a superior air power at the eleventh hour and the fifty-ninth minute. It was their determination and vision, to which must, however, be coupled German blunders, which gave the R.A.F. the initiative in the air surprisingly early in the war. Through years of frustration they had persisted and not in vain.

Nevertheless, the British Air Staffs of the inter-war years are certainly not above reproach and the doctrine with which the R.A.F. entered the war in 1939 suffered from grave defects. This doctrine was the product of operational experience gained in the First World War and observed in the Sino-Japanese and the Spanish Civil Wars. It was the product of experiments and air exercises, of scientific inventions and aeronautical developments. It was also the product of imagination. Owing to the limited experience available and the policy of financial stringency imposed by the Government, it was necessarily a theoretic doctrine, and owing to the superiority of the German Air Force it was not a free development. It is now necessary to reconstruct the elements which went to the making of this doctrine and to analyse the reasoning which supported it. For this purpose, it is essential to think, not only in terms of strategic bombing, but in the whole panoply of air power.

At the root of the British doctrine was the belief that the bomber will always get through, but among the branches was the hope that it would not. Britain had become a pacific power who in war had everything to lose and nothing to gain. The air force doctrine of offence did not therefore easily accommodate with the national policy of defence. By the time war was declared in September 1939, the truth of the doctrine that the bomber will always get through would have been fatal to Britain, not to Germany. This is somewhat anticipating the main argument, but we shall presently see how the need for defence influenced the plan for attack and also and what is more important, how the prospects of successful defence might have, but did not, alter the methods of attack.

While Germany lay prostrate before 1933, Britain did, however, have few immediate fears of attack and it was in this period that the doctrine of the offensive was permitted a free development. Now if the bomber was always going to get through, this supposed one or more of three eventualities. Either the bombers must be so fast relative to the fighters that they could not be successfully engaged in the air by the enemy air force, or they must be so heavily armed and perhaps armoured as well that they would be invulnerable to fighter attack. Or failing these two possibilities, they must be capable of night flying and rely upon the darkness to give them the same immunity from attack which superior speed would have given them in daylight. If the bomber was going to get through, then clearly it must either fight its way through, or it must get through by evasion. In either case it would have to reckon first and foremost with the air defences of the enemy and included in these defences it must also reckon with anti-aircraft guns, searchlights and perhaps balloon barrages as well. If the bombers could reach the target neither by fighting nor evading, then clearly, they would need a fighter escort to convoy them through the danger zones.

Now it was not really reasonable to suppose that the bomber could be relied upon to attain higher speeds than the fighter. The very fact that a bomber carried bombs and a fighter did not would make this improbable. Experience in the Great War by both sides had already indicated the inequality of the bomber with the fighter in combat and later developments confirmed this impression. It did not take an expert to forecast that a Messerschmitt 109 fighter would be able to fly circles round a Whitley or even a Battle bomber. The tendency of bombers in the Great War to turn from day to night attack had been significant, but this did not exhaust the possibility, or in American eyes the probability, that the bomber might be so heavily armed and armoured that its disadvantage in speed would be amply compensated in superior strength and fire power, especially if the bombers were concentrated in strict formation.

An aircraft can, however, lift no more than a given weight and the more of that weight given over to armour, ammunition, guns and gunners, the less remains for bombs. While theoretically feasible, the armed bomber was at least in appearance uneconomical. This left the more promising prospect, especially for a country with limited resources, of evasion by night. Passing unseen through the darkness the bomber would surely prove an impossible target for the enemy fighters and anti-aircraft guns alike.

The general impression was therefore that fighter escorts were neither necessary nor desirable and the Chief of the Air Staff, Lord Trenchard, ruled that "we ought to rely on bombers to defend themselves". This historic and grave decision had the advantage of offering the bomber force a larger share of the limited resources of the nation than would otherwise have been the case. No definite opinion was expressed as to whether these self-defended bombers would be able to fly in daylight or not. Circumstances and time would solve this problem and meanwhile the bomber force must be equipped for either eventuality.

Even if the bombers could get through at night, the question of what they could do when they got there was still unsolved. The Handley Page four-engine bomber of 1918, which had been designed for night flying, was not in time to provide any of the answers to this question. Broadly speaking the problem was the extent of the moral havoc they would cause among the peoples of the nation being attacked.

Its solution depended upon the numbers of bombers which would be engaged in the operations, the precision with which they could navigate to their targets, the accuracy with which they could discharge their loads and the destructive effect which their bombs would have. It also depended upon the resilience of the enemy's organisations for repair, protection and relief and ultimately upon the resilience of the enemy people themselves. Some of these problems were material and could be measured or estimated by referring to past experience of war, or experiment in peace. Some were psychological and could be solved only by guess work and the rules of probability.

Now it was in the solution of these problems that some clear thinking and exhaustive experiments were needed. The two basic requisites for a bomber, second only in importance to the obvious necessity that it should be capable of flight, are clearly that it should be able to find its way, or navigate and that it should be able to hit its targets. Before the war, however, these problems were not seen in their full magnitude. Their solution was regarded more as a matter of course than as one of exhaustive scientific research and operational experiment.

Navigation was regarded simply as a matter of observation, not as a complex science. At the Air Ministry there were Assistant Directorates for aircraft, for engines, for armament and for instruments, but there was none for navigation. In the squadrons there were no special posts for navigation specialists and in January 1933, out of the 1,346 officers of the R.A.F. between the ranks of Flight Lieutenant and Group Captain inclusive, only 38 had passed the ordinary specialist course in navigation. It was not until 1937 that anything was done about this and too little was then done. The real problem of navigation was, in fact, not squarely faced until 1941.

As far as bomb aiming was concerned, there was a great deal of discussion, but scarcely more action. Various improvements to bomb sights were introduced, but bombing experiments and training were usually carried out in daylight at medium altitudes. Thus, the aircrews gained little or no experience of bombing from high level or at night and the Air Staff were able to formulate no realistic, nor even remotely accurate, idea of what the aiming error would be in war.

It is true that in January 1934 a Bombing Committee had been established under the chairmanship of the D.C.A.S. to study the whole problem. This committee failed, however, to make a valuable contribution and in 1937 too much time was still being spent discussing the tactics to be employed by single engine light bombers which were even at the time obsolescent.

The solemn fact therefore has to be recorded that while the Air Staff were designing a long-range bomber force, the problem of how those bombers would get to their targets was practically ignored and the question of how they would, having got there, hit them, was though much discussed, hardly investigated. It scarcely needs the after-knowledge which is now available to realise that this was extraordinary negligence, but in the light of that after-knowledge it is possible to assert that the course of the war in the air would have been infinitely more favourable if these problems had been seriously tackled. Necessity is the mother of invention, but until the necessity had been proclaimed, science could hardly come to the aid of a force which was presently to be lost in the dark.

In the mounting crisis after 1937 and particularly after the Munich crisis, when Britain was imminently threatened with war against a superior air power, Lord Trenchard's doctrine of the offensive had been temporarily suspended. Britain's hopes of survival were centred upon Fighter Command, a force consisting of short range and purely defensive aircraft. The development of the eight-gun Hurricanes and Spitfires, their tremendous speed and the radar early warning devices which would serve them, all gave good grounds for believing that the attacking German Air Force could be defeated when the test came. This hope was vindicated in 1940. By 1938 the evidence did, in fact, suggest that the aeroplane was a defence against the aeroplane, at any rate in daylight.

If, however, the British fighter could defeat the German air offensive, could not the German fighter equally defeat a British air offensive? By 1938 it was evident that if indeed the aeroplane was not a defence against the aeroplane, then Britain would be defeated long before her own bombing offensive could mature. Either the doctrine behind Fighter Command in 1938 was groundless or the doctrine behind Bomber Command, the same doctrine which had once been behind the whole Air Force was groundless. They could not both be right.

If this had been recognised, or rather if the 'fighter doctrine' of 1938 had been accepted as a bomber doctrine as well, then the Brutish Air Staff would before the war have achieved a conception of air power which was, in fact, obscured until 1944. Let us therefore examine the implications of the fighter doctrine further. If the eight-gun fighter was capable of defending Britain, of maintaining a superiority in British air, then it was obvious that the German air offensive could only succeed after Fighter Command had been knocked out. If German strategy ran a true course the first objective would be the Royal Air Force and the second would be British industry, the British ports, British morale or whatever appealed to German Intelligence as the best strategic target. If the German Air Force tried to obtain its ulterior or strategic objective before it had destroyed the opposing air force, then "the angry buzz and hot pursuit that (would) immediately" follow would be "far from conducive to an undisturbed and methodical execution of the programme laid down".

Whether Britain happened to be ahead in 1938 in fighter and radar development or not should not have obscured the fact that what would be the task of the German Air Force would in turn be the task of the Royal Air Force. The prelude to a successful bombing offensive by Bomber Command would be the defeat of the German Air Force, the attainment of air superiority over Germany. The nation which would win the war would not, as Lord Trenchard believed, be the nation which could stand bombing the longest. It would be the nation which could first destroy the enemy air force.

The three questions which the British Air Staff therefore had to ask themselves were, firstly, how can the German air offensive be defeated? Secondly, how can the German Air Force be defeated? Thirdly, how can Germany be defeated?

The time to ask these questions came in 1937 when the Chiefs of Staff set in train preparations for war with Germany. The Chiefs of Staff did not, however, see the problem in this light. The air force, they suggested, would require three principal plans, the first to assist the Navy, the second to assist the Army and the third to destroy the German war economy. Now even in this general instruction the object was confused with the objective. How was the Royal Air Force to carry out any of these roles while the German Air Force remained in superior being?

It is true that the Chiefs of Staff did talk about "counter air force action" and they did suggest that plans should be made to attack German aerodromes and German aircraft factories, but clearly the idea was to impede the German air offensive rather than to facilitate the Bomber Command attacks. This confusion of the object, the destruction of the German war economy, assistance to the Navy or assistance to the Army, with the objective, was projected into the Western Air Plans which followed and which formed the basis of Bomber Command's action in war.

The first problem, the question of how to defeat the German air offensive, was in the last years of peace the main preoccupation of the

British Air Staff. The possibility of an unrestricted bombing offensive by the German Air Force seemed to offer the greatest and certainly the most imminent threat to Britain. The imagination of H.G. Wells and Douhet was now capable of translation into a cold probability.

In 1936 the Joint Planning Committee reported that the German attack might, within 24 hours, reduce the activities of the Port of London to 25 or 30% of normal. In another three days similar disasters might befall all the ports from the Tyne to Southampton. In another 10 days all British ports might be similarly blasted. If the attack was directed at British morale, it seemed probable that London might expect 20,000 casualties in the first 24 hours of the war. Within a week 150,000 casualties might have occurred. Telephones, railways, electrical services and food distribution would be rendered chaotic. Many millions of people would have been forced to leave their homes. The nation might demand surrender.

The only real answer, the J.P.C. believed, lay in the British ability to mount a "counter-offensive of at least similar effectiveness". But in July 1939 it was estimated that Germany had 1,750 bombers ready to attack England. The R.A.F. had fewer than 500 with which to reply.

This was the stimulus which had been afforded to the development of Fighter Command. This was the reason for which the Air Staff had to suspend the doctrine of the offensive, still affirmed in the J.P.C. report of October 1936, but partly abandoned in the expansion scheme of 1938 which gave Fighter Command first priority. Nevertheless, to rely upon 'close defence' alone was obviously a dangerous expedient, which only the force of circumstances had imposed upon the Air Staff. The doctrine of the offensive was really not so much abandoned as overwhelmed.

All the same, Lord Trenchard's teaching was not entirely neglected even at this critical stage. Bomber Command must also take part in the Air Defence of Great Britain. A plan must be made "to assist our direct defences by the employment of our air striking force to bring about an immediate reduction in the scale of German air attack".

To achieve this, Bomber Command might attack a variety of targets ranging from German bomber aerodromes, aircraft plants and fuel supplies to Headquarters Staffs and Training Organisations, but the only targets which seemed encouraging were the aircraft plants and of these the airframe plants seemed easier targets than the engine plants. The location of all the thirteen airframe assembly plants upon which the German bomber force was supposed to depend was known. All were within the range of R.A.F. bombers and it was supposed that they could all be totally destroyed by the discharge of 1,820 500lb. G.P. bombs from high level or 910 from low level in daylight.

If this fantastic plan was really capable of fulfilment, then clearly Britain would have been knocked out of the war long before her bombers could reach Germany. If bombs were really as destructive as this, if bombers could be navigated so accurately and bombs dropped so precisely and indeed if it was necessary for so few of them to reach their target, then the prospects of 'close defence' were grim. A German victory was certain.

A little investigation into bombing accuracy, a few sensible experiments with 500lb. G.P. bombs, some thought about the vulnerability of Wellingtons and Hampdens to German fighter attack, a straightforward navigational exercise would have immediately shown the whole conception to be at least as fantastic as Sir Edgar Ludlow-Hewitt, the C-in-C Bomber Command, in any case believed it to be. Above all, an application of Fighter Command's prospects to Bomber Command's problems would have given the same answer. Even with the limited and in many cases unnecessarily limited, knowledge of the day, the plan for Bomber Command's participation in the air defence of Great Britain was at least as futile in theory as it proved to be worthless in action. Indeed, as time went on less and less confidence was placed in it and more and more reliance fell upon Fighter Command to devise a successful close defence. Thus, as far as the air defence of Great Britain was concerned, Fighter Command became the key.

Fighter Command alone stood between Britain and the lurid fate which the Joint Planning Committee had forecast in 1936. If the aeroplane was not a defence against the aeroplane, then Britain would perish, but if it was such a defence, then, on the further W.A. plans which were made, Bomber Command would perish, for surely if Fighter Command could defeat the German air offensive, then the German equivalent could equally defeat the British air offensive.

This reasoning might have brought the Air Staff to the second major problem which confronted them, the question of how to defeat the German Air Force, that is, the problem of how to attain a general, as opposed to a purely local, air superiority. This was the crux of the whole proposition of air power and it took five years of war, five years of trial and error, five years of colossal German blunders, five years of aircraft production and five years of superior training to solve it.

This was in fact to prove the fundamental element of war, not only in the air, but of war in every theatre and every medium. That the British Air Staff should not have mastered the most expeditious methods of attaining this air superiority before all this experience had been gained was inevitable, but the fact that the Air Staff did not recognise the need for command in the air as a pre-requisite to effective strategic bombing was tragic.

It is one thing to enter a war with basically sound doctrines and strategy but to lack the tactical and technical means of carrying it out. It is quite another thing to enter the war with a basically unsound doctrine. The doctrine will father the tactics, the equipment and the technique of the force. Only what can be done will be done and a false doctrine, having fostered its own equipment, then dictates the wrong strategy even when this is known to be wrong. Put most simply, an air force designed for night bombing cannot instantly switch to day bombing, any more than an air force designed for short range attacks can suddenly switch to long range attack.

The need for the destruction of the German Air Force was seen only as a need to defeat the German air offensive in the opening phases of the war. The broad conception and hope was that Fighter Command would defeat the German 'knock out blow' and thus gain time for Bomber Command to mount an offensive of at least equal intensity. Then it would be possible to return to the doctrine of the offensive and the nation which could stand the bombing the longest would win the war. Thus, the fighter doctrine was a stop gap idea intended to guarantee Britain during the awkward period while her bomber force was less powerful than the German bomber force. That any fighter force could impose a permanent stop upon any bomber force was not imagined. Ultimately the bombers would win.

The development of the R.A.F. bombing offensive would gradually throw the German Air Force on to the defensive, just as the threat of a German offensive had already in 1938 thrown the R.A.F. on to the defensive. Once it was on the defensive the German Air Force would mount a diminishing attack on England. The R.A.F. attack against Germany would increase and the relative positions of the air forces in 1938 would, perhaps by 1941, be reversed. For this plan the essentials were an efficient defence in 1939 and 1940 and the means of formidable attack in 1941 and 1942.

This was not mere wishful thinking. The Hurricanes and Spitfires supported by radar gave the prospects of successful defence at the beginning. The 'giant' bombers, the Stirlings, Halifaxes and Manchesters, projects which had been maturing since 1936, seemed to offer the prospects of formidable attack in 1941 and 1942. Britain's future, even in 1938, was not without hope. Meanwhile the Hampdens, Wellingtons, Whitleys, Blenheims and even Battles would have to do what they could towards gaining the initiative in the war in the air. Offensive plans for Bomber Command were therefore the key to the Air Staff's policy.

Now there were two respects in which Germany was obviously vulnerable to air attack. The first was in the heavy concentration of a large proportion of her basic industry in one relatively small area, the valley of the Ruhr. The second was in the domain of her oil supplies. It was upon these two points that the hopeful attention of the British Air Staff was riveted. The Air Ministry Intelligence organisation had gathered some very striking information about the Ruhr. No less than 51% of the entire industrial population of Germany lived there.

By far the greater part of many of Germany's basic industrial products came from the Ruhr[9] and if the Ruhr could be paralysed, "the German economic system could not function and she would become impotent to wage war on a large scale in less than three months". There were several ways in which this "the greatest and most centralised industrial area in the world" might be paralysed by bombing attacks. The reservoirs and dams might be destroyed with the object of cutting off supplies of water essential for industrial and domestic purposes alike and also of causing flooding. The canals might be breached with the object of delaying the arrival in the Ruhr of essential raw materials and dislocating the distribution of Ruhr products. Attacks might be made on fuel and power supplies with the object of bringing industry to a standstill.

That this obviously attractive strategic theory might also be tactically feasible and technically within the grasp even of the small Bomber Command with which Britain would enter the war was suggested in the C-in-C's reception of the plan. Sir Edgar Ludlow-Hewitt was of the opinion that the aim, that is the paralysis of the Ruhr, could be achieved by the dispatch of about 3,000 sorties and the sacrifice of no more than 176 bombers. The only worry which seems to have assailed Bomber Command Headquarters was the question of whether the bombers would be able to take a direct route across the Low Countries. If they could not, then it might be impossible to sustain the attack.

In greater detail, Bomber Command H.Q. thought that the aim could be most easily achieved by concentrating upon the Ruhr coking plants. The destruction of these would, the plans section of Bomber Command said, bring Ruhr industry to an "immediate standstill". The bombers would, it was predicted, have no difficulty in finding and hitting the coking plants by day or night. All the 26 important coking plants could, the Air Ministry was told, be put out of action by no more than 78 low level sorties.

To make assurance doubly sure, Bomber Command thought this should be supported by attacks on electricity supplies. Destruction or even reduction of electricity supplies would have immediate effect both "materially and morally". Owing to their small size, these targets would, however, have to be attacked by day and owing to the defences, from high level. All the same 38 squadron attacks could destroy the nineteen most important electricity stations. The destruction of water supplies might be tried when heavier bombs were available.

This extraordinary optimism, which contrasted so significantly with Sir Edgar Ludlow-Hewitt's more general pessimism about the other plans, could hardly fail to make a profound impression, even if the Air Ministry were not quite so sanguine themselves. Accordingly, the C-in-C was told on 17 January 1939 that the Air Staff could say "quite definitely" that, in the event of immediate war, Bomber Command would undertake resolute attacks against power targets in the Ruhr. Thereafter the C-in-C's enthusiasm began somewhat to cool.

Germany's oil position, though apparently not quite so vulnerable as the Ruhr industrial area, offered another promising offensive plan for Bomber Command. Like all the other European great powers, with the exception of Russia, Germany lacked an indigenous supply of oil adequate to meet her peace time, let alone her war time, requirements. The four-year plan was doing something to ease the position but it was clear that the synthetic plants and the natural oil wells of Germany could supply no more than about twenty per cent of her probable war time consumption. Her war effort would therefore depend upon stocks and imports from abroad.

Roughly two-thirds of Germany's peace time oil imports came from North and South America. Under one fifth came from Rumania. Great Britain, however, owned "practically the whole" fleet of tankers and with the command of the sea which she might expect, it would not be difficult in war to cut Germany off from overseas oil supplies. For continued imports Germany would therefore have to rely upon Poland and Rumania.[10] Polish supplies would not exceed 150,000 tons per annum, but in Rumania there was enough oil to meet German needs. The problem here would be one of transport and the limiting factor would be the capacity of the Danube which could scarcely carry more than one million tons a year. Stocks which would cushion the war effort against a diminution of imports, at any rate for a time, were variously estimated to be between about three and five million tons.[11]

It was therefore reasonable to assume that for Germany a decisive shortage of oil would follow the destruction of stocks, production capacity and refining capacity.[12] Unless Germany could import extraordinarily large quantities from Rumania, the effects of a bombing offensive against oil should be seen within about three months.

The planning machine accordingly went into action and a second major offensive plan for Bomber Command was produced. Thirty-two targets were selected which consisted of the sixteen major synthetic plants, the fourteen major refineries and two independent tank farms. All but nine of these targets could easily be reached from England, but it was thought that the remainder might require bomber bases in Poland. Nevertheless, if endurance was the sole consideration, all the targets with "the possible exception of Stettin" could be reached by home-based bombers.

It was not thought possible to estimate the weights of bombs which would be required to destroy synthetic plants or refineries. The damage would depend on the extent to which the plants proved to be self-destructive. It was therefore left to later and less cautious estimates to determine the number of sorties which the plan would demand. Some of the targets, for instance Leuna, were thought large enough to warrant night attack.

The oil plan, known as W.A.6., did not have quite the attraction of the Ruhr plan, numbered W.A.5a. There was always the fear that Rumanian supplies might defeat it, but here at least the Air Staff believed they had two plans which offered Bomber Command, even in its early days, the prospect of decisive independent and strategic victories.

With these two plans the Air Staff might well have rested content, but they were permitted no such luxury. To the military, if not to the air force mind, the destruction of lines of communication seemed to be a significant part of the role which air power could play in war. Indeed, in the independent and strategic plans the significance of transport had not been overlooked. In the Ruhr plan, for instance, Intelligence had pointed to the desirability of impeding the inflow of raw materials and the outflow of products to and from the Ruhr. In the oil plan the significance of blocking the Danube was obvious. As early as 1936, however, the Air Staff had been advised by a Cabinet Committee that a general attack on transport was unlikely to cause sufficient damage to affect industry seriously. What might be harmless to the industrialist might all the same be fatal to the general and an attack on military lines of communication was one of the most obvious ways in which Bomber Command might discharge the duty, laid upon it in 1937 by the Chiefs of Staff, of assisting the Army.

The French in particular with their natural concern about the approaching German invasion, were especially enthusiastic about such a plan and the British War Office was sufficiently interested to sketch a bombing plan for the prevention or delay of a German advance through the Low Countries. A great many theoretical discussions and some singularly ill-conducted experiments were carried out with the object of determining what should be attacked, viaducts, moving trains in cuttings or on bridges, moving trains on open lines, moving trains in small stations, open lines in cuttings, or open lines not in cuttings, traffic centres and so on. The War Office enquiries encountered formidable delays at the Air Ministry and very little agreement could be reached between the French and the British Staffs on the subject. From time to time the Air Ministry displayed a reviving interest in the prospect of industrial dislocation arising from transport attacks.

From the welter of international and inter-service argument there did however emerge three possible lines of action for Bomber Command. In order to do something to meet military demands and apparently impressed by the reported break-down of German communications during the seizures of Austria and Czechoslovakia, the Air Staff decided to introduce a variant to the Ruhr plan. This variant, known as W.A.5b., provided for a limited and harassing attack against communications in the Ruhr. Besides perhaps contributing to their own strategic aim there, the Air Staff considered that the advance of the German army would be "hampered" by this action.

The French were not, however, so easily satisfied and in April 1939 the Army Staff (3rd Bureau) presented a note outlining an ambitious plan to make and maintain 100 cuts in open railway tracks with the object of checking the German army. The Air Ministry reminded the French that 1,490 tons of Japanese bombs dropped on 718 sorties over a period of 103 days had suspended traffic on the Canton-Kowloon railway for only ten days. The British War Office disagreed with the French not only about the targets they had chosen but about the areas they had selected, and this plan, known as W.A.4a., was overtaken by the war before the stage of argument had been passed.

All the same the military and air force delegates of Britain did assure those of France that, in the event of a German advance through the Low Countries, the primary role of the R.A.F. Bomber Command would be to stem it. These confusing discussions and imperfect plans for attacks on transport have a dual significance. In the first place they indicated one of the auxiliary functions which would undoubtedly fall upon the independent force and in the second place they were, like the Ruhr and the oil plans, the prelude to the greater events which were to follow. As we shall see in time, it was at the area of the Ruhr, the industry of oil production and the activity of transport that strategic bombers were to strike their decisive blows.

If, however, various possible auxiliary activities were a threat to what the Air Staff regarded as the central task of the bomber force, that is the strategic and independent attack, they were by no means the only threat. Another threat was raised by the so-called illegality of bombing. From the beginning of the First World War the Germans believed that in the submarine they possessed a weapon with which they might bring Britain to her knees. Yet they did not start unrestricted submarine warfare until 1917 and the first result of their action was to bring America into the war against them.

There were two reasons to explain why the German government forced their submarine commanders to hold their hands for three years. The first was that the German U-boat fleet was not until 1917 large enough to offer the prospect of decisive success. The second was that by sinking merchant ships without search or warning, Germany would undoubtedly be charged by enemies and neutrals and especially by the U.S.A., with contravening international law. She would be told she was no longer a civilised nation. Thus, new coalitions might be formed against the German Empire. Germany could therefore not afford the risk of provoking new enemies until she was certain that the submarine would dispose of Britain and perhaps also isolate America.

These decisive consequences, the Emperor was advised, could be expected in 1917 and the unrestricted submarine war began in 1917. Now if Germany, like Britain, had also depended upon a merchant fleet for her existence and if Britain had also possessed a formidable U-boat fleet, it is inconceivable that Germany would ever have stimulated this kind of warfare.

Bombing presented a strictly similar case. There was, it is true, no international law of the air, but the bomb was widely regarded as a more or less illegal weapon. The League of Nations had sought ways of outlawing the bomber and the British government had given its support to the Beneš resolution designed for this purpose. The negotiations had, to the relief of the Air Staff, come to nothing, but the idea continued to prevail that to bomb civilians would be a dastardly act. Much prominence had been given in the British press to the German bombing of Guernica and the Italian bombing of Barcelona. The democracies proclaimed these killings as murders. Clearly, however, if civilians were sacred and only "military targets" could be attacked, then strategic bombing could never be applied, for round all strategic targets were civilians, 6,000,000 of them in the Ruhr, 8,000,000 of them in London. Civilians were indeed a possible strategic target themselves. No bombing of civilians meant in effect no strategic bombing.

To support the so-called and variously interpreted but actually non-existent laws of air warfare was therefore to deny the strategic bomber its function in war. If, however, by doing this, Britain might attract powerful neutrals to her cause, the sacrifice might be worthwhile, for it would surely be only temporary. If in addition by refraining from any "illegal" act in the air, she encouraged Germany to do the same, she might have discovered an extremely cheap way of averting the much-dreaded German 'knock out blow'.

When, therefore, on 21 June 1938 the Prime Minister publicly proclaimed in the House of Commons that it was against international law to bomb civilians, that targets attacked must be "legitimate military objectives" and that due care must be taken to spare civilians in the neighbourhood of these military objectives, he committed a very statesmanlike and discreet act. After all, only in the previous February the Air Staff had expressed a wish, about which it may be assumed they did not consult Lord Trenchard, for an international agreement by which "air forces, while they may remain valuable ancillaries to surface forces, cannot in themselves be a decisive factor in war". Seldom can the Air Staff have more nearly approached the attitude of mind which generally prevailed at the Admiralty.

France and Britain therefore agreed between themselves that they would take no "illegal" action in the air until the Germans did. Thus, they hoped to gain a further breathing space while German air superiority was at its greatest. German ambitions in the East, heightened by the British guarantee to Poland, gave a more solid assurance that there might well be a "gloves on" period in the west after the declaration of war.

This curious situation, inspired, alas, more by weakness and fear than by moral rectitude or sincerity, produced a number of "legal" plans for Bomber Command designed to provide an employment for the force while the period of restricted bombing should last. It also made the Air Staff willing enough to prepare an ambitious plan to destroy the German fleet, for at least there could be no doubt that a battleship at sea was a legitimate target, it being so unlikely that there would be any civilians in the neighbourhood. The only significance of this plan known as W.A7a. or Plan "K" was that it was carried out and was in fact to be the first war operation of Bomber Command.

One other "legal" plan is worth noticing because it revealed the extraordinary view of German morale which already pervaded Britain. This was the plan to drop propaganda from the air, known as W.A.14. The supposition was that Hitler's regime was so unstable and the German public so nervy and impressionable that it might well prove "that skilfully dropped propaganda, distributed by aircraft, may prove a more potent weapon than bombs".[13] At one time the Air Staff were even poring over a specification for the "ideal leaflet bomber". The jejune mixture of threats, bribes and cajoleries which the projected leaflets contained hardly justified the hope and it took some sharp words from the D.C.A.S. to restore some sense of proportion. Nevertheless, the conception of German morale which helped this plan lingered, as will appear, with disastrous results for Britain.

It is now possible to summarise the policy with which the R.A.F. entered the war and to suggest whither it led. The doctrine of the offensive, the doctrine that the aeroplane is not a defence against the aeroplane, was modified in the British mind by the supremacy of the Luftwaffe. Most promising weapons to afford the means of a successful close defence in the air had been devised, but the principle remained that ultimately the only way to deal with the German Air Force was to mount a counter offensive of equal and later superior intensity.

The idea was for the R.A.F. to rise from the defensive position in which it would have to enter the war, to strike blows which would cast the Luftwaffe onto the defensive and which would in themselves destroy the core of the German war effort. The function of Fighter Command and the restricted bombing policy was to gain the time in which to build the 'giant' bombers. At the same time, it was not possible to think exclusively in terms of the independent offensive, for it was not only in the air that Britain's position was unfavourable. Desperate measures might be necessary to save the situation on land, or to advance the cause of Britain at sea.

These considerations made the R.A.F.'s war policy reasonably obvious. In so far as the independent offensive was concerned the bombers must hold their hands as long as possible, they must gain the greatest possible strength before they struck. Fighter Command must defeat the initial German attack. As far as the auxiliary offensive was concerned the action of the bombers, on the other hand, would have to be controlled by the events of the battlefields. In other words, Bomber Command must conserve its forces, if possible until the 'giant' bombers were ready. Then it must strike at the heart of Germany.

But where did this policy lead? Obviously if the Luftwaffe could be thrown onto the defensive Britain would gain substantial advantages. Her own danger of destruction by the Luftwaffe would be abated. A concentration of German air power on the defence of the Reich would deny the Wehrmacht at least a proportion of its air support, but the crucial question was would this defensive alignment of the German Air Force, once it had been enforced, be an adequate achievement for the British bombers themselves? Would they be able to get through these defences to strike those mortal blows at the Ruhr, at oil supplies or transport which the W.A. Plans envisaged? If they flew by day, would they in the absence of superior speed be capable of fighting their way to the target and back again? If they flew at night to evade the German fighters, would they be able to find and hit their targets?

There was absolutely no evidence to suggest that bombers could fulfil either task with success. The relatively slow bomber armed with .303 machine guns would obviously fall a victim to the much faster German fighters armed with larger guns. It soon did. There was nothing in the yet undeveloped science of air navigation which suggested that bombers, even if they could evade the fighters by night, would succeed in finding their targets, let alone hitting them. Much bitter experience of war was to be required before these two lessons were learnt, yet even before the war began there did lurk behind the scenes a possible evasion of these issues.

If the combination of German close defence and navigational problems made it impossible to strike precise blows at specific points in the German war economy, it still had to be asked whether in fact it was necessary to strike precise blows at all. In 1918, when confronted with the same problem, Major General Trenchard had said that the moral effect of bombing stood in relation to its material effect in the proportion of 20 to 1.

British fears of the German Air Force had centred as much, if not more, upon the probable reaction of the British people as upon the effects upon the ports. The belief that bombers could quickly spread panic among populations was the leading impression of the inter-war years. The thought that the German people would be especially susceptible to this treatment suggested that the weakest point in the German war economy might lie not in the Ruhr industry or the shortage of oil, but in the people themselves. It was after all the fathers of these people who had collapsed in 1918. If therefore the small precise targets could not be hit, then missing them might prove at least as effective as hitting them. The German people, massed in their great cities could not be missed, even in the dead of night.

This argument was in time to be exposed by the German people as an error of judgement of the first magnitude, yet it arose from an even more fundamental misconception. The idea of attacking areas instead of targets derived its attraction from the possibility of succeeding at night, from the opportunity, which it offered more than did any other bombing policy, of evading the German defences. Morale was in fact the one target admirably suited to the methods of the guerre de course in the air.

The German Air Force having once been thrown on the defensive, it was believed, need never be defeated. Germany herself could be destroyed while her air force searched the dark skies in vain for the British bombers. The offensive air force, unlike any other weapon of war, need not, if this theory was correct, fight the defending air force. It would grapple directly with the nation. If this was so, then the conquest of the air had introduced to the art of war a revolution. If it was not, then the principles of air power could have been discerned in the teachings of naval and military history.

The war of 1939–1945 has answered these questions.

Part I

The First Bombing Offensive, 1939–1941

Chapter 1

The Collapse of the 'Knock Out Blow' Theory and the Origins of Attritional Bombing

With whatever doctrine the R.A.F. entered the war on 3 September 1939, there was one inescapable conclusion which dominated the councils of the British Government and Air Staff. If a 'knock out blow' from the air was indeed coming, it would be the Luftwaffe and not the R.A.F. which delivered it. The German Air Force was supposed to be ready for war. Bomber Command was little more than a shadow force.

This had a sobering effect on all calculations and Britain was unlikely to submit herself voluntarily to an unequal test in the air. Her interests would best be served if the outbreak of the bombing war could be delayed, if she could conserve the small bomber force which she possessed and use it as the cadre of the much bigger force of the future, which could deal out at least as much destruction as the Luftwaffe. When therefore the Wehrmacht turned east to crush Poland, the British were well content to carry out only the restricted bombing which, with the French, they had planned for this event.

It seemed certain all the same that Germany would presently turn the full weight of her armed strength against the Western Powers. The British Army was as yet only a bare nucleus of the force which was to come, and the Royal Navy could not immediately or directly get to grips with the enemy. The main hope of countering this impending danger therefore lay in the French Army and the British bomber forces. So long as German eyes were turned eastwards, the policy of restricted bombing seemed not only possible, but it also seemed to be obvious wisdom. As soon as Germany turned westwards, there must, the Chiefs of Staff advised the Government, be no shrinking from "using all that we have got". In that case British bombers must be used "at all costs in the manner which holds out the best hope of obtaining decisive results against Germany".

These were bold words and they meant, in effect, that a German invasion of France would instantly be countered by an all-out R.A.F. attack upon the Ruhr. Since the German invasion would almost certainly come through the Low Countries, where the Maginot Line curiously ended, the bombers would be able to take a direct route to their target, and one of the principal difficulties of the plan, the need to fly round neutral air, would have been removed.

Even so, the Ruhr attack would still be a formidable undertaking, which the French believed might do more harm than good. Neither the Supreme Commander, General Gamelin, nor General Vuillemin believed that the attack would have any effect upon the advance of the German army. General Vuillemin thought it would be folly to do anything to provoke a German bombing attack on French industry, which he regarded as much more vulnerable than German industry. General Gamelin felt that the less bombing that took place, the greater would be the prospects of a French victory on land in the Spring of 1940.

Such bombing as did occur should, he thought, be directed against columns of troops, lines of military communication and aerodromes. The French Generals, thinking in terms of purely military strategy and imbued with a defensive outlook upon the war, regarded the bomber as a weapon of army co-operation. The British Air Staff on the other hand, looking at Germany from across the water, persevered with their belief in the independent and strategic role for bombers, which they had always believed to be the ultimate expression of air power.

Nevertheless, by the time the French had agreed to the principle of a strategic bombing attack upon the Ruhr in the event of a German invasion of the Low Countries, other and even more formidable objections to the plan were beginning to disclose themselves. In order to hit small targets like power stations, which the Ruhr plan demanded, the bomber force would have to make the attack in daylight. In order to achieve the surprise, which the Ruhr plan envisaged as essential to success, the bomber force would have to commit its whole strength to a single attack. The more Sir Edgar Ludlow-Hewitt, the C-in-C Bomber Command, thought about this enterprise, the less he liked it. The indications were, from the little experience of air operations which had yet been gained, that the bomber was no match for the fighter in combat.

Hopes that a fleet of bombers flying together in daylight would be able to protect themselves against hostile fighters had already received a rude shock. There had been two high level actions on 14 and 18 December 1939, in which Wellington bombers had been attacked by Messerschmitt fighters. On both occasions half the bombers had been shot down. At low level there was the grim experience of 4 September 1939 when the low flying force of Blenheims attempting to attack the German fleet off Wilhelmshaven, had all been destroyed by light anti-aircraft guns.[1]

If the greater part of Bomber Command was launched against the Ruhr, the C-in-C thought it highly probable that half the entire force might be lost. Quite apart from the immediately paralysing effect this would have upon further bombing operations, the effect upon the expanded and re-equipped force of the future would be disastrous. The small bomber force of 1940 with its Hampdens, Wellingtons, Whitleys and Blenheims was to be the nucleus of a much greater force of Stirlings, Halifaxes and Manchesters. The loss of half the best crews of 1940 would deny the Bomber Command of the future half of its potential leaders.

A concerted strategic air attack upon a first-class industrial power was something which had never yet been attempted. The proposed R.A.F. offensive was certain to be experimental in nature. No one could say what the consequences would be either for the industries which suffered the attacks or for the bombers which carried them out. The Ruhr plan would involve the R.A.F. in a gamble with the highest stakes, for it was evident that nothing less than the whole future of Bomber Command hung in the balance. The C-in-C was already convinced that the "speculative amount of damage" which might be inflicted on Germany was no justification for such a risk.

Thus, it appeared that, in the case of the Ruhr plan, the probable tactical dangers far outweighed the possible strategic advantages. More specifically, the problem of whether large scale daylight bombing could be carried out at all now had to be faced. It seemed essential to find another plan for Bomber Command, a plan which would not involve committing the whole force to a single enterprise on a single day, a plan which might be carried out at night, if indeed the German fighter opposition proved to be as deadly as early indications had suggested, and yet a plan which offered the chance of decisive strategic results comparable to those promised by the Ruhr plan.

Though the Air Staff were reluctant to abandon the Ruhr plan, at least as a measure to be taken in the critical emergency which might follow a German invasion of the Low Countries, discretion was the better part of valour. Even if the Air Staff had not yet admitted it, the 'phoney war' had sufficed to kill the idea of a British 'knock out blow' against Germany. It had also struck what proved to be a mortal blow at the British plan for daylight bombing. As an alternative to the Ruhr plan, the oil plan seemed to enjoy many advantages, especially for an offensive which was bound to be experimental. It would enable Bomber Command to feel its way into the war because it did not envisage one single decisive attack.

On the contrary it was thought that the destruction of oil plants could be sought over a considerable period and the offensive could therefore be carried out bit by bit as circumstances permitted. Oil plants were also larger targets than power stations, and could therefore be attacked from a higher altitude, or perhaps even at night. In addition to these tactical advantages, there was also a powerful strategic sanction for the oil offensive, for if the Ruhr was Germany's most vital and vulnerable industrial area, oil certainly represented a dangerous bottleneck in her whole war economy.

By the end of March 1940, when Sir Charles Portal had succeeded Sir Edgar Ludlow-Hewitt as C-in-C Bomber Command, the intention of attempting a daylight offensive had been abandoned, and the Air Staff were thinking more and more of the oil attack as the principal strategic task for Bomber Command. If, however, some doubts had been cleared away, many others remained. Opinion before the war had been generally sceptical about the possibility of carrying out precision bombing at night, yet the oil attack would certainly call for precision bombing.

Then there was the unknown question of what the Germans, armed with the initiative in the air and on land, would do. No one yet knew the extent to which Bomber Command might get drawn into the impending battle on land or the war at sea. The efforts of the Advanced Air Striking Force in France and the efforts of Costal Command and the Fleet Air

Arm, designed to help the Navy, might not prove adequate to protect the independent role of Bomber Command. Indeed, the air defence of Great Britain herself might demand wider activities than Fighter Command alone could perform. All these problems remained unsolved when, on 9 April 1940, Germany invaded Denmark and Norway.

The attack on the west had begun, but still the German bombers were held in check. For a few uneasy weeks the period of restricted bombing survived. Nevertheless, the time had come for the Air Staff to proclaim a bombing policy which would be needed soon enough. If the Germans invaded the Low Countries in an advance towards the French frontier, then, the C-in-C was told on 13 April 1940, Bomber Command would be expected to attack German communications leading west. The targets would be columns of troops on the move and marshalling yards in the Ruhr.

These, however, would be "harassing" attacks, and the main weight of bombs was to be dropped on German oil plants. This plan was known as W.A.4c. If, on the other hand, the Germans did not invade the Low Countries but it did become advisable to start unrestricted bombing, then Bomber Command would be free to concentrate on a strategic offensive against oil plants, coking plants, electricity plants if they could be seen, and other self-illuminating targets.

These two plans for two eventualities had two common factors. In either case the offensive would be carried out at night, and in either case there would be attacks on oil. Through all the vicissitudes of the tremendous events now breaking upon Europe, the British Air Staff never abandoned this faith in the principle of strategic bombing. The R.A.F. was never completely swallowed by the consuming demands of defence which beset Britain for many years to come. All the same this faith in strategic bombing was a blind faith, and the course of the bombing offensive was to be repeatedly marred by the clamour of defence.

At dawn on 10 May, the German army, with the Luftwaffe in close attendance, swarmed over the Low Countries towards France. The barriers were down and five days later, the War Cabinet having given their approval, 99 aircraft of Bomber Command were dispatched to the Ruhr to attack oil and railway targets. True to its tradition Bomber

Command took to the offensive. After more than twenty years of thought, but practically no experience, the strategic bomber at last moved from the realm of speculation to that of action. By destroying Warsaw and Rotterdam the Luftwaffe had invited a terrible retribution. This first R.A.F. strategic attack on the night of 15 May was the beginning.

The Wehrmacht, fresh from its victories in Poland and Norway, swept into France like an avalanche. This time there was no Battle of the Marne. The British Expeditionary Force was pushed into the sea at Dunkirk. Paris fell and France capitulated on 17 June 1940. Hitler, with his armies now occupying the Channel ports, sought a quick decision against his last enemy. The Luftwaffe was flung against Britain and an invasion was daily expected to follow. The unchecked series of German victories, however, ended abruptly in the Battle of Britain under the guns of the R.A.F. Fighter Command and Germany was forced to seek a longer drawn out conflict in the Atlantic while her main forces recoiled, turned about and looked for further victories in the east.

During 1940 Britain endured through three great defensive struggles, the Battles of France, Britain and the Atlantic, but at the same time her bombers began a fourth struggle, the Battle of Germany. Even without these defensive battles to sap the strength of Bomber Command, the first phase of the bombing offensive would have been difficult enough. With them, it became practically impossible.

The first difficulty threatening the bombing offensive now beginning was inherent. This was the difficulty of identifying precise targets at night. It was hoped that oil plants might be found and successfully bombed in conditions of moonlight, but it was never expected that success could be achieved in total darkness. If therefore the decision to bomb at night did not apparently mean the abandonment of precision bombing altogether, it did limit the time in which it could be carried out to nine or ten nights in the month, and even on these nights there might well be no coincidence of good weather and moonlight. From the outset therefore the oil plan was something less than the design of a whole bombing offensive. Unless Bomber Command was to be diverted from its strategic role, or was to be partly idle, other forms of attack would have to be considered as well.

In 1940 the problem of idleness was, however, the least of those which confronted the force. The C-in-C Bomber Command was told on 19 May 1940 to concentrate his effort during the moon periods against oil and railway targets in and around the Ruhr, as had been arranged in plan W.A.4c. All the same the Chief of the Air Staff had made it a condition that this policy should only be carried out subject to the promises of direct support for the French army, made in Paris by the Prime Minister, being honoured. Thus, Bomber Command found it difficult to get at the German oil plants, not only because of the dark nights, but because there were so many other tasks to perform.

The collapse of France removed one diversion and created another and greater one. All the same this catastrophic event had increased the strategic attractions of the oil offensive. The Lloyd Committee, which had been formed to consider the German oil position, calculated that Germany and Italy would be unable to balance their oil budget. They would therefore be compelled to draw on their stocks. No oil producing territory had been conquered, but the field of military and industrial activity had been greatly extended. The oil which had been captured in France and elsewhere would therefore do no more than delay a crisis which was in any case inevitable. For these reasons the Lloyd Committee concluded that oil represented "a very weak link in the economy of the European system under German hegemony".

The immediate issue of the war did not, however, depend upon whether Bomber Command could destroy the German oil plants or not, but upon whether the Luftwaffe could gain command of the air over Britain, so that the German army could land to enforce peace terms. Years of thought had been devoted to the prospect of this German air attack on Britain which was now beginning.

A great deal had been done and the R.A.F. did possess in Fighter Command a force worthy to play the principal part in one of the decisive battles of the world. The plans for 'close defence' were worthy of their brilliant execution by Hurricanes and Spitfires during the Battle of Britain. On the other hand, no convincing plan for the participation of Bomber Command in this struggle had ever been evolved. Nevertheless, it seemed necessary that Bomber Command should take part in the battle and on 20 June the C-in-C was told in a directive that his primary task was to be the reduction in the scale of the German air attack on Britain. The oil offensive could continue only to the extent which this principal aim would permit.

Bomber Command was thus thrown decisively on to the defensive in an attack, which, as was generally recognised, had practically no chance of success. The force of events had driven the Air Staff to this gloomy decision and the attack on the German Air Force remained the chief task of Bomber Command throughout the summer and until the end of September, by which time it was clear that Fighter Command had won its battle.

Even then it was necessary to switch the attack, at least for a time, to the invasion ports. These attacks on German aircraft production were aimed at airframe assembly plants and aluminium plants as well as at stores and depots. It should have been obvious, and it was presently recognised, that Germany had acquired large stocks of aluminium in France. It was known that airframe assembly plants were easily and quickly repairable and that in any case Germany possessed several reserve plants which could instantly make good any loss of production which did occur. Thus far had German predominance in the air driven the growth of British bombing policy from the natural course of its development.

It was only when the Battle of Britain was over and when an "off season" for the German invasion approached that the Air Staff was once more able to contemplate an offensive bombing policy. All the same, one difficulty followed another and the season which made invasion unlikely also promised more difficult flying weather. There would be fewer and fewer nights on which precision bombing could be attempted. While the Air Staff were still resolved to persevere with the oil offensive, the genesis of a new idea was beginning to form in their minds. Bomber Command might attempt a direct attack on the morale of the German people.

There had already been some attacks on Berlin, and at the end of October a most encouraging report had been received about their effects, through the British representative in Belgrade. Although the attacks had been only "sporadic", they were said to be causing a daily fall in the morale of the citizens. The "cocksureness which every German felt after the victories in Holland, Belgium and France" was apparently "steadily disappearing". This remarkable news excited the approbation of the War Cabinet, and it was hoped that Berlin might be bombed as often as possible.

German cities would present targets which the bombers should be able to find on moonless nights or in conditions of indifferent weather, when no other form of bombing was profitable. The directive of 30 October 1940 spoke of the need to concentrate the bombing offensive upon two principal target systems, German oil and German cities. Oil was to be regarded as the more important target and the Deputy Chief of the Air Staff particularly emphasised to Sir Richard Peirse, who had succeeded Sir Charles Portal as C-in-C, that all other objectives were to be treated as secondary and were only to be attacked when tactical reasons made it impossible or unprofitable to bomb oil plants.

The ultimate significance of this decision was concealed in 1940 by the belief that the oil offensive could be carried out at night in the light of the moon. So long as this belief persisted, the genesis of the area bombing policy, which had now appeared, seemed to be no more than a promising sideline.

A more important tendency was the increasing Air Staff desire to concentrate the bombing offensive, which so far had been torn, not only between the needs of defence and the hopes of offence, but also between the many conflicting views of the course which the offensive should take. Already in July 1940 the Air Staff had diagnosed in the dispersal of the offensive one of the principal explanations of ineffective bombing. Nevertheless, they had so far shown themselves quite incapable of resisting the many and varied demands made on Bomber Command, or indeed of living up to their own maxims themselves. On the very day that the directive of 30 October was issued, with its emphasis upon oil as the primary objective, the Air Ministry sent a signal to Bomber Command saying that the "maximum effort" was to be devoted to attacks upon morale, particularly Italian morale. Three days after the Deputy Chief of the Air Staff had written his letter of 10 November to the C-in-C pressing him to depart from the oil attack only on tactical grounds, the Air Ministry sent a signal asking for a maximum effort against Italy.

The tragedy of this nebulous situation was thrown into particular relief by the fifth report of the Lloyd Committee on the German oil position which was circulated on 16 December 1940. The major conclusion of the Committee was that the Axis oil position was "sufficiently important and sufficiently weak to justify a heavy effort against the strategic points". The obvious implication was that the oil offensive should be intensified. Meanwhile, however, the Committee pointed out that Germany was working "ceaselessly to increase her synthetic production, to organise a great increase in transport from Rumania, and to develop the widespread use of substitute fuels". The obvious implication was that the oil offensive, if it was to be effective, should be intensified and that without delay.

The Chief of the Air Staff told his colleagues, the Chiefs of Staff, that the seventeen major synthetic plants in Germany could be put out of action by an average of ninety-five bomber sorties per night on nine nights in the month, over a period of four months. This would, of course, still leave Germany in possession of her imports from Rumania, and the Lloyd Committee had already emphasised that the only way to get a "quick death clinch on the whole enemy oil position" was by the simultaneous destruction of the synthetic plants and denial of Rumanian imports. Nevertheless, it was calculated that the destruction of these synthetic plants would deny the Germans a potential production of nearly one and a half million tons of oil in six months. This would indeed be a serious, and possibly fatal, blow.

The argument for a concentrated oil offensive seemed unimpeachable. If successful results could be achieved, the strategic prospects of the offensive were dazzling. Equally the probability that success could be achieved was indicated by the reports already to hand on what the few and minor attacks carried out so far had already apparently achieved. The Chiefs of Staff therefore had no hesitation in recommending to the Cabinet that Bomber Command should be concentrated against oil targets on every night when the phase of the moon and the condition of the weather was agreeable. Only when the moon and weather were unfavourable should Bomber Command pursue its secondary aim, the destruction of German morale by bombing German cities.

The Collapse of the 'Knock Out Blow' Theory   13

So strongly were the Chiefs of Staff impressed by the prospects of the oil offensive that they went further and recommended – the naval, the military and the air force chiefs all agreeing about this – that the only permissible diversions should be against enemy ports at times when invasion seemed imminent, or against German naval forces if favourable opportunity was presented. Despite the Prime Minister's sceptical attitude to "cut and dried" calculations, Cabinet acceptance of this advice came swiftly from the Defence Committee and on 15 January 1941 the Air Staff were able to issue the most pungent bombing directive they had yet written.

This was a triumph for the advocates of independent strategic bombing, for those who knew the advantages of concentrated bombing and for those who pointed to Germany's weakness in the domain of her oil supply. It was none the less a short-lived triumph. After about seven weeks of adverse weather in which practically no oil attacks could be undertaken, the returning calls of defence exhausted the hopes of offence once again. On 9 March 1941 Bomber Command, at the insistence of the Prime Minister, was called away from the Battle of Germany and thrown int the Battle of the Atlantic.

The oil offensive, which the Battle of the Atlantic ended almost before it had begun in March 1941, marked the end of the first phase of the development of bombing policy. When the conditions for independent bombing returned, the Air Staff had new evidence before them and entirely different circumstances were seen to prevail. It would, all the same, be a mistake to regard the first bombing offensive, which began on 15 May 1940 and ended on 9 March 1941, in isolation from the events and decisions which followed. It is true that the Air Staff, like the bombers themselves, were struggling in the dark to a greater extent than at any subsequent stage. So little was known and so much had to be guessed. It is also true that the first bombing offensive was largely a theoretical enterprise, in the making of which hours of discussion may well have exceeded hours of flying. Many of the beliefs and hopes of 1940 had to be abandoned in 1941 and 1942, and the twin-engined bombers of 1940 were, in the years to come, to give way to an "all heavy" force of four-engined bombers. Revolutions in the scale and technique of bombing were to take place, which, in 1940, would have seemed almost beyond comprehension. Even so, many of the decisions taken in 1939 and 1940 were binding. The determination to maintain the strategic function of heavy bombers, even in the most unfavourable conditions, proved to be abiding. The decision to bomb at night was one which the R.A.F. alone never proved capable of reversing.

These two decisions alone determined the general course of bombing policy in the future. The foundations off the whole bombing offensive were firmly and irrevocably laid in this first phase. If at times the more spectacular events of later years are inclined to overshadow this first humble attempt to decide a war by strategic air power, it is well to bear this in mind.

Chapter 2

The Failure of the First Bombing Offensive: An Analysis of the Principal Assumptions on Which Hopes of Success Rested

The R.A.F. attacks on oil in 1940 and early 1941 failed to achieve any appreciable effect upon the German war potential. The inability of Bomber Command to mount the offensive in sufficient strength, due first to the defensive diversions of 1940 and then to the adverse weather of 1941, was the apparent cause of this failure, but the operative explanation lay deeper than any temporary embarrassment in 1940 or unkind chances of the weather in 1941. The first bombing offensive foundered upon miscalculations which contributed to the basic elements of the policy.

The two principal assumptions underlying this policy were, firstly, the strategic conclusion that oil represented a weak link in the German war economy which might be broken by bombing, and secondly, the tactical calculation that Bomber Command was capable of causing sufficient damage to have this effect. Now if either of these basic assumptions proved in the event to be groundless, the offensive was certain to fail and it would at once appear that the inability to adhere to the offensive because of diversions or weather was only important in so far as it concealed more important factors.

The first task is therefore to examine the strategic intelligence which suggested the desirability of the oil offensive. It is true that in 1940 Germany consumed about 2,000,000 tons of oil less than the British experts had anticipated because of the inactivity between the conquest of Poland and the attack on the West, and also because of the rapidity with which France was overrun. Not only was the swiftness of German victory economical in oil consumption, but the victories were so complete that large quantities of oil fell into German hands. In fact, the initial conduct of the war seemed to have justified Hitler in ignoring his advisers who had shown apprehension about Germany's oil position at the beginning of the war.

Nevertheless, saving oil was not producing oil. As far as production was concerned, the German position was even weaker than the British experts calculated. They expected that 1,080,000 tons would be produced in the first six months of 1941 by the hydrogenation plants and a further 370,000 tons by the Fischer Tropsch process. Actually, the two processes produced respectively 941,088 and 232,769 tons. The British estimate of German crude production was correct to within 5,000 tons. Actual German imports of oil in the same period were considerably less than the amounts calculated by British Intelligence.

It was suggested that the Germans might import over one and a half million tons of oil from Rumania. In fact, they imported no more than 644,160 tons. Similarly, the British overestimated the imports from Russia by about 100,000 tons. The British experts did not overlook any foreign source of oil with the minor exception of 232,200 tons imported by Germany in the whole of 1941 from countries other than Russia and Rumania.

The British assumption that the German stock position was perilous is also borne out by the fact that during the first half of 1941 German consumption exceeded production and imports. There was, in fact, a decline in stocks from 2,537,800 tons on 1 January 1941 to 1,779,496 on 30 June 1941.[1]

Finally, the British oil experts were right when they suggested that it was important to proceed with the oil offensive as quickly as possible because the position would begin to improve for Germany in the course of 1941. In the event, imports from Rumania began to increase steeply after April 1941 until, at their peak in August, more than 300,000 tons were brought in, which was more than six times the amount imported in January 1941. Synthetic production showed a less spectacular, but none the less impressive increase. The average monthly production from hydrogenation plants in the first six months of 1941 was 156,848 tons as compared with a monthly average of 194,155 tons in the second half of the year.[2]

Thus, the Air Staff assumption that oil represented a weak link in the German war economy, but that it was a link which was gradually being strengthened was in accord with the facts. Certainly, the intelligence experts were not right in every detail, but equally certainly the gist of their advice was sound. So far from overstating the case for an oil offensive, they did in many instances somewhat understate it. The failure of the offensive was in no way due to the strategic intelligence upon which it was based.

Bombing policy cannot, however, be determined by strategic considerations alone. Air power is not a theoretical force which can be applied at any point at any moment. The best strategy backed by accurate intelligence will come to nought if the tactical methods and technical means are inadequate for the task. If therefore the technical limitations of the force available are realised, then the strategic task which is set should be commensurate with the means, but if these limitations are not realised, then the whole strategy will be vitiated, and the effort will be largely wasted, except from the point of the view of the lessons which are learnt and acted upon in the future. This was the case with the first bombing offensive. The strategy was sound, but the tactical and technical assumptions which had suggested that the task could be performed were unrealistic and so the whole plan broke down in inevitable failure.

The principal miscalculation, upon which the first bombing offensive foundered, was that which suggested that the average bombing error at night would be no more than three hundred yards. From this flowed many unfortunate consequences, not the least of which was the failure to believe and follow up such evidence as did become available to show that the results of the bombing were profoundly unsatisfactory. Those in authority had such a strong impression that the bombing would, in fact, achieve this high degree of accuracy that they found it very difficult to believe the truth.

The importance of the three hundred yard aiming error calculation was far reaching. If a more realistic bombing error had been accepted, then the probability nomograms, which were used to calculate the necessary weights of attack, would presumably have shown that oil targets could not be attacked successfully by Bomber Command in 1940 or 1941 at night. The inception of the oil offensive therefore owed a great deal to this miscalculation. The belief that it was succeeding, and so the decision to continue it, rested almost entirely on this miscalculation.

Therefore, the calculation that the average aiming error of Bomber Command on moonlight nights would be three hundred yards was the cardinal assumption which underlay the policy of the first bombing offensive. Yet this assumption was reached without evidence, indeed, against evidence and against the conclusions which had been reached before the war, when the tendency was to exaggerate, not to minimise, the capabilities of bombers.

Changes in organisation at the time of the Munich crisis had brought the planning of Bomber Command prospective war operations more directly under the central control of the Air Ministry. The Staff Officers responsible for planning had been confronted with the need for making certain tactical assumptions, including some about the accuracy of bombing. Without such assumptions they would not have been in a position to make realistic plans. To solve this problem, a conference had been held at the Air Ministry on 30 November 1938 with A.C.A.S. in the chair. Representatives of the Air Ministry planning, tactics, operational requirements and intelligence sections were present, and the C-in-C Bomber Command with members of his Staff also attended.

The object of the conference, as the chairman explained, was to reach agreement on those tactical assumptions necessary to the making of bombing plans, with the object of ensuring "that plans produced would be capable of implementation". The problem of bombing accuracy found a place on the agenda beside those of penetration and range. In the course of discussion, the conference agreed to accept the figure of three hundred yards as the average standard of accuracy which would be achieved in high level attacks by day.

It was further agreed that "a standard of accuracy for night bombing cannot be estimated", but it was thought "that night attacks would not achieve appreciable results against 'precision' targets". It is to be presumed that the assumption of a three-hundred-yard day error was the result of the various bombing trials and experiments which had been carried out, and the failure to estimate the night error was certainly due to the lack of night bombing trials. It had, in fact, proved impossible to obtain figures for bombing accuracy by night under realistic conditions, because regulations prohibited practice bombing of an unlighted target at night.

The day error of three hundred yards was accepted as the tactical basis of the W.A. Plans which followed, and similarly, when the plans envisaged night bombing, the impossibility of getting good results against precision targets was pointed out. After the outbreak of war, the leaflet raids and reconnaissance flights which were carried out over Germany provided a source of evidence. A report on night bombing prospects, based on actual experience of night flying over Germany gained by No. 4 Group, was submitted to Bomber Command by the A.O.C. in October 1939. The whole question of night visibility depended, the A.O.C. No. 4 Group explained to Bomber Command Headquarters, on whether there was moonlight or darkness, whether the target was self-illuminating or blacked out, what the weather was like, and how strong the defences were. Assuming the weather was clear, it had proved possible on moonlight nights to see large areas of water from above 12,000 feet and small areas of water from below 6–8,000 feet. Roads, afforested areas, villages and small towns could not be distinguished from above 4–6,000 feet, and separate buildings could not be seen from above 3–4,500 feet. It would not be possible to fly low if the targets were defended, and from this the A.O.C. concluded that oil plants were "unsuitable targets" for moonlight attack. They could not be seen. On dark nights only self-illuminating targets were visible.

The A.O.C. No. 4 Group went on to suggest that it would therefore not normally be possible to sight the target on a night raid, and that the best way of bombing it would be by making a timed run from a recognisable landmark. This he hoped would produce accurate results. This belief was, however, evidently not shared by everyone. As an Air Ministry paper was soon to suggest, precision bombing by night would be "largely a matter of chance". This paper emphasised the radical differences between day and night bombing. "By day", it said, "selected objectives can usually be identified and attacked with reasonable accuracy. By night this is not so".

Between the production of these ideas and the beginning of the first bombing offensive an extraordinary and mysterious thing happened. Without any new device or fresh evidence to justify it, the average bombing error which had been estimated for day attacks, that is three hundred yards, was translated into a night bombing error for moonlight conditions. This estimate of three hundred yards was assumed in the course of the attacks on oil in 1940. It was used both as a means of calculating the weights of attack necessary to achieve the aim, and also as the yardstick of damage assessment.

Even as late as December/January 1940–1941, when the oil directive was being prepared, the three hundred yard aiming error remained as the "all important basis" of the calculations made. It was subsequently claimed by the Air Ministry that there was at the time "no concrete evidence" that this estimate was "other than a correct estimate", but it is hard to accept this claim in view of what the A.O.C. No. 4 Group had reported as early as October 1939. If the logic of his argument had been followed to the end, it should have become obvious that the estimate was far from correct. In any case no explanation was offered of how a rather flattering day bombing error was translated into a night error.

While these calculations, or rather miscalculations, about bombing errors had been proceeding, little or no attention had been paid to another and perhaps even more pressing problem, that of navigation. The first necessity was to find the target and the second to hit it. Even assuming that the crews could have seen their targets clearly at night, a precision bomb sight would be of little avail if the bomber was still fifty miles or more away from the target. In the absence of anything better, reliance had to be placed upon astro and Radio Direction Finding navigation as the only checks upon Dead Reckoning. Both these methods were profoundly unsuitable for operational flying, which could not be carried out on an even keel and steady course. Even under ideal conditions the fixes obtained by these means would never be exact and would frequently be inaccurate by twenty miles or more. Thus, the wind calculations would be wrong and the error would become cumulative.

Considerable navigation errors should therefore have been expected in night flying. These evidently were not, however, expected. Even the A.O.C. No. 4 Group, who had shown a most realistic attitude to the question of night visibility, does not appear to have anticipated difficulty in reaching specific landmarks in Germany for the final dead reckoning run into the target.

The consequences of the bombing error miscalculation and the failure to recognise the problem of air navigation at night must now be examined. When it is realised that the C.A.S. was deceived into suggesting to his colleagues of the Chiefs of Staff Committee that the oil offensive could be successfully accomplished by an average of ninety five sorties per month, that in turn the Chiefs of Staff were deceived into recommending the oil policy on this basis to the Defence Committee of the War Cabinet, then the magnitude of the mistake by miscalculation and default can be seen. The real trouble would appear to have been the failure to interpret rationally such limited evidence as did become available early in the war, the dilatory attitude towards the collection of further reliable evidence, and the complacent reliance upon false data. It was this reliance upon false data which preserved the illusions, once created, for an unnaturally long time.

The only reliable means of measuring the immense gap between expectation and realisation in the matter of bombing and navigating accuracy was the camera, but the authorities, confident of success and short of cameras, were content to rely upon much less sound evidence about the results which were being achieved. It was not until much later that the photograph, taken by the bomber to show its position at the time of bombing, and by the reconnaissance aircraft to show the condition of the target after it had been bombed, began to exercise a decisive influence upon the conduct of bombing operations. Then and then only were the counsels of realism to begin to weigh against those of illusion. Then the strategy and tactics of the first bombing offensive were to be abruptly and necessarily abandoned. The effective cause of failure in the first bombing offensive was therefore the inability of the bombers with the equipment which they possessed to find and hit the targets, but nearly a year of fruitless effort had to be expended before this was realised.

In the light of these observations it is now possible to proceed to an examination of the methods by which the illusion of accurate bombing and so the hopes of success in the first bombing offensive were sustained, and how only at the end of the year the whole structure of the offensive began to collapse under the impact of the first photographs.

The principal architect of continuous illusion, who had many accomplices, was the oil adviser to the Commander-in-Chief, Bomber Command. To him was committed the unenviable task of acting as a substitute to the almost non-existent camera. His was the imperfect eye through which the progress of the oil attack was seen.

The C-in-C Bomber Command obtained the services of Mr. Dewdney as his oil adviser as a result of a request which he made to the Air Ministry at the end of July 1940. He said that the services of an expert would be especially valuable to him in view of "the lack of information of the results of our bombing attacks, and the very small number of photographs which it has been found possible to take of objectives which have been bombed". By September Mr. Dewdney felt that he had collected enough evidence to make a first report to the C-in-C, and the memorandum which he submitted is of the greatest interest, for in the clearest terms it shows the methods which were adopted.

There were, according to Mr. Dewdney, six types of evidence to be considered before estimating the results of the attacks on oil plants. Direct evidence would be provided by reconnaissance photographs, pilots' reports and intelligence reports originating in Germany. Indirect evidence would be provided by analysing the results of German attacks on similar targets in Britain, examining oil samples from German aircraft shot down on British territory and considering the probable effect of the total weight of R.A.F. bombs dropped in relation to the size and type of the German target. Of these heads of evidence, the memorandum went on to point out, the first, that is photographs, were few in number and small in size. Those which were available revealed, in Mr. Dewdney's words, "disappointingly little apparent damage", but this was not accepted as a warning.

Much larger scale photographs of British targets which had been attacked by the German Air Force apparently showed much less damage than had in fact been caused, and it was expected that a "cautious upward revision" in the damage assessment of enemy targets which appeared to be more or less undamaged on small photographs would become possible after sufficient comparisons had been made between photographs of known damage in Britain and unknown damage in Germany.

Pilots' reports suffered from serious limitations. They only referred to a strictly limited time, and the pilot might have been deceived by appearances. A very impressive oil fire might, in fact, involve only a small quantity of oil. Intelligence reports from Germany were of course likely to be exaggerated and vague. Of the other types of evidence, Mr. Dewdney clearly felt that the most important was a mathematical calculation of the probable damage, worked out from the weight of bombs which had been dropped, taking the accepted aiming error as the basis. "However little damage appears in a photograph", he said, "an objective must have suffered damage in proportion to the weight of bombs dropped over it and this factor must be considered when assessing damage".

It was assumed that the attacks would be made from high level, and therefore that the average error in bomb aiming would be three hundred yards. It was further assumed that each bomb would cause complete destruction within a radius of twenty-five yards[3] from the point of explosion, and that the bombs would be dropped in sticks of four at fifty-yard intervals. Finally, the aim was stated to be to effect 75% destruction of the targets. Thus, if the calculation was to be used for planning, the necessary wight of attack would be 260 bombs for a target 10,000 yards square, 318 bombs for a target 160,000 yards square, and 530 for a target of half a million square yards.[4]

Similarly the amount of damage which had already been caused could be calculated by comparison of the ideal figures with those which had actually been achieved. The calculation was therefore obviously unsound. It would, for instance, make complete nonsense if the assumed bombing error of three hundred yards proved to be wrong. If, however, the calculation was to be accepted as a more reliable means of damage assessment than the photograph, even if it was a small photograph, then it was worse than unsound, it was positively dangerous. Yet it is clear that Mr. Dewdney did set more store by the calculation than any other single type of evidence. He was thus able to advise the C-in-C that he agreed with the Ministry of Economic Warfare that the results of the oil attack as far as it had proceeded in September 1940 were "satisfactory".

Thus, it appears that the mathematical method was to be the principal means of assessing the results of the bombing and therefore the basis of bombing policy. The other types of evidence were to be ancillary to this. They would provide checks upon the mathematical method, not alternatives to it. Thus, more photographs were wanted, but they were to be looked at critically, almost suspiciously, pilot's reports were to be improved in scope and accuracy if possible and German raids on British oil were to be used as a check on British raids on German oil.

The first task seemed to be to improve the content of the pilot's reports. As a result of Mr Dewdney's memorandum of 4 September 1940, the Senior Air Staff Officer, (S.A.S.O.) Bomber Command circulated a note to the Bomber Groups pointing out that in the absence of photographs the main source of information about the results of the attacks on oil would have to come from the pilot's reports. The importance of these reports being accurate was therefore stressed. The crews were expected to report on the size of the explosions, their colour, the appearance and colour of the smoke and so on, which they caused or witnessed.

A few days later the S.A.S.O. sent the Group Headquarters a questionnaire for the guidance of intelligence officers in collecting information from the operational crews. This questionnaire, which had been prepared by Mr. Dewdney, showed more precisely the type of information which was wanted. For instance, if the target map had no details, how did the buildings run and where were the chimneys in relation to the buildings? If the chimneys were hit, were they the ones near the distillation columns, the concrete boxes or the power house? These and similar questions must have brought a smile to the faces of the flying men who were actually supposed to pick out these details as the passed rapidly over the targets at considerable speed and height in the dark, even if there was a moon. It is indeed surprising that Bomber Command Headquarters allowed the questionnaire to pass to the Groups, especially as this was done by the S.A.S.O. (A.V.M. Bottomley) who had himself less than a year before forwarded to the Air Ministry without unfavourable comment the report by the A.O.C. No.4 Group, enlarging upon the impossibility of seeing individual buildings at all, let alone their chimneys.

Even more surprising is the absence of immediate representations from the Groups on the subject of night flying and the difficulties of seeing much if anything. Perhaps the Groups, and within the Groups, the squadrons, were reluctant to be the first to admit the truth. So, the operational crews must have rubbed their eyes and looked again. It was not until February 1941 that Mr. Dewdney was convinced by personal conversation with these crews that it was "the exception for the target itself to be visible to the bomb aimer during an attack because of searchlight activity and the height to which the aircraft are forced by flak", a point which, as has been seen, he could equally well have learned in October 1939. Even then it was an extraordinary thing that the Commander-in-Chief, Bomber Command, should have received this piece of information from a civilian adviser. As a check upon the mathematical calculation, the pilot's report was therefore of little more value than the calculation itself.

Another, and intrinsically a much sounder, method of checking the mathematical calculation would have been derived from photographs. The tasks of taking and interpreting photographs, which were eventually to be discharged with great distinction by the Photographic Reconnaissance Unit (P.R.U.) and the Central Interpretation Unit (C.I.U.) were, however, during the first bombing offensive still in a state of arrested development. The nucleus of what was to become the P.R.U. was still uneasy as an official part of the R.A.F. The official mind clashed with the unorthodox imagination of its original sponsors, and while protracted disputes about who should have control of the organisation, the Air Ministry, Bomber Command or Coastal Command, were going on, the photographs which were taken remained small in size and few in number. Of these, many necessarily were of no value to the strategic bombing offensive. There was only a small force of aircraft and men to cater for wide requirements with equipment inadequate both in quantity and quality.

Similarly, the nucleus of the future Central Interpretation Unit was in a raw condition. The Air Ministry had only begun to interpret its own photographs in March 1938 and it is therefore not surprising to find that the early activities of the intelligence section, which was charged with this task, so recently taken over from the army, were conspicuously unsuccessful at the time of the first bombing offensive. Bomber Command, which was interpreting its own pictures, was meeting with little more success, but a civilian organisation, the Aircraft Operating Company Limited, seemed to hold out better prospects.

For various reasons, this Company had been pressing its services on the Air Ministry ever since the Munich Crisis, but they had, unfortunately, been turned down with equal persistence. Eventually in February 1940 the success of the Wild apparatus in dealing with the small photographs which were available, and which had been designated as useless by the

Air Ministry, drew official attention to the Company, and after that it was gradually absorbed into the Service.

Thus, the foundations of the P.R.U. and the C.I.U. were, if not 'well and truly', at least laid. The benefits which were to flow from their work in the course of time, did not amount to much in the first bombing offensive. Thus, as a check upon the mathematical calculation of bombing error, photographic reconnaissance of bombed targets was not an operative element. This is not to say that there were no photographs which might not have provided a clue. As Mr. Dewdney had remarked in September 1940, a study of the photographs which had been taken of the bombed oil plants revealed "disappointingly little apparent damage". This, however, he took to be reflection on the photographs, not upon the accuracy of the bombing. The shock of the truth was yet to come.

Meanwhile, as a possible means of assisting in damage assessment, and as a certain means of revealing navigation errors, the camera, carried by the bomber, was still in desperately short supply. As late as the 13 January 1941 the C-in-C Bomber Command felt it necessary to make a direct appeal to Lord Beaverbrook, the Minister of Aircraft Production. The C-in-C explained that officially the establishment was four cameras per squadron.

There were at the time twenty-five operational squadrons of heavy bombers, and eight more were due to become operational in the near future. There were also nine medium squadrons. Thus, the number of cameras should have been 168. Actually, there were thirteen modified cameras and nine unmodified in service. Six more were due to arrive within the next week, and after that none were expected for a fortnight. To this extent it was unlikely that the navigation error was going to be revealed by photographic evidence produced by the operational squadrons. It was, however, even more unlikely that errors being made by navigators in the final and vital stages of their training would come to light, for at the operational training units there were no night cameras at all.

Substantially, then, the mathematical calculation of probable damage, based upon a theoretical bombing error, stood alone as a means of determining the course of the first bombing offensive, and on 22 October 1940 Mr. Dewdney produced another memorandum which was to have important consequences.

Since September he had had many discussions with various experts, and as a result he was able to reach certain assumptions about the vulnerability of oil plants, and the speed at which they could recover from bomb damage. Whether these assumptions were correct or not, is not in the afterlight a matter of great importance, for they of course assumed that bomb damage was being inflicted. The basic element of the damage assessment which Mr. Dewdney now produced was still the mathematical calculation of the damage inflicted on the plants derived from probability nomograms. These nomograms in turn depended on the assumption that the average aiming error was three hundred yards.

From this Mr. Dewdney estimated that the loss of synthetic production, which had been inflicted on the German synthetic plants by bombing between 15 May and 5 October, amounted to about 100,000 tons. This estimate, he thought, was "conservative" and though he was not prepared to guarantee the estimates which followed about the condition of the individual plants,[5] he did feel confident that the overall loss really did amount to at least 1,000,000 tons. This figure represented a loss of 15% of the nominal output of the plants concerned.

Now this reduction in output was not in itself likely to have a decisive effect upon the German war machine, but if it was related to the effort which had been expended by Bomber Command, it was likely to have a marked influence on the course of the bombing offensive. Mr. Geoffrey Lloyd's Committee accepted Mr. Dewdney's estimate and showed that this result had been achieved by the expenditure of only 539 tons of bombs. Therefore, a mere 6.7% of the total bombing effort had apparently destroyed a potential 100,000 tons of German oil. If this was so, and the Lloyd Committee did admit that the estimate was tentative, then the argument for intensifying the attack was almost irrefutable, especially as Mr. Geoffrey Lloyd's Committee had now given expression to the 'Dewdney method' at Cabinet level. In fact, the fifth report of the Lloyd Committee which had embodied these estimates was to prove the decisive argument in favour of the policy which found formal expression in the January oil directive.

While, however, these discussions about the intensification of the oil offensive were taking place at a high level, evidence came to light which threatened the whole basis of the policy which was being decided. On 24

December 1940 "excellent" photographs were at last taken of Scholven and Gelsenkirchen which showed both plants to be working and "apparently undamaged". The lesson came too late to save the Defence Committee of the Cabinet from going on record with a policy which was now indicated as impracticable, but the photographs did cause a stir in the Air Ministry which eventually spread upwards to the Chiefs of Staff and the Cabinet. In fact, they were the death blow to the plan of the oil attack, to the strategy of precision bombing at night.

Mr. Dewdney at once realised that a large proportion of the bombs, which he had previously assumed had been finding their targets, had in fact fallen elsewhere. It was "quite evident" to him that "the average aiming error in at least some of the sorties" had "greatly exceeded" three hundred yards. It was "very desirable that a figure as close to the practical truth as possible should be adopted".

A telling blow had been struck at theoretical calculations and unreliable evidence, but its full weight was not at once registered. Revolutions occur suddenly, but their effects can only be slowly discerned. There could, however be no return to the ancien régime after the Gelsenkirchen and Scholven photographs. The Air Staff were now in a more critical frame of mind and great changes in bombing policy were impending.

Part II

The First Lessons of Experience: A New Design for the Bombing Offensive, 1941

Chapter 3

The Transition from Precision Attack to Area Bombing

On 9 July 1941 a bombing directive was issued which carried Bomber Command back into the Battle of Germany after its long defensive diversion in the Battle of the Atlantic. Already the German army had invaded Russia, and, apart from the continued threat to her shipping in the Atlantic, Britain enjoyed a much greater freedom from the pressing needs of defence than had been the case in 1940. All the same the resumed bomber offensive did not last long, for six months after it had been launched it exhausted itself. The steady toll which the German defences exacted from the attacking British bombers began to threaten the future of the force and in the winter of 1941 the need to conserve bombers became the first consideration.

This continued emphasis on the need to conserve the force showed that Bomber Command in 1941 was still an investment for the future. In fact, the second bombing offensive was envisaged as the first instalment of a massive and long drawn out assault on Germany, which was only to reach full smaturity in the spring of 1943. When the war began British Ministers had proclaimed that it would last for at least three years, but the disasters of 1940 had made that seem an understatement. Yet the first bombing offensive had, at least in theory, been designed to produce quick results. It had been an application of the 'knock out blow' theory. Circumstances had militated against the success of that offensive but there had been enough bombing by both sides to show some of the limitations from which the bomber suffered. The plans for the first bombing offensive had been largely based upon theoretical assumptions, but the plans for the second could rest, at least in part, upon lessons learnt.

The most important of these lessons was that night bombing, particularly in the moonless periods, could not approximate in accuracy to day attacks. Thus, the bomb dropped at night was a much less destructive weapon than had been expected, when it was aimed at a small target. If, however, it was aimed at a target which was so large that it could scarcely be missed, then there seemed every reason to suppose that confidence in the ultimate efficacy of strategic bombing need not be reduced. Oil targets were small and therefore extremely difficult to hit, except in the best conditions of light and weather which were rare.

The problem was to define a new programme for Bomber Command which could be carried out by a force which was small in size, inaccurate in aim, and blind in the dark, but which was in the future to be greatly improved not only in size, but also in quality. This, then, was the problem which confronted the Air Staff and Chiefs of Staff when, during the months in which Bomber Command was absorbed in the Battle of the Atlantic, they were searching for a new policy.

When in March 1941 Bomber Command was diverted from the oil offensive to the Battle of the Atlantic, the prospects of carrying out the January directive had already become bleak. In the first six weeks of the full-scale oil attack the C-in-C had found it possible to direct his bombers against the synthetic oil plants on not more than three nights because of the bad weather. The prospects of shorter hours of darkness in the spring and summer lent little hope of improvement. The Prime Minister's March ruling was therefore no more than a coup de grâce signifying the end of an offensive in which confidence was already waning.

A more important explanation of this declining confidence in the oil plan, was the dawning realisation that the bombers were technically incapable of destroying the oil plants. This had been impressed upon the Air Staff by the photographs of Scholven and Gelsenkirchen. There was as yet no conclusive evidence about what the bombers could achieve, but there was at least some clear indication of one of the things they could not do. Thus, empirical methods were beginning to supplant the doctrinaire element in planning.

It was obvious that the average aiming error at night was much greater than three hundred yards, and under normal weather conditions, the Bomber Operations Directorate of the Air Ministry concluded, it was probably in the region of a thousand yards. In the best conditions of moonlight, they still hoped that the error might be no more than six hundred yards, but even during this period, which would in any case last for only about a quarter of every month, it would be necessary to have excellent weather conditions as well. If these estimates were still optimistic, they were sufficiently realistic to show that the oil offensive could not be continued. The targets were too small. For tactical reasons alone a new bombing policy would have to be worked out, and larger targets would have to be sought.

Even so the conception of selective bombing died hard, and the Air Ministry persisted in the search for a target which was at once vital to Germany and limited enough for the R.A.F. The belief that it would still be possible to bomb with an error of no more than six hundred yards suggested that it would be tactically possible to hit railway centres. The idea of attacking German transport was not new. There had been various plans before the war, and in the autumn of 1940 the D.C.A.S. had thought that this might be "one of the most important contributions" which could be made to the disruption of the German economy. In the following January the Chiefs of Staff had shown that they shared this view.

At the time, however, the idea of attacking transport had been in discredit because of the abortive attempts which had been made against Hamm, Soest and Osnabrück in 1940. To reject the plan on this evidence seemed to the D.B. Ops. unreasonable in April 1941. He pointed out that these 1940 attacks had been on a slight scale. In fact, the average scale of attack in the period from June to December 1940 had worked out at about two aircraft per target. On the heaviest raids it seemed that only about eight bombs could have hit the target, and on the average only about half a bomb. The "much heavier loads" which could be carried in 1941, amounting to as much as twenty tons of bombs per target, would, he believed, produce very different results.

Also, since these early attacks on German transport, Hitler had extended his activities over nearly the whole of Europe and into Africa. He was compelled to shoulder heavy responsibilities in Italy. He was confronted with the "most gigantic task of economic management ever attempted". The interchange of goods from unaccustomed sources by unusual channels to peoples of varying degrees of hostility would, it seemed, tax German ingenuity and resources to the breaking point. Transport might indeed prove to be one of the "weakest links in the German economic chain".

Although the bombing of the German transport system might appear to be an enormous task far beyond the resources of Bomber Command in 1941, there was a concentrated area of activity in and around the Ruhr which seemed to offer a short cut to success. The isolation of the Ruhr by the successful bombing of its railways would, the D.B. Ops. claimed, have the same effect upon Germany that the severance of the lines of communication across the Atlantic would have for Britain. Thus, the attack could be brought within the scope of the small force which Bomber Command had ready to strike.

According to the British Railway experts, an attack amounting to twenty tons of bombs should put a junction out of action completely for a week, and it would result in reduced railway operations for a much longer period. Thus, it seemed possible to isolate the Ruhr by the destruction of its most important railway centres during one moon period. This estimate was, as was admitted at the time, based upon a calculation, and not upon direct evidence. There had not yet been a comparable attack on railways by the R.A.F. or the Luftwaffe. The inference was that the task might be stiffer, but in any case, it did seem to be a promising employment for Bomber Command. The task appeared to be tactically possible, strategically profitable, and commensurate with the size of the Command.

This plan would not, however, provide full time employment for Bomber Command, for the railway attacks could only be carried out when there was a coincidence of moonlight and good weather. Thus, it appeared that "approximately three quarters of every month" could be considered as "only suitable for the blitzing of cities and towns or large targets on the edge of water". This suggested the desirability and indeed the inevitability of undertaking an attack on the morale of the German people. Quite apart from the tactical arguments which compelled the consideration of such a plan, there was a powerful body of opinion which favoured its adoption on strategic grounds.

There was a strong conviction in the minds of responsible men in Britain that German morale was a potential source of weakness to the nation at war. There could be little doubt that Hitler had been right when he claimed that the German army had been stabbed in the back in 1918, it did not seem unreasonable to suppose that the same result could not be obtained by bombing. The psychological results of bombing were of course impossible to calculate in advance of the event, but the supposition was that they might be catastrophic.

Before the war the British had been seriously alarmed that the Luftwaffe might succeed in knocking Britain out of the war by a concerted attack upon her larger cities, and the danger of morale breaking down had been thought at least sufficiently serious to justify defence schemes at R.A.F. aerodromes against "angry or frightened mobs of civilians". The resilience of the British people under the attack of the Luftwaffe in 1940 and 1941 had somewhat chastened these alarmist views, but it was believed in Britain that German morale would not show the same firmness. "All the evidence goes to prove", the Ministry of Information reported in December 1940, "that the Germans, for all their present confidence and cockiness will not stand a quarter of the bombing that the British have shown they can take".

This kind of advice had not greatly interested the Air Staff while they still believed that they could achieve decisive results by the oil offensive. When that hope collapsed, however, it became the living material of a new plan. Sir Robert Vansittart could, then, have scarcely chosen a more opportune moment than the end of February 1941 to send to Sir Archibald Sinclair a memorandum which had been written by a former German Staff Officer and war pilot urging the attack on morale.

This German ex-officer said that Britain must not hesitate to adopt the methods of total war, and to regard German morale as a "military objective of the first importance". It was not a question merely of taking reprisals but of damaging the war capacity of the opponent, and finally of destroying it. Hitler's prestige, he thought, would be seriously undermined if the German people suffered seriously in the war. He thought that the German Government had exposed their own weakness in launching an attack against British morale. They had expected their enemy's morale to be as weak as that in their own country. Britain would, the German ex-officer suggested, miss her best opportunity if, on the other hand, she assumed that German morale was as sound as her own. She should, he urged, strike at German morale.

At the Air Ministry these comments were received sympathetically, and it was thought that they fitted in generally with the direction in which Air Staff thought was moving. In fact, the C.A.S. had only just drafted a note expressing no confidence in the oil plan and proposing that when the offensive was resumed the attack should be switched to industrial cities. Indeed, the Ministry of Information and Sir Robert Vansittart were not alone in urging the Air Staff to this course of action. The Ministry of Economic Warfare and the Political Intelligence Department were competing with each other to expose the weakness of German morale, and their recommendations were supported by public and private individuals alike. The reasoning of these arguments was often obscure and sometimes hysterical,[1] but it was nevertheless beginning to exercise a decisive influence upon bombing policy.

There was therefore a powerful strategic sanction for the plan to make a direct attack upon German morale, and tactically this seemed to be the only task which Bomber Command could perform during the dark period of the month, which was after all the greater part of the month. All the same it had to be remembered that a severe German attack had failed to break British morale, and even if every allowance was made for the greater weakness of Germany in this respect, it was obvious that a colossal effort would be needed to achieve the aim.

The D.B. Ops. thought that it would be many months until the force was large enough to undertake the task, and he feared that it might never be big enough to make the attack sufficiently widespread.

The D.B. Ops. might be pessimistic about this, but not so Lord Trenchard. To him the problem was simple. The R.A.F. must be expanded until Bomber Command could deal a crushing blow to German morale. The evidence of two wars suggested to Lord Trenchard that Germany was peculiarly susceptible to bombing, and it was here that the R.A.F. "should strike and strike again". If ships at sea were attacked then 99% of the effort would be wasted, for 99% of the bombs would fall into the sea. If targets in occupied territory were bombed, then 99% of the effort would be worse than wasted, for the bombs would kill and disturb old friends and allies. If, however, targets in German cities were bombed, then 99% of the bombs would contribute directly to the destruction of German morale. This form of attack should be mounted every night, even if on occasion it was possible to send only one machine. The offensive should be carried to every quarter of Greater Germany from the near West to Berlin, Munich, Stuttgart and eventually Vienna as well in the East.

To achieve this, Lord Trenchard was prepared to admit, would require a large force and would be a costly adventure. The casualties might amount on occasions to 70% of the first line in a month and four to five hundred per cent reserves would be needed behind the front line. The production of long-range bombers would have to enjoy absolute priority, and men would have to be found to fly them, if necessary, at the expense of the Fleet Air Arm, the Army Co-operation squadrons, Fighter Command and the Photographic Reconnaissance squadrons. The diversion of this great force on to invasion ports as required by the army, on to naval targets as required by the Admiralty, or on to oil targets in Rotterdam, as suggested by the Ministry of Economic Warfare, would have to be rejected.

Lord Trenchard had little doubt that if the bombers went often enough and in great enough strength to Germany, the morale of the country could be broken. Meanwhile the Army and Navy would have to face the fact that they could make no contribution to victory until Bomber Command had cleared the way. Thus, by aiming at, or rather missing, targets in the German cities, Bomber Command could, in the view of Lord Trenchard, make its greatest contribution to victory.

Considerations of defence, or rather of survival, made it impossible for the Chiefs of Staff, burdened with the responsibilities of office, to adopt wholeheartedly the adventurous and single-minded attitude which had characterised Lord Trenchard's views, but they did agree with him in his principal diagnosis when they recorded their view that "the most vulnerable point in the German nation at war is the morale of her civilian population under air attack".

The Chiefs of Staff did feel that Lord Trenchard's paper was, as the First Sea Lord put it, "a complete overstatement". Many of the diversions which Lord Trenchard had hoped to eliminate would have to be maintained. In particular, air co-operation in the Battle of the Atlantic would have to be continued. Defence would have to be provided for, before offensive action could be taken. Not only would it be impossible to concentrate the entire effort of Bomber Command against Germany, but it would also be impossible to accord long range bombers unconditional priority in construction. It would still be necessary to maintain a strong Fighter Command and Fleet Air Arm. In other words, the Chiefs of Staff agreed with Lord Trenchard that the most promising target for Bomber Command was the morale of the German people, but they disagreed with his suggestion that the Command could be so rapidly expanded that the task could be undertaken as a primary aim at once.

They therefore suggested to the Prime Minister that this attack on morale should be adopted as the long-term aim of the force which would come to fruition when the force had, in the course of time, expanded to the necessary dimensions. In the meantime, as a short-term policy, the main target for Bomber Command should be the German transport system. The attack on transport would, they pointed out, be a contribution to the long-term aim of reducing morale.

This advice was accepted by the Defence Committee of the Cabinet towards the end of June and so the way was open for the resumption of the offensive, the beginning of the second bombing offensive.

In the new directive, which was sent out on 9 July 1941, the C-in-C was therefore told that the weakest points in the German system lay in her civilian morale and inland transport. The main attack was to fall on the Ruhr area, where the immediate object was to disrupt the railway system, and the long-term aim was to smash morale. Nine railway centres were chosen for attack, and it was hoped that the destruction of these would isolate the Ruhr from the rest of Germany. These attacks were to be carried out on the rare occasions of moonlight and good weather. On the other nights the bombs were to be aimed at the towns which contained these railway centres. Morale attacks were also to be aimed at Hamburg, Bremen, Hanover, Frankfurt and Stuttgart to prevent a concentration of the German defences.

Thus, in theory at least, Bomber Command was enabled to keep up an almost continuous offensive, for the targets which had been selected were the tactical complement of each other. On good nights the railway centres would be bombed and on dark nights the city centres would be the focus of the attack. These targets were also regarded as strategically complementary, for it was believed that the attack on the railways, though primarily aimed to achieve economic effects, would also impose a strain on morale, for everyday life depended on the smooth functioning of transport. Also, many of the bombs aimed at the railways would clearly fall on the built-up areas near them.

The attack on the city centres, though primarily intended to reduce morale, would also, it was hoped, increase economic strain. Apart from the need to perform certain diversionary functions, notably against German capital ships and U-boat construction yards, and the need to spread the German defences, the theory was that most of the attacks would fall on the highly concentrated area of the Ruhr. This was, in effect, a re-creation of the Ruhr plan, on which such high hopes had been placed at the beginning of the war.

Thus, Bomber Command was to strike in the war of two fronts, the front of economy and the front of morale. Indeed, it did not appear that there was any other route to victory for Britain. The German army consisted of about two hundred and fifty divisions, ninety of which were available for operations anywhere. This army had the support of a powerful air force, and Germany was in control of the greater part of Europe. In days gone by Britain had been able to exploit her strength at sea, and had succeeded in using inferior numbers of her troops against the outlying forces of her enemy. Thus, for instance, Wellington had been able to build up his forces in Spain against the Napoleonic armies, and eventually he was able to cross the French frontier.

The advent of the aeroplane and the mechanisation of transport had changed all this, and in 1941 it appeared that there was nowhere on the Continent that the British, even if they could achieve a landing, could prevent the Germans concentrating rapidly and driving them back into the sea. The action at Dieppe in the following year pointed the lesson. Nevertheless, it was obvious that if Britain was to defeat Germany, she would have to occupy some portions of the Continent. If she was incapable of defeating the German army in the field, the only way to do this was so to undermine the economic strength and the morale of her enemy so that a landing would ultimately become a practical proposition of war.

For this purpose, the blockade alone would not suffice. The extent of German land conquests gave her a certain immunity from this type of warfare. Through France she gained access to the resources of French North Africa, and through Russia she had been able to draw on the resources of the Far East, South America and even the U.S.A. Her military and political prestige was such that in the event of difficulties she would be in a strong position to meet them. Spain, for instance, she could probably have brought within her orbit by no more than an ultimatum, and in any case there was nothing Britain could do if she decided to invade that country. In 1941 Britain and not Germany was the country in danger of defeat by blockade and as Lord Trenchard had said, the sea was for Britain a source of danger as well as of strength.

This indicated that the first blows to achieve victory would have to be struck by Bomber Command, and this was the responsibility which was recognised in the July directive. All the same it remained questionable whether Bomber Command was technically capable of performing this role. In the course of the second bombing offensive it became increasingly obvious that the plan to isolate the Ruhr was based on assumptions which were still too optimistic about the tactical abilities of the Command. In particular the belief that it would be possible to bomb with an error no greater than six hundred yards was a wholly unrealistic deduction.

In time the fact had to be faced that the bombers of 1941 were not capable of any type of precision attack at night. It was no more possible to dislocate railway centres than it was to destroy oil plants. About five to six thousand tons of bombs were dropped to establish this, and after October the transport attack began to wither away. By February it had ceased almost entirely, and it was only in March 1944 in very different circumstances that it was resumed. Like the oil offensive it was doomed to early abandonment and late revival.

The failure of the transport attack of 1941 was the death rattle of the conception of the "knock out blow" The stark fact was that Bomber Command was neither large nor efficient enough to achieve quick and decisive results. It then appeared that the bombing offensive would have to be long, sustained and of increasing weight. Bomber Command was to be the agent, not of a "knock out blow" but of a war of attrition. The

Air Staff were no longer looking for decisive results in 1941, or even 1942. They were now looking to 1943, in which year they hoped to deploy no fewer than four thousand bombers.

For the time being at least, then, precision attack was out of the question. This meant that the morale attack had to assume responsibility not only for the destruction of the German will to make war, but also for the destruction of the German means to do so. Thus, the war on two fronts was to be waged by one means: area attack, and the success of the bombing offensive was now seen to depend either upon effective area attack, or upon the introduction of technical aids to make the resumption of precision bombing feasible.

The technical failure of Bomber Command to succeed with precision attacks did not, however, do more than accelerate the acceptance of a strategy which had already been planned for the future. Already at the end of July the Chiefs of Staff had declared the intention to proceed to "a planned attack on civilian morale, with the intensity and continuity which are essential if a general breakdown is to be produced". If the force could be sufficiently expanded, they felt confident to forecast that "the effect will be shattering". No less confident forecasts had been made about the prospects of the oil offensive and the attack on transport, and these high hopes did not ensure the future of the morale offensive. Nor on the other hand was the morale attack likely to be rejected on its early results, which would necessarily be small, for it was recognised in this case that the results would not come for some considerable time.

The future of the morale offensive depended rather upon whether its strategy could be expressed in convincing terms, and whether the tactical means and technical aids to make area bombing effective could be devised.

The details of the area bombing technique were worked out in the late summer and early autumn of 1941 and, for the first time, actual experience and photographic evidence formed the principal basis of the discussion. The German Air Force had been attacking British cities and towns, Coventry, London, Portsmouth, Birmingham, Liverpool and many others. The material damage here could be seen, the psychological effect and the industrial dislocation could be calculated.[2] The number of German bombers employed could be ascertained, if not exactly at least approximately. Their tactics and technique could also be considered. Photographs of R.A.F. damage in Germany were becoming increasingly available. Comparisons could be made, conclusions drawn, and from them calculations for the future could be attempted.

Working on these lines an "index of activity" in English towns after air attack was reached. This index covered the psychological as well as the material damage. Production in a factory might be stopped or slowed down because its gas, water, or electricity supply was cut off, or because its workers absented themselves as a result of nervous strain, lack of food, or fatigue. If therefore it could be decided to what level this index of activity had to be reduced, then an examination of German bombing in Britain should indicate the amount and type of effort required to perform the task. For this purpose, the German attack on Coventry on the 14/15 November 1940 was considered.

The original estimate of this German attack had suggested that its weight had worked out at about one ton of bombs per five hundred of the population and this estimate was based on the assumption that 90% of the German force actually reached the target area. This figure had been reached by counting the aircraft plotted over the target at the time, and it was obviously inaccurate, since a single aircraft might have been plotted several times.

Evidence which subsequently came to light from work done by the Bomb Census Organisation suggested that in average conditions not more than 20–30% of the German force actually reached their targets. In good weather the proportion would be higher. For instance, when Birmingham was bombed in good conditions on 9/10 April 1941, it was suggested that 37% of the force reached the target. The conditions on 14/15 November 1940 were similar to those of 9/10 April 1941 so it seemed reasonable to assume that 40%, not 90% of the German force despatched had actually attacked Coventry. This meant that the weight of the attack worked out at about one ton of bombs per eight hundred and not per five hundred of the population.

The reduction in the "index of activity" at Coventry had been 63% on the morning after the raid and recovery took thirty-five days. The reduction at Coventry corresponded to proportionate drops in the activity of other English towns which had been bombed. It had to be admitted that the cumulative reduction in the index of activity resulting from successive raids was difficult to calculate, but it seemed reasonable to assume that the level of activity would become progressively lower after each succeeding attack, provided sufficient time for recovery, that is about thirty days, was denied the town. After the fourth or fifth monthly raid on the Coventry scale, the index of activity should be reduced to nil and after six raids, it should be "beyond all hope of recovery". The ideal would therefore seem to be to deliver six "Coventry" raids in six nights, but since this was hardly possible, it would be better to deliver the six attacks over six months at regular intervals. Even this would limit very greatly the number of towns which could be attacked at all, and in practice it was thought it might be preferable to attempt the partial destruction of a larger number of towns rather than the complete destruction of a smaller number.

A compromise would be to deal with one particular area of towns at a time. The author of this suggestion must have had the Ruhr in mind, though he did not actually mention it. These calculations and observations indicated the number and frequency of attacks which should be made, six in not more than six months, and also the scale of attack required, one ton of bombs per eight hundred of population.

The next problem was to determine which German towns should be attacked. The object was to destroy a sufficient number of towns to ensure that Germany's power to continue the war was demolished. Forty-three towns were selected with a total population of fifteen million, approximately 20% of the total German population, and it included the majority of places with a population of over 100,000. The complete reduction of the index of activity in all these forty-three towns would, it was felt, certainly prove decisive.

Here then, apparently, was a certain way to victory, but the force to accomplish the task still had to be created. Another problem remaining to be solved was therefore the size of the force which would be required. Assuming that 25% of the bombers despatched would actually attack the target, the weight of bombs to be lifted would therefore have to be four times as great as that required to do the necessary damage. It was also assumed that each squadron in Bomber Command with sixteen I.E. aircraft[3] could operate one hundred sorties per month at all times of the year, and further that the average bomb lift of each bomber in the 1942/3 force would be three tons. Thus, the force required would be:

Tonnage to be dropped monthly on the 43 towns populated by 15,000,000 people at 1 ton per 800 persons.	18,750 tons
Tonnage to be lifted from base, assuming 25% of aircraft will actually attack.	75,000 tons
No. of Squadrons (16 I.E.) at 3 tons per aircraft.	250
Total number of heavy bombers.	4,000

These figures were indicative, not precise. It would still be necessary to bomb diversionary targets. Squadrons might fail to operate one hundred sorties per month, but the Lancasters and Stirlings might carry more than three tons each. "We certainly cannot do with less bombers", the report ended, "We may well need more." If these assumptions were correct, then the war could be won by the monthly discharge of 18,750 tons of bombs on the selected targets for a period of six months, and it is perhaps not out of place to point out here that Bomber Command claimed to have dropped 147,000 tons on towns in 1943, 204,000 in 1944 and over 478,000 tons in the whole war.

If, however, there was much to be learnt from the German air raids, because, for the British, it was so much easier to examine the results of them, there might also be lessons which the German Air Force could teach the R.A.F. by virtue of greater efficiency, and possibly greater experience.

A comparative study of photographs of German towns bombed by the R.A.F. and British towns bombed by the Luftwaffe with forces of approximately the same size showed that the British towns were much more seriously damaged. The Air Staff believed that the British high explosive bombs used on these raids were at least as efficient as the German ones, but the fact that the German bombers carried a much higher proportion of incendiary bombs than did the R.A.F. seemed to be extremely significant. The German proportion of incendiary to H.E.

bombs had been as high as 60% and averaged about 30%, whereas the R.A.F. proportion averaged 15%, though on occasions it rose to 30%.

The German technique was to open the raid with a fire-raising attack and then to follow up with high explosives. The R.A.F. normally mixed the incendiaries evenly with the H.E. bombs. Certainly, these German tactics seemed more profitable than the British. Responsible members of the London Fire Brigade affirmed the difficulties associated with saturation fire raising tactics.

The Vice Chief of the Air Staff was not convinced that incendiary bombs were the sole explanation of the German Air Force's greater success. He thought the German firefighting services were better prepared than the British and he thought the R.A.F.'s failure to attack often enough, or in great enough strength, against a single target was an important factor. Nevertheless, he took "no great exception" to what had been suggested, and he did not object to these views being put before the C-in-C Bomber Command, and this was done of 29 September 1941 when the C-in-C was invited to try out the technique on the first opportunity. The C-in-C said that he agreed generally with the idea of incendiary attack, but he pointed out certain disadvantages.

He said that he had tried the technique of opening with a fire-raising attack in the winter of 1940–41, but had abandoned it because of the difficulty of ensuring that the fires were started in the right place.[4] He was also not convinced that German technique was superior to British, and he declared that a report by the Central Interpretation Unit showed that the damage inflicted on Münster, Aachen and Kiel compared favourably with that done to Coventry, Bristol and Southampton.

No one in a responsible position seemed to doubt the wisdom of the strategy of morale bombing. Criticisms of the new technique, now being worked out for area bombing, were hesitant, and as no one seriously entertained the possibilities of causing an immediate break down of German morale, the future of the whole plan seemed assured, at least until either it was found that the necessary numbers of bombers could not be built or until they had been built and had delivered their loads.

The policy of area bombing was therefore likely to survive for a very long time, unless it could be rapidly destroyed almost at its inception. Such a threat did arise, also at the end of September, when the C.A.S.

suggested that it might be more profitable to revert to the old idea, which had not been intentionally tried in practice, of spreading the offensive far and wide over Germany. This he felt might result in much greater psychological effect and not much less material damage than the concentrated area policy. At least, the C.A.S. thought it was worth trying during the winter months as an experiment, and it seemed to be one way of evading the "unpleasant fact" that 75% of the bombers dispatched were failing to attack the intended area targets.

According to the advocates of concentrated area bombing, in whose ranks was the V.C.A.S., this was a heresy, one which Lord Trenchard had fallen into earlier in the year, and one which the C.A.S. had himself always condemned up to now. The V.C.A.S., who had the D.C.A.S. and the D.B. Ops. behind him, told the C.A.S. that he felt "very strongly" about this matter. He believed that it was possible to achieve material and psychological damage only by concentrated attacks. The German raids had proved this, he thought. Scattered German raids in July and August 1940 had stimulated British morale, but a few months later concentrated raids were causing serious concern to the Ministry of Aircraft Production because of the absenteeism which followed. If they had been able to obtain an even greater concentration, the breaking point of British resistance might have been reached. German morale could not be so dissimilar to British that its destruction required the maximum dispersal whereas the destruction of British morale required maximum concentration. In any case the 75% of the bombers which failed to find their concentrated targets would equally fail to find their dispersed targets. The thing to do was to look for ways of improving the concentration of bombing, not for alternatives to it.

If, however, the C.A.S.'s suggestion had been accepted, it would have been no more than formal recognition of what was already happening. Bomber Command crews were already dropping their bombs where they could rather than where they intended to, particularly in bad weather.

For instance, on the night of 1/2 October 1941 when Bomber Command was supposed to be bombing Karlsruhe and Stuttgart, they were reported over Aachen, Eupen, Malmédy, Coblenz, Neuwied, Kreuznach, Frankfurt-am-Main, Wiesbaden, Limburg, Darmstadt, Mainz, Worms,

Trier, Offenberg, Saarpfalz, Nuremburg, Erlangen, Bamberg, Bayreuth, Coburg, Pegnitz, Aschaffenburg, Schweinfurt, Würzburg, Regensburg, Weiden and Chemnitz. Certainly, if area bombing was to be the policy of the future, there was some considerable room for improvement! For the advocates of dispersed bombing there would be compensations for a long time to come, even if their views were rejected on the policy level. It is clear, however, that the V.C.A.S. won his argument and the Air Staff set their faces against dispersed bombing. On 19 October the C.A.S. told the Prime Minister that the C-in-C was aiming to concentrate his bombers at the rate of one hundred an hour in the moon periods, and at eighty an hour on dark nights.

The strategy of morale bombing was accepted, the tactics of concentrated area bombing were approved. It remained to expand the force to proportions commensurate with the task, and it was this last consideration which resulted in a delay of three months in the application of the offensive. In November the Prime Minister ruled that the Bomber Force must be conserved. The casualties could not be borne. The attack must be delayed.

Many inspired ideas, calculations, guesses, and some not so inspired, had now gone towards making a policy for Bomber Command. Henceforth the bombing offensive was to unfold logically and almost inevitably. The crisis of decision had been passed. Only the future could deliver a verdict on what was one of the most fateful decisions in the annals of warfare.

Chapter 4

The Weapon More Accurately Measured and the Origins of Strategic Misconception

"It is not reasonable to speak of the air offensive as if it were going to finish the war by itself. It is improbable that any terrorization of the civil population which could be achieved by air attack would compel the Government of a great nation to surrender.

"Familiarity with bombardment, a good system of dug-outs or shelters, a strong control by police and military authorities, should be sufficient to preserve the national fighting power unimpaired. In our own case we have seen the combative spirit of the people roused, and not quelled, by the German air raids.

"Nothing that we have learned of the capacity of the German population to endure suffering justifies us in assuming that they could be cowed into submission by such methods, or, indeed that they would not be rendered more desperately resolved by them. Therefore, our air offensive should consistently be directed at striking at the bases and communications upon whose structure the fighting power of his armies and his fleets of the sea and of the air, depend. Any injury which comes to the civil population from this process of attack must be regarded as incidental and inevitable."[1]

Thus wrote Mr. Winston Churchill, not in 1947, but in 1917. It is true that great advances had been made in the field of air warfare between 1917 and 1941, and that the bombing which was carried out in the First World War can only be compared to that which was done in the Second as the infant can be compared to the young man, but Germany was the same country and the Germans were the same people in both wars. If defeat in 1918 had bowed the heads of Germans, surely the victories of 1940 had re-created memories of 1870. Yet it was in 1941 that the first decisive steps were taken towards the policy of seeking victory by the direct bombing of the German people. Moreover, this was at the very time that the realisation was dawning that the bomber was not such an efficient weapon as had been believed before the war.

As has already emerged, the explanation of this apparently curious tendency was the realisation that Bomber Command, with its 1941 standard of efficiency, could not attack anything other than large targets with any prospects of success, allied with the strong belief, shared by those in the highest positions, that the German people were ready to break down, panic or even revolt under the impact of really intensive bombing.

Strategically the attack on morale appeared to be the most effective contribution which bombing could make to German collapse. Tactically it seemed to be the only contribution which it could make, at least until new bombing and navigation aids were ready. In this chapter it is therefore intended to examine the development of those empirical methods of assessing the tactical and technical capabilities of the bombers, which had their origins in the Gelsenkirchen and Scholven photographs taken at the end of the first bombing offensive. This is important because, as has been seen, the new evidence which was produced played a major part in the formation of the tactics of area bombing, and so the strategy of attacking German morale.

After this it will be possible to turn to an examination of the basis of this strategy, to trace the growth of strategic misconception about the state of Germany and the stamina of her people. Only when these basic elements in the bombing offensive have been mastered, will it be possible to proceed, in the later chapters, to see how the offensive matured into the mighty assault which was presently to engulf every corner of Germany, to absorb such a large proportion of the productive and fighting capacity, not only of Britain but of the U.S.A. as well, and to see what effect this effort had upon the fighting capacity of Hitler's Europe.

The immediate problem therefore to examine the tactical sanction for area bombing, which was fully justified in so far as it showed that nothing else was possible for the bomber at that time, and also the strategic sanction for the morale attack, which, as an independent strategic conception, rested on a much less sure foundation.

It has already been seen how the oil offensive was abandoned, when it was at last recognised that the average bombing error was greater than six hundred yards. The new offensive began with the assumption that a six-hundred-yard bombing error was something reasonable to expect in good weather and moonlight. This assumption had been the basis of the railway plan. As the offensive developed, however, it gradually became apparent that the crux of the problem did not lie in bomb aiming at all, though that difficulty remained, but in navigation. Not only the Air Staff, but the Government as well, began to see that a large proportion of the bombers were not finding their way to the targets at all.

In other words, 1941 saw the recognition that the immediate task was to devise means of getting the aircraft over the appointed area, not of trying to identify particular targets in that area. The term, target area, came to mean an expanse of seventy-five square miles. The object was no longer a plant or even a railway junction. It therefore became obvious, before the second offensive was over, that nothing could be gained by persisting with the plan of attack on the German railways outlined in the July directive.

It was the agency of photography which, following upon the shock it had registered when the pictures of Gelsenkirchen and Scholven were examined, brought about this revolution in tactical appreciation. The camera was, in this period, the most important single factor exerting influence on those who had to say what the bomber could do, and what should be done if its performance was to be improved.

The Gelsenkirchen and Scholven photographs had done more than put the oil offensive out of court, they had put the whole school of experts out of effective business. The destruction of the principle of calculating bomb damage and tactical possibilities by mathematical means was followed by a great access of interest, not unnaturally, in the more reliable but less easily available photograph.

As will presently be seen the R.A.F. had to pay a heavy price for the failure to grapple earlier with the problem of air photography, and night photography in particular. But already there was some evidence upon which to work. The Gelsenkirchen and Scholven photographs were reconnaissance pictures taken in daylight after the bombing attacks. They showed that the bombers had failed to destroy, or even to damage the target, they did not explain why. This was a question which could be answered by photographs taken by the bombers at the moment they delivered their bombs. These would show approximately, if not yet precisely, where the bombs had fallen, and so would show the difference between the position in which the navigator thought the aircraft was and the position in which it actually was.

This method of analysis would not of course be of much value, if the bombs had been missing the targets by a matter of hundreds of yards. It would, however, be of great interest if it showed that the bombers were missing the targets by a matter of several miles or even tens of miles. Lord Cherwell became interested in this possibility, and he invited Mr. Butt to conduct an examination of night photographs taken by the bombers to see what could be deduced.

On 18 August, Mr. Butt submitted his report to Bomber Command. It was based on the research he had been doing during the previous fortnight, and he explained that he had made no attempt to study day reconnaissance photographs, which he had neither the time nor the skill to interpret. Nor had he attempted a comparative study of damage in British and German towns. These tasks, he thought, should be undertaken by qualified experts, but he felt confident that their conclusions would confirm what now appeared in his report.

The report was based on summaries of operations and other documentary records as well as photographs taken by the bombers themselves. Several of these documents were found to have been inadequately completed, and the photographs themselves were subject to certain errors, caused by banking of the aircraft at the time of exposure, delay in launching the flare, and changes in speed, height and direction at the vital moment. Mr. Butt therefore frankly admitted that his figures might be subject to some correction. Nevertheless, he felt confident that the broad picture which he presented was correct.

He had collected the bulk of his evidence from about six hundred and fifty photographs taken during night bombing between 2 June and 25 July 1941. They related to twenty-eight targets, forty-eight nights and one hundred separate raids.[2] For the purpose of argument, the report assumed "target area" to be an area within five miles of the aiming point. An analysis of 633 photographs purporting to show the target, the target area or the supposed target area, showed that 113 or 18% were outside the target area, 194 or 31% were within the target area and 326 or 51% could not be plotted.

The Photographic Interpretation Section at Bomber Command felt certain that all those photographs which could not be plotted were in fact outside the target area, and Mr. Butt was willing to accept this verdict on the grounds that a section, which he said had examined 750,000 prints, should be in a position to judge. Assuming then that this represented a fair sample, which Mr. Butt thought it did, since it covered more than one in ten of the sorties which had claimed to have attacked the target, it was possible to conclude that, of the aircraft which thought they had attacked the target, only 31% had actually done so by the evidence of the camera. It was true that nearly half of these photographs had not been taken simultaneously with the bombing, but in each case the position of the photograph had been stated by the crew. These were therefore included as being equally good checks of navigation. Even if they were excluded, they did not materially alter the figure of 31% of actual attacks.

This was, however, only 31% of the aircraft which claimed to have attacked the target. Since only 66% of the aircraft which were dispatched claimed to have attacked the target, this meant that from the total number of bombers sent to the targets only one fifth had actually attacked them. It was therefore possible to suggest that, in the period under review, out of the total of 6,103 bombers which had been dispatched and from which 4,065 claimed to have attacked, in fact, only about 1,200 had really done so. Even worse, many of the aircraft in this one fifth would, in fact, have dropped their bombs in open country because of the very large size (seventy-five square miles) which had been assumed for the target area.

Even these gloomy figures were not, however, the whole story. If the French targets, which were easier to find, were excluded from the calculation, then it appeared that one quarter, not one third, of the bombers claiming to have attacked their targets actually did so. Considering the problem from the point of view of the easier and the more difficult targets, the following ratios were calculated:

Germany all targets	100
French Ports	215
German Ports	125
Ruhr	25

After considering statistically the effects of moonlight, haze and cloud upon the accuracy of bombing, the report concluded with the suggestion that this should be the starting point for more intense research. Day photographs should be examined, for from these, a check upon the numbers of bombers which had attacked their targets could be worked out. Comparative work should be done on the differences between the damage in Britain and the supposed damage in Germany, and a special statistical officer at Bomber Command should be empowered to carry on this type of work.

Meanwhile, the report pointed out that night photographs were the best means of checking navigation errors, which seemed now to appear as a problem of the first importance. The camera was really the only reliable means of finding out the navigation error, for the camera did not make mistakes, was not deceived by appearances and was not subject to human strain. "Conclusions drawn from photographs should be completely reliable." When the automatic cameras were available, it should then be possible to cut out even such human error as did occur in the use of the simplified cameras.

Lord Cherwell read the report and found it depressing. He at once addressed the Prime Minister on the urgency of doing something to improve the accuracy of navigation in Bomber Command. The implication of what had been revealed did not evade Mr. Churchill who told the C.A.S. "This is a very serious paper, and seems to require your most urgent attention. I await your proposals for action."

The C.A.S. replied a week later admitting the "supreme importance of improving our navigational methods" which he regarded "as perhaps the greatest of the operational problems confronting us at the present time." He proposed to grapple with this problem be expanding the newly formed Operational Research Section at Bomber Command, endeavouring to improve the standard of astro-navigation, by training expert fire raising crews to indicate the targets, by developing marker bombs, both pyrotechnic and radio, by investigating A.S.V. as a possible aid to navigation, and by the development of the new radar navigation aid called Gee.[3]

The Butt report had not only drawn attention at the highest levels to the appalling inaccuracy of night navigation, but it also resulted in vigorous action to overcome the difficulties associated with navigation. This was a problem which had hitherto been largely neglected, and this neglect had given rise to a feeling among navigators that the force in which they served was a "pilot's air force."

Now at last after two years of war something better was promised. The C.A.S. in his minute to the Prime Minister had shown the whole future design of the force. He had forecast the function of the Path Finder Force, he had indicated the future marker bombers, he had promised Gee and he was going to investigate the possibilities of another radar aid, which eventually emerged as H2S. Only Oboe was required to complete the basic radar devices which were later to show the way to targets. Indeed, the only suggestion made by the C.A.S., which had no future, was the intention to improve the standard of astro-navigation. Yet until the first radar aids did come into service, there did not seem to be much else that could be suggested. This concentration on the fundamental problem of navigation at the highest level, and the realisation which it implied of the very poor results which were being obtained by the 1941 force was irresistible. The optimists, who had until now advanced almost unopposed, suddenly found themselves fighting a rear-guard action, which presently ceased altogether.

When he read in the Butt report that only one in five of the aircraft which he had dispatched had actually reached their targets, the C-in-C's reason was inclined to reject the evidence of Mr. Butt's eyes. "I don't think at this rate", he wrote, "we could have hoped to produce the damage which is known to have been achieved."[4] The A.O.C. No. 4 Group was later to go further than this when he said that "the lack of a photograph of the precise target should not be regarded as conclusive proof that the aircraft failed to attack its proper objective".

The inference was that the blame might reside with the camera, not with the navigator. All the same the seriousness of the problem itself, and the recognition it had received in high quarters, precluded any possibility of disposing of it by sophistry. Nor can it be said that Bomber Command, shocked as they undoubtedly were by the report, made any serious effort to do so. They did, of course, draw attention to points in the report which they considered showed them in an unnecessarily poor light. The S.A.S.O., for instance emphasised that the weather in June and

July had been particularly unfavourable for bombing, and that a sample of 10% of the sorties flown could not be accepted as an entirely reliable means of assessing the results of the whole force. He underlined this last point by suggesting that the Squadron Commanders would tend to give such cameras as were available to the crews in which they had the least confidence.[5]

On the contrary, Bomber Command displayed a commendable vigour in following the implications of the report. Immediate plans for the establishment of an Operational Research Section were going ahead and the C-in-C sent the Groups under his command a summary of the Butt report on 13 September and went on to speak of the "urgent need for improved navigation". He exhorted his Group Commanders to take a "very close" interest in the performance of the operational navigators and in the training of new navigators. A detailed investigation of the problem, conducted by an officer from Bomber Command at the stations, however, revealed that very little could be done until the new radar aid was introduced to service. The first step in solving a problem is, however, to recognise it, and this at least had now been taken.

The introduction of Gee into operational service was not such a simple problem as it might have appeared. The Air Staff were alive to the fact that the Germans would not be slow to devise counter measures, which Lord Cherwell had gone so far as to suggest would ultimately leave us "as badly off as we are now". It was therefore obvious wisdom that the risk of having the secret unravelled should not be taken until a force of impressive size could be equipped.[6] The Air Ministry thought that it would be possible to equip twenty squadrons early in 1942, and that after February, supplies would make it possible to keep those squadrons equipped. After May 1942 full production would be achieved. There was therefore going to be a rather alarmingly long interval during the remaining months of 1941, when little or nothing could be done to solve the navigation problem. This indeed may have been an argument for the conservation policy which was, as has already been seen, about to be laid down.

The immediate need, as Mr. Butt had already pointed out, was to collect more evidence, so that the conclusions which had already been reached could be checked and expanded. The main source of this further evidence would of course lie in more photographs and better photographs. Here, however, there were great difficulties and a substantial legacy of previous neglect to be overcome. Circumstances demanded the operational use of night cameras before their technical development had been completed.

When, therefore, the need arose, there were no cameras entirely suitable ready for mass production. There was also disagreement on the specification of the ideal camera for night photography, which made it impossible immediately to remedy the situation. There was also a good deal of muddled thinking about the functions of night photography. Some felt that it was required for damage assessment. The A.O.C. No. 5 Group was even prepared to record the view that night photography used as a check upon navigation was dangerous. It would "revive the prejudice amongst crews", he said, "of regarding the camera as the official spy – a prejudice which we have been at such pains to kill".

Bomber Command fortunately stuck to the opinion, which they had expressed as early as April, that the object of carrying night cameras was for "the primary purpose of establishing that they (the bombers) reached their proper objective."

Now if the object was to check navigation error, then the simplified night camera, which could be produced in reasonable numbers at reasonably short notice, would provide adequate if not perfect results. If on the other hand the object was to assess damage, then the simplified camera was not adequate, for fires could not be plotted on its pictures. Obviously much better damage assessments could be made by day photographs, taken of the target as a whole after the attack by aircraft of the P.R.U., which was now beginning to produce better results.

Nevertheless, Bomber Command refused to accept the logic of this argument, even though it was of their own making. They insisted that it was necessary to be able to plot the fires. Accordingly, to the dismay of the Directorate of Photography at the Air Ministry, they insisted on having the automatic night camera, whose performance was still unreliable, and whose large-scale production had not begun at all.

Despite frequent requests to relax this attitude, Bomber Command insisted for some time upon accepting only a limited number of the simplified cameras, and even these they took with a bad grace. It was not until 31 August that Bomber Command finally agreed to accept the simplified camera, for by that time they had found out that fires could not be plotted on photographs taken by the automatic camera. Thus, the introduction of night photography was slowed down, and many pictures proved to be valueless because of the erratic performance of the automatic camera. Bomber Command was right to insist on the need for improving the cameras, but it was wrong not to accept such cameras as were available until this had been done.

Thus, by the end of 1941 the revolution which had been begun by the Gelsenkirchen and Scholven photographs, and which had been secured by the Butt report, was complete. Sufficient evidence had come to light to give a true picture of the inaccuracy of night bombing. Earlier theoretical methods of calculating tactical possibilities had been disposed of. There was still a great deal to be done, but what was most important had already been done. The period of tactical delusion was at an end. Whatever other implications it may have had, the most important achievement of this revolution was to justify the decision to abandon precision bombing at night. Area bombing alone was tactically worth thinking about, and even that required a greater degree of accuracy than could readily be obtained. What effect the future radar aids would have upon this conclusion only the future could tell but it is certain that at its inception nothing tactically more ambitious than area bombing was feasible.

It now remains to consider the strategic assumptions which seemed to justify the attack on morale, for without a strategic sanction it is inconceivable that the area bombing could ever have been undertaken.

Ever since almost the first days of military aviation there had been speculation about the effect bombing might have upon civilian populations. Bombing in the First World War had not been sufficiently extended to provide any factual solution to this gnawing problem. As the scope of aerial warfare was seen to develop, so the field of speculation about its results was broadened. H.G. Wells conjured from his fertile imagination a horrific picture of what could happen. Giulio Douhet saw the possibility of France falling in three days under the bombing of four of her cities. He believed that a "people who are bombed today as they were yesterday, who know that they will be bombed again tomorrow and see no end to their martyrdom, are bound to call for peace at length".

On a more serious level, British experts envisaged the possibility of catastrophic casualties in the cities of Britain in the very first days of the war, rather as a Congressional Committee in the United States of America had been told that 40,000,000 Americans might be killed in the first hours of atomic warfare. Intensive air raid precaution propaganda, rumours from Spain and colourful accounts in the press brought the fear of bombing into the hearts and homes of the masses. These fears, after the experience of the Second World War, may seem almost hysterical, but at the time they seemed very real. It is today difficult to estimate precisely what was the effect of bombing on the German people. How much more difficult it was to estimate what this effect would be before the bombs had fallen.

Yet when British leaders adopted morale bombing as a policy, many bombs had already fallen. London, Coventry, Bristol, Southampton, Hull and Glasgow had already apparently given the lie to Douhet. The shock had been great and the damage grievous, but the people remained in their occupations. The war effort was, surprisingly, almost unimpeded. This proved that the German Air Force, which was the most powerful in the world, had failed to break the morale of the British people. This was either a great victory for the British people, or a revelation that bombing was not nearly so terrible a weapon as had been supposed. In the view of British experts, it was neither. The German bombing had failed because it was not heavy enough, not long enough sustained. It proved that the German Air Force had not been powerful enough. Douhet had not been wrong in principle, but Göring, had underestimated the stamina of the British people.

What then were the prospects of the R.A.F. succeeding where the Luftwaffe had failed? They still seemed good enough if the offensive was mounted in sufficient strength and efficiency. No one can prove conclusively even today that it would have been physically impossible to bomb the Germans into submission. All that can be said is that the blow which was struck failed to do this. The real test is, however, not so much whether the aim could be achieved by unlimited forces, but whether in practice the prospects of doing so within the limitations of reason justified the attempt.

Let us therefore examine the chief ideas which inspired the British to attempt this gigantic task. First and foremost, there was the difficulty, and, if the offensive tradition of Bomber Command was to be maintained, the impossibility of doing anything else. But there were other sanctions of a less compelling nature. It was not categorically suggested that Germany could be knocked out by the same proportionate bombardment that the British had already withstood, but it was claimed that the Germans would not show the same stomach for the ordeal. The Nazi régime was thought unstable, the people disillusioned, fearful. A greater effort by far than the Luftwaffe had attempted would therefore surely make the R.A.F. their conquerors. The emphasis may have been on the greater effort required, which was a realistic deduction, but the belief that German morale was more vulnerable than British was a dangerous assumption, which subsequent events have disproved. Nevertheless, it was an assumption which existed at the conception of the attack on German morale, though Mr. Churchill had warned against it more than twenty years before.

Much of the information which the British received about the instability of the Nazi régime came from ex-German citizens whom that same régime had driven into exile, often after terrible persecution. It would have been unreasonable to expect these people to present a realistic and unbiased picture of Nazi prospects in Germany. Their views were bound to be coloured by past fears and future hopes.

Hitler was a figure comparable to Napoleon in that he covered his people with the glory of conquest. He vindicated them from the bitterly resented stigma of defeat. His control over his people was considerably more effective then Napoleon's; Himmler was as efficient as Fouché, Goebbels was certainly more loyal than Talleyrand. The invention of wireless and the mechanisation of transport had extended the tentacles of Government far beyond anything known to Napoleon. Yet Napoleon's power had proved astonishingly resilient even after great military disasters.

Indeed, these disasters may have strengthened his hold on the French people. In the case of Germany, the Nazi régime retained its grip on government till the eve of an all-engulfing collapse. The stresses of bombing, not mortal in themselves, may even have strengthened the position of the régime. The pledge that British bombers would never reach Germany was indeed shown to have been absurd, but the crisis when it arose made a naturally submissive people more submissive. In Britain the crisis of Dunkirk had closed the ranks of the country, and people had voluntarily accepted a greater degree of governmental control than ever before. The probability that the Germans would react in the opposite sense was therefore hardly based on historical reasoning.

It was believed, however, that the Germans, unlike the British, did not have their hearts in the war, that they were unwilling to make sacrifices and that when the vision of rapid and almost bloodless victory receded, they would instantly react under the impact of further hardship caused by bombing. Subsequent events were to reveal this assumption as groundless. The Germans continued the struggle against hopeless odds long after defeat had become inevitable. They showed themselves to be stoical in adversity and resolute in defeat. The British view of the morale of the German people, so confidently expressed by Lord Trenchard and shared by nearly all those who occupied an important position, was one of the major strategic misconceptions of the war.

Some explanation of how this misconception arose may be provided by the belief that the Germans were suffering under a severely depressed standard of living, and that their war effort from the earliest days was absorbing every ounce of their strength. In fact, this was not the case at all. Dr. Wagenfuehr has subsequently pointed out how reluctantly any drop in the civilian standard of living was permitted. "In other words, intoxicated by early military successes, people considered it unnecessary to devote all energies to increasing armament, believing that a lesser effort would be sufficient."

In fact, according to the indices of civilian expenditure on consumer goods, the British standard of living declined much more precipitately than the German. In 1940, according to this analysis, the standard of living in Germany remained at the 1938 level, while in Britain it had declined by 13%. Similarly, the Germans did not see the necessity for total mobilisation, or the need to exact the last ounce from their people, until much later than the British. As a striking example of German adherence to their peace time economy, the numbers of domestic servants in Germany remained substantially unchanged throughout the war, whereas in Britain their number was probably reduced by two thirds. Again, in the first two years of war the number of German women in productive work declined by about half a million, and subsequent increases barely raised their number above the pre-war level.

This may have meant that Germany was living in a fool's paradise, and that her comparative lack of effort in the first two years of the war cost her dear when greater tasks had to be faced. Clearly Germany underestimated the power of her enemies, notably of Russia, while Britain greatly overestimated the effort Germany was making. The true position may therefore have ultimately been a decisive factor in German defeat, but at the same time it did provide a great slack both in economy and morale which could be taken up in time of emergency. British Intelligence did not perceive this slack, and therefore gravely exaggerated the extent of German exhaustion. This was the second principal strategic misconception which contributed to the plan of morale bombing.

The implications of this misconception were far-reaching in their effect upon the bombing offensive. These reflections do not, of course, prove that the policy of bombing German morale was necessarily wrong. They do, however, suggest that the task of breaking morale in Germany was a stiffer proposition than was generally recognised. They indicate that the main assumptions underlying the strategy were unreliable and, in some cases, clearly wrong. Whether those misconceptions would prove fatal to the success of the offensive, only the offensive itself could demonstrate, and this was still, in 1941, a thing of the rather distant future.

The failure of Bomber Command to break the morale of the German people must have been due either to the fact that the Germans were invulnerable to that form of attack, in which case the chief blame must rest with the intelligence which suggested the contrary, or to the fact that, though the German people were vulnerable, the attack was not sufficiently heavy or sustained. In that case responsibility for the failure would rest mainly on those who diverted the force to alternative targets, or upon anyone who continued to exaggerate the capability of the bomber. These were complex questions, which it is desirable to indicate here, but only to answer at a later stage.

The bombing offensive against German morale cannot be dismissed simply as a failure or a success. Between these two extremes there could be many degrees of achievement. Morale could be reduced without being destroyed. There are also many other factors to be considered. The pursuit of the primary aim might, for instance, result in secondary achievements. An attack on morale might result in industrial dislocation. These two aims came in fact to be closely identified. The main object here has been to indicate the foundations on which the conception of morale bombing rested. Later chapters will take up the question of what was built on these.

However insecure these foundations may appear to have been in the strategic sense, there was always, at least in 1941, the compelling fact of the bomber's limitations to be borne in mind. In war, as Moltke remarked, one must do what one can, not what one ought.

Part III

The Crisis for Bomber Command, 1942

Chapter 5

The Attack on German Morale

The third year of the war brought a crisis for Bomber Command which threatened its continued existence as an independent weapon. For two years it had been almost the sole means by which Britain, bereft of allies and hard pressed on every front on land, on the sea, and in the air, could conduct offensive operations against an enemy who seemed to enjoy an otherwise unchallenged supremacy. But the British bombing of Germany had failed to reduce the German oil production and supplies, it had failed to dislocate German transport and, if it had been a source of encouragement to British morale, it had not yet had any perceptible effect on German morale. Judged by any standard it had achieved practically nothing, and judged by the standard of what it had been thought before the war could be achieved by bombing, its performance had been lamentable. The time had come to decide whether better results could be achieved in the future.

Many of the difficulties which had in 1940 and 1941 prevented Bomber Command from achieving decisive results were now already solved, or at least on the way to solution. The introduction of Gee, which was imminent, would alleviate the problem of night navigation, and perhaps of bomb aiming as well. The lessons of experience and the products of scientific research promised to introduce a more successful phase into the annals of air warfare. Incendiarism, yet to be tried on a large scale by the R.A.F., seemed to offer a more serious threat to Germany than high explosives.

More efficient four-engine bombers, including the Lancaster, were coming into service to replace the famous but by now obsolete Wellingtons, Hampdens and Whitleys. Last but not least, the experience of the first two years of war had taught the Air Staff many lessons, both tactical and strategic. Whatever else they did, they would hardly repeat the mistakes of thinking that German's oil plants could be wiped out by a few bombers in a few months. Nor would they trust calculations of damage without the evidence of the photograph to support them.

Apart, however, from these improved prospects for Bomber Command, the whole war situation had undergone a remarkable change in recent months. In June 1941 Hitler had embarked upon another Blitzkrieg. He had dealt a staggering blow at Russia, but this time, despite phenomenal achievements, his enemy did not collapse. During the winter Russia had fought back strongly, and at the beginning of 1942 she confronted Germany as a formidable enemy and Britain as a powerful, if remote, ally. Then in December Japan had attacked the American Fleet at Pearl Harbor, and Hitler had declared war upon the U.S.A. Thus in 1942 Hitler no longer faced a resolute, but isolated enemy. He faced a grand alliance, whose unity, if not entirely voluntary, was likely to last at least as long as he did.

These events which ultimately proved so favourable to Britain and disastrous for Germany were not necessarily so favourable to Bomber Command. America, now at war with two first class military powers, began to absorb her own armaments production. In particular, American bombers which would in other circumstances have found their way on to R.A.F. aerodromes would now find their way onto American aerodromes from where they would be flown by American crews. The prospects of the Air Staff ever deploying four to six thousand British bombers became remote indeed.

If, however, Bomber Command therefore had to face a more meagre future, it also had to face a certain loss of prestige. With the Russian army already in the field and the American army on the way, it could no longer claim that it was the sole means of ultimate victory. Plans for a continental invasion and the subsequent development of major operations in the west became a real military possibility and a diplomatic necessity. If Bomber Command could win the war in the meantime so much the better, but it would not receive that unconditional support which it might have counted on in different circumstances.

So far from enjoying the monopoly of offensive operations, the Air Staff now had to convince those in authority that Bomber Command could make a useful independent contribution to victory. If this could not be done, then the force was threatened with extinction or at least with demotion to the role of auxiliary weapon. This was the real hour of crisis for the advocates of the independent bomber force, and 1942 was the year in which they came to grips with their critics.

The Air Staff were resolved to attempt the gigantic task of breaking German morale by concentrated area bombing, and we have already seen that this resolve was the product of despair and hope; despair at the failure to destroy selective targets by precision attacks, and hope that, with the technical advances which had been made, city centres would prove to be easier and more vulnerable targets than railways, oil plants and factories had shown themselves to be.

The strength of the case was its ambiguity. It was difficult to say how the Germans would react to the impact of concentrated bombing. It was impossible to say that precision bombing might not suddenly become a practical possibility. In addition to this, the machinery, both administrative and productive, for this offensive was already in motion. On the whole it would be easier to maintain the old idea than to reverse it at this late stage, especially as there was no immediate prospect of landing on the Continent and so proving to the Russians that they were not fighting alone.

These arguments, strong as they seemed to those who were in any case inclined to advocate the continued bombing offensive, offered loopholes to those who did not. There was, for instance, a complete lack of concrete evidence to show the validity of the argument. In fact, all the evidence showed the failure of independent bombing both British and German. If this was due merely to bad strategy, inadequate strength and undeveloped technique, strength was still relatively weak, and the new strategy and improved technique had not yet established anything, for the simple reason that they had not yet been tried. To the bewildered arbiters it seemed impossible to give judgement. In the absence of factual proof, the prospects of the bomber offensive seemed to be a matter of opinion, not of jurisdiction. Indeed, this was not a crisis which could be solved by words. Deeds alone would suffice, and this the Air Staff was not slow to appreciate. The trial of this case was therefore to be conducted over the towns and cities of Germany.

"We Allies", Mr. Churchill wrote in July 1942, "have the Air Power. In the days when we were fighting alone, we answered the question: "How are you going to win the war?" by saying "We will shatter Germany by bombing." Since then the enormous injuries inflicted on the German Army and manpower by the Russians, and the accession of the manpower and munitions of the United States, have rendered other possibilities open. We look forward to mass invasion of the Continent by liberating armies, and general revolt of the populations against the Hitler tyranny. All the same, it would be a mistake to cast aside our original thought which, it may be mentioned, is also strong in American minds, namely that the severe, ruthless bombing of Germany on an ever-increasing scale will not only cripple her war effort, including U-Boat and aircraft production, but will also create conditions intolerable to the mass of the German population".

This was the role of Bomber Command, as it appeared to the Head of the British Government, and if its duties seemed slightly less exalted than they had been when "we were fighting alone" they exceeded what many believed to be possible and some desirable. When Mr. Churchill wrote these words the Thousand Bomber Raids had already taken place, and the bombing offensive against German morale was already under way. The offensive had not, however, been begun without considerable opposition.

During the winter of 1941–1942 the bombing offensive had petered out, and soon after the Cabinet decision to conserve the force had been made known, the C-in-C received a further direction from the Air Ministry. This informed him that his "primary task" was to be the attack on the three German capital ships which were lying at Brest. Until Gee was ready for operational use, this delay in the offensive against Germany was not likely to be so distasteful to the Air Staff. They might have no great confidence that the bombers would succeed in destroying the *Scharnhorst* and *Gneisenau*, but they also knew their limitations in the bombing of Germany.

By the end of January 1942, the position was different. The failure to destroy the German capital ships was becoming embarrassing. Gee which was now ready to go into operational service would make the task no easier, but it would greatly facilitate the bombing of Germany, for which it had been designed and over which its transmitters were about to send waves. The time had come to consider the resumption of the bombing offensive.[1]

The Air Staff accordingly gave their attention to the preparation of a case for the return of the Battle of Germany. Apart from the impending introduction of Gee into service, which was important not only because it offered such improved prospects of success, but because it was urgent that the greatest benefit should be got from it before the Germans devised counter measures, there were several other arguments which could be brought forward in support of the claim that Bomber Command should now resume the offensive.

Germany had suffered severe reverses in Russia during the winter, which, it seemed likely, would have had a depressing effect upon the morale of the previously victorious nation. This would therefore seem to have been an excellent opportunity to drive home the lesson that Germany had other enemies as well as Russia. The hard-cold weather was considered to be ideal for the new incendiary technique which had been devised, but not yet tried on any scale. It was also hoped that the resumption of the offensive would enhearten the Russians to whom it must certainly have seemed at the time that they were fighting single-handedly.

The decision to attack morale as the primary target had already been taken, and indeed the offensive had been begun in 1941, but the idea of attacking precision targets on favourable occasions was not abandoned. The range of Gee seemed to indicate that the best area targets to attack would be in the Ruhr. This was the case which the Secretary of State for Air put to his colleagues on the Defence Committee on 9 February 1942.

The C.A.S. had no illusions as to the probable opposition which these suggestions would arouse. This opposition was not, however, at the time sufficiently vociferous to prevent Cabinet approval of the suggestions, perhaps, as the C.A.S. had suggested, because of the dazzling prospects which Gee seemed to offer. It was therefore possible for the Air Staff to issue the February directive.

On the very day that this directive was issued, 14 February 1942, the Prime Minister had written to the Secretary of State for Air and the C.A.S. "The Brest question has settled itself by the escape of the enemy" and he had added that he was "entirely in favour of the resumption of full bombing of Germany". Once more the conditions for independent offensive bombing seemed to have returned, as they had done almost exactly a year before in January 1941. The third bombing offensive was about to begin, but the directive which initiated it was unlike any previous directive, in that for the first time the question of bombing policy was approached principally from the point of view of what could be done. Indeed, the directive was called at Bomber Command the "T.R.1335 directive". Gee, a technical aid, was in fact one of the best elements of the policy which was now decided.

The principal focus of the attack which was about to develop should, the directive explained, be the "morale of the enemy civil population and in particular, of the industrial workers". This was to be assailed by area bombing, and the targets were carefully selected with the anticipated range of Gee (350 miles) in mind. The four primary targets in the Ruhr selected were Essen, Duisburg, Düsseldorf and Cologne. There were a number of other alternative industrial areas indicated, some within and some beyond Gee range. The main attack was, however, to be on the Ruhr, and within the Ruhr, Essen was thought to be the most important target. The directive looked beyond area bombing and went on to point out that it was possible that the results of Gee would be good enough to reintroduce precision bombing. A number of precise targets were therefore indicated for this event.

Bombing directives were not intended to be precise executive orders. They were more in the nature of statements of general policy, which it was left to the Commander-in-Chief to interpret as best he could in the prevailing tactical conditions. They were usually followed by signals and letters modifying them from time to time, and they are not an accurate guide to the course of operations which were actually carried out. Not infrequently they were somewhat vaguely worded even as statements of policy.

This February directive must, however, be ranked as one of the most important documents of the bombing offensive. It marked the beginning of business-like war against Germany in the air. The ultimate object of Bomber Command was as ambitious as ever, but the futile hopes of 1940 and 1941 had been abandoned in the light of experience. The increasing appreciation of the difficulties of night bombing brought a tone of much greater realism to deliberations about bombing policy than had been apparent before, and it is significant to note the change of emphasis in the definition of the aims of the morale attack.

The Background to the Bombing Offensive   71

The idea of attacking the German people with the object of scaring them into surrender, though it was not abandoned, now gave place to the idea of destroying their houses and amenities, and if possible, their lives as well, with the object of disrupting the industrial system of the nation. If this could be accomplished, then Germany would have been forced and not scared into surrender. The target was the people in their homes and the C.A.S. wanted it made clear to the C-in-C that the built-up areas of the towns, not the docks or the factories, were to be the aiming points.

If, however the February directive represented a policy of much increased tactical realism, it was still a strategic gamble, and there were many who doubted if it was a gamble which would come off. There was, in fact, a feeling of marked uneasiness about the bomber offensive in what the Air Ministry described as "unofficial circles". This feeling was reflected in the House of Commons. The Government, which had been recently reconstructed was passing through stormy waters, for the war situation was bleak. "Within a month after the announcement that the great coalition had been formed, there were alarming evidences that it was about to be knocked to pieces by the blows delivered by the reinforced Germans in Africa and the staggering procession of Japanese conquests southward and westward.

The manifold accomplishments of the Arcadia Conference[2] appeared to be so many melancholy scraps of paper.[3] Mr. Churchill described the fall of Singapore, which surrendered to Japanese forces on 15 February, as "the greatest disaster to British arms which our history records".[4] Everywhere the Japanese were pressing forwards towards what must be recorded as one of the most rapid conquests of an empire. The *Prince of Wales* and the *Repulse* had been sunk, and the American fleet lay in ruins in Pearl Harbor. If the tide had turned in Russia and the Middle East, the situation was still dangerous on both those fronts. And as if to rub salt into these wounds the *Scharnhorst*, *Gneisenau* and *Prince Eugen* had escaped from Brest on 11 February and thence sailed up the Channel and back to Germany under the gallant, but largely ineffective, attacks of the R.A.F. and the Fleet Air Arm. It is therefore not surprising to find that Parliamentary nerves had become somewhat frayed. There was hopeful speculation in Berlin about the impending fall from power of Mr. Churchill,[5] and to Goebbels the inclusion of Sir Clifford Cripps in the Government was a cause of particular celebration.[6]

Whether this appointment would be equally a cause of celebration for the British Air Staff became extremely doubtful as a result of a significant statement which the new Lord Privy Seal made in the Commons on 25 February 1942, when he was summing up at the end of a two-day debate on the war situation.

"Another question which has been raised by a great number of Members", he said, "is the question of the policy as to the continued use of heavy bombers and the bombing of Germany. A number of Hon. Members have questioned whether, in the existing circumstances, the continued devotion of a considerable part of our effort to the building up of this bombing force is the best use that we can make of our resources. It is obviously a matter which is almost impossible to debate in public, but, if I may, I would remind the House that this policy was initiated at a time when we were fighting alone against the combined forces of Germany and Italy, and it then seemed that it was the most effective way in which we, acting alone, could take the initiative against the enemy.

"Since that time, we have had an enormous excess of support from the Russian armies, who, according to the latest news, have had yet another victory over the Germans, and also from the great potential strength of the United States of America. Naturally, in such circumstances, the original policy has come under review and is, indeed, kept constantly under review. I can assure the House that the Government are fully aware of the other uses to which our resources could be put, and the moment they arrive at a decision that the circumstances warrant a change, a change in policy will be made."

The possible implications of this statement, guarded as it was and obsolescent as it proved to be,[7] could not be missed, and there was an instant reaction from the R.A.F. Delegation in Washington. Here it was felt that the statement might be taken to mean that the British Government had lost confidence in the independent bomber offensive as a principal means of "wearing down and undermining German resistance", which they had so recently expressed at the Washington War Conference.

The *New York Times* had reported the speech, and the R.A.F. Delegation feared that it would strengthen the hands of those Americans who were pressing their Government to concentrate on the war against Japan in contradistinction to that against Germany which Mr. Churchill and President Roosevelt had agreed at the Washington Conference should receive first consideration. It might have also had an adverse effect upon the American production programme for heavy bombers. "Unless authoritative reaffirmation of our belief in the Bomber Offensive is supplied immediately", the Delegation's telegram ended, the "effect both on strategical and production planning here may well be irremediable".

The Air Ministry reply which was sent out just before midnight on 28 February was reasonably confident in tone. There was a growing feeling in unofficial circles, it said, that heavy bombers should be directed more against naval targets and less against German industry and transport, but the policy strategic bombing, indicated in the February directive, had received the approval of the Government and this, it was stated, held the field. The Lord Privy Seal's remarks should not therefore be taken to indicate a change of policy, which the Air Ministry thought would be impossible without throwing the whole production programme out of gear. Defence bombing alone could not win the war, and so the Air Ministry saw no reason to fear that this would be a serious threat to the offensive against Germany, especially as the Russian situation had produced "one of (the) strongest arguments for intensifying (the) bombing of Germany". The Secretary of State for Air would, the message concluded, be making a declaration during the debate on the Air Estimates which was shortly to take place, and this, it was hoped, would provide the necessary "authoritative reaffirmation" of the Government's belief in the heavy bomber as a strategic weapon.

The debate on the Air Estimates, held in the Commons on 4 March, therefore provided Sir Archibald Sinclair with a convenient platform from which to express this "authoritative reaffirmation", but it also necessarily presented the opportunity for the critics to make themselves heard. It is significant that the Secretary of State for Air in the course of his speech gave considerable attention to the auxiliary co-operation which the R.A.F. had been affording to the Navy in the Atlantic and to the Army in the Middle East. He spoke particularly of the efforts which had been made by Bomber Command to contribute to the Battle of the Atlantic. The attacks on the *Scharnhorst* and *Gneisenau* at Brest provided him with some useful, if rather selective, figures.

At length he came to the controversial question of the bombing offensive against Germany. He spoke of the new aircraft, the Stirlings, Manchesters, Halifaxes and Lancasters, which were coming into service, and said that it was intended "to resume the bomber offensive against Germany on the largest possible scale at the earliest possible moment". Talk about the "futility of bombing" he regarded as "dangerous". The R.A.F. aircrews, he said, were well armed and inflexibly determined, "they are the only force upon which we can call in the year 1942, to strike deadly blows at the heart of Germany".

Sir Archibald Sinclair's comforting remarks about the effectiveness of R.A.F. co-operation with the other services did not, however, reassure Mr. Garro Jones, and the promise of an increased offensive against Germany disquieted him considerably. "We know", Mr. Garro Jones said "that these heavy bombers cannot operate except from extreme altitude or by night. In the former case they cannot hit their targets: in the latter case they cannot find their targets, and have not found them, unless they were zones and not targets".

This suggested to Mr. Garro Jones that night raids should be directed against the morale of Germany, and that when it was desired to destroy a specific industrial target, it should be attacked by day with the proper escort of fighters. In neither case did he think that the un-versatile heavy bomber was the ideal weapon. Like the German Air Force, the R.A.F. should be equipped with bombers which would be capable of being used not only for these strategic attacks, but also for naval and army co-operation. He thought that the Air Staff policy which had resulted in the production of these long-range bombers, suitable only for strategic and independent bombing, had proceeded from the desire to keep the R.A.F. independent. The Air Staff, he thought, feared that if they provided machines effective for co-operation, they would be absorbed into the other services. There followed a sharp attack upon the most famous protagonist of the independent bomber force, Lord Trenchard, which was certainly a shot on the target for one who shared Mr. Garro Jones' views.

Thus, in a few words, Mr. Garro Jones summed up many of the problems with which the Air Staff had been grappling since the beginning of the war. He did, however, sum them up from a different angle. Clearly, he had no confidence in the success of an independent and strategic bomber offensive. He believed that the primary role of the Air Force was to provide the support for the army and navy which had normally been the principal task of the German Air Force. Here then was a possible alternative employment for the resources which were then being used to build up the heavy bomber force, an alternative which Sir Stafford Cripps may have had in mind.

Mr. Garro Jones' argument had for the Air Staff a double sting. In the first place it was impossible to refute it by pointing to the past. So far, the strategic bombing offensive had been an almost acknowledged failure, whereas the auxiliary efforts of the German Air Force had been a triumphant success. The desire to imitate a successful enemy had an obvious appeal. To claim that the future of the strategic bomber offensive would be very different to its past was liable to appear to its opponents as no more than a pious hope. Secondly, the argument did not spring merely from a politically irresponsible member of parliament. It was backed by more expert opinion.

The Royal Navy bore a heavy responsibility for the safety of Britain during the war. In the war against Germany their principal task was to keep open the supply line across the Atlantic. This was, as the Germans had recognised, Britain's life line, and if, by their operations over, on and under the sea, the Germans could break it then Britain would surely have starved. The huge American armaments production would, from the point of view of the war in Europe, have become so much rubble. Thus, in preventing the defeat of Britain the Navy had a gigantic task, but in bringing about the defeat of Germany the Navy had an equal responsibility. Without American supplies in men and materiel there could have been no Allied invasion of the continent, and there could have been no bombing offensive from the United Kingdom without imports of oil and machinery.

This great struggle, which was called the Battle of the Atlantic, was waged throughout the war with fluctuating fortune, but always it demanded the greatest vigilance of the Royal Navy to avoid calamity and especially in 1941 and 1942. Seldom can there have been a battle when for so long the issue was in doubt and in which the stakes were so high. It is therefore hardly surprising to find that the Admiralty looked beyond their own resources to continue the struggle.

We have already seen how in addition to the sustained assistance of the R.A.F. Coastal Command, they constantly demanded and frequently obtained the services of Bomber Command. These calls from the Admiralty had in 1940 and 1941 made nonsense of the strategic bombing offensive against Germany, but at the beginning of 1942 the Battle of the Atlantic was still at a critical stage. The entry of Japan into the war had vastly enlarged the sphere of naval operations, and the loss of the *Prince of Wales* and *Repulse* had seriously diminished naval resources. In the circumstances it was hardly likely that the Admiralty would relax its demands on the bombers which the Air Staff now wanted to direct in the greatest possible strength over Germany.

The First Lord of the Admiralty had no objection to the resumption of the bombing offensive against Germany, provided that "certain immediate Naval requirements of long range G.R.[8] aircraft" were met.[9] The First Lord's point was that the Battle of the Atlantic must still come first and the bombing offensive against Germany second. There must be no return to Lord Trenchard's idea of "unconditional" support for the strategic bombing offensive. Only on this condition was he willing to give his approval to the policy of the February Directive. Meanwhile Professor Blackett of the Admiralty carried the naval case further, with less authority but more pungency. He had no confidence in the independent bombing offensive. On the evidence of the past two years he had formed the opinion that it could not make a significant contribution to victory. The bomber force, he argued, should therefore be halved and the effort so released should be harnessed to the Battle of the Atlantic.

These comments represented something more than the First Lord of the Admiralty's claim that the Battle of the Atlantic was of greater urgency than the Battle of Germany. They were a direct challenge to the view that the independent bomber force was a potentially war winning weapon.[10] Thus the issue was something more than a petty inter-service dispute. Obviously, the Battle of the Atlantic could not be lost and the air force had a responsibility for ensuring that it was won, but if Professor

Blackett's view was correct, the air force had no independent role. It could only operate by the side of the army or the navy. In this case it would be folly to continue to pour resources into the building of an independent bomber force which could achieve nothing.

The real issue was not so much whether the bombing offensive could be afforded, as for instance it could not be afforded between March and July 1941, but whether it was worthwhile at all. This had been the real dispute between Sir Archibald Sinclair and Mr. Garro Jones in the House of Commons, and now it was still the dispute between Professor Blackett and another Professor, that forceful champion of the Air Force and close associate of the Prime Minister, Lord Cherwell.

On 30 March 1942 Lord Cherwell addressed a minute to the Prime Minister. In refreshingly simple, if somewhat fallible, terms he expressed his view of what strategic bombing could achieve. One ton of bombs dropped on a built-up area would demolish between twenty and forty buildings, and turn from one to two hundred people out of house and home. This, Lord Cherwell claimed, was proved by careful analysis of the German attacks on Birmingham, Hull and other British towns. Each bomber which was put into service would on the average have an operational life of fourteen sorties and the average bomb load of these bombers would be three tons. Thus, each bomber could drop forty tons of bombs in its life time.

If these bombs were dropped on built up areas, they would make four to eight thousand Germans homeless. It was planned to build ten thousand heavy bombers before the middle of 1943.[11] If therefore only half the load of these ten thousand bombers was dropped on the built up areas in fifty-eight German towns, each containing more than 100,000 people, they would destroy the great majority of the homes of one third of the entire population of Germany. "There seems little doubt," Lord Cherwell concluded, "that this would break the spirit of the people."

This attractively straightforward argument proved decisive. The crisis had burst. At the end of September 1941, the Prime Minister had warned the C.A.S., "It is very disputable whether bombing by itself will be a decisive factor in the present war… The most we can say is that it will be a heavy and I trust a seriously increasing annoyance." At the beginning of April 1942, the Prime Minister told the Secretary of State for Air, "We are placing great hopes on our bombing offensive against Germany next winter, and we must spare no pains to justify the large proportion of the national effort devoted to it." Between these two pronouncements lay the Cherwell Minute.

Yet Lord Cherwell had produced no new arguments, and anything he did say could equally well have been said in 1941, when as we have already seen the real crisis of decision had been passed. Lord Cherwell had affirmed that Bomber Command could, given the right orders and adequate material, win the war by strategic bombing. He took a heavy responsibility when he said this, and the critics continued to doubt if he was right. The reason that Lord Cherwell's minute was decisive was that these critics, though they might doubt his wisdom, were unable to offer an alternative to what he suggested.

Defeat in the Battle of the Atlantic would mean defeat for Britain, but defeat for Germany in the Battle of the Atlantic would not necessarily mean defeat for Germany in the war. Bomber Command remained for Britain the only weapon with which, at least for the time being, she could strike offensive blows at Germany. Thus, the Government sought no more than a mandate to proceed with something which they had already decided to do. Lord Cherwell provided that mandate.

All the same the critics remained and it seemed desirable to seek further for a resolution of the doubts which still existed. Accordingly, the Prime Minister invited Mr. Justice Singleton to conduct an independent enquiry into the prospects of the bombing offensive. Mr. Justice Singleton presented his report on 20 May 1942. If it was hoped that this report would reach general conclusions of decisive value about the prospects of the bomber offensive, then it must have been a great disappointment. In fact, it never got beyond the stage of detailed observations about the difficulties still standing in the way of the bombers.

It analysed these difficulties, the chief of which Mr. Justice Singleton concluded was still the problem of target finding, but it could not say firmly whether they would be overcome or not. This meant of course that it was impossible to say what overall effect the bombing offensive was going to have upon Germany. The report indulged in nothing more than cautious speculation about this crucial issue. It was, in fact, a significant commentary on the whole problem that it was impossible to reach any general conclusions. The report therefore had the merit, not of solving the problem, but of demonstrating that it could not be solved on the evidence which was available.

It did, however, precipitate a crisis which had been simmering since the February directive had been introduced between the Admiralty and the Air Ministry. The First Sea Lord, Sir Dudley Pound, argued that the Singleton report offered no hope of the bombing offensive achieving really significant results within the immediate future. This was exactly what Mr. Justice Singleton had reported. Meanwhile the "gravity" of the position in the war at sea was increasing "day by day". This, the First Sea Lord thought, was a clear indication that the air force should play a larger part in naval war.

The C.A.S. felt that the First Sea Lord's quotations from the Singleton report were "to put it mildly, highly unrepresentative". Other quotations, he suggested, could equally well be used to produce quite different conclusions. This was also quite true, for the Singleton report, having itself failed to reach general conclusions, did not contain the evidence upon which they could be formed by others. It was easy to argue about the Singleton report, but impossible to arbitrate. Thus, the argument remained at the stage it had reached before the Singleton report.

The C.A.S. did not think the situation at sea was as grave as the First Sea Lord had suggested. He found that naval construction would soon overtake sinkings, and in any case he claimed that Bomber Command would be better employed in attacking German naval construction, rather than ships at sea. This was, however, an argument the truth of which he could not prove. The real strength of the C.A.S. case lay in his assertion that after three years of war it was time to think not only in terms of avoiding defeat, but in terms of achieving victory. It was therefore necessary in his opinion for the First Sea Lord to prove conclusively that the war at sea really was as critical as he suggested, and that only if this could be done would it be justifiable to make further inroads on the offensive weapon of Bomber Command, which was in any case still shrinking and not expanding.

Eventually both sides gave some ground and an agreement was reached under which the Admiralty reduced their demands and the Air Force agreed to meet them. This, of course, had an injurious effect upon the first line strength of the Command, but it did resolve a crisis which had been assuming dangerous proportions for both sides.

By now, however, the real issue, that is, of what Bomber Command could achieve against Germany by strategic bombing, was being put to the test, not round the council table but in the field of action. The advocates had waged a successful campaign against their critics at home. It remained to be seen whether their success would be justified by events in Germany. 1942 would not solve this problem, for Lord Cherwell had thought in terms of a period up to the middle of 1943, and Mr. Justice Singleton had envisaged 1942 as an introductory period.

Nevertheless, it would be possible to see more clearly the prospects for 1943 after the battles of 1942 had been fought. The spate of words died down. The time for action had come. Sir Arthur Harris, who was appointed to succeed Sir Richard Peirse as Commander-in-Chief of Bomber Command on 20 February, was a man of action.

Mr. G.M. Young likes to divide historic figures into two groups: those who make a noise and those who make a difference, but Sir Arthur Harris made both a noise and a difference. Before proceeding to examine the tasks which lay ahead of the new C-in-C, and the way in which he performed them, we must pause to measure the weapon itself, for the weapon still had serious limitations, the chief of which was its limited strength.

From the point of view of the expansion of the Command in number of aircraft, 1942 was a disappointing year. At its end there were sixty-three bomber squadrons established as against the fifty-seven which had been established in January 1942, but the number of operational squadrons on 31 December was exactly the same as it had been on 1 January. On both dates there was forty-nine.[12] The numbers of operational aircraft upon which the C-in-C could call did not increase during the year, and in some months showed a decrease.[13]

The explanation of this failure to increase the numbers of machines in Bomber Command was fourfold. Firstly, British production of bombers fell short of expectation. Secondly, the prospect of large numbers of machines reaching the R.A.F. from America ended with the President's declaration of the principle that American aircraft should be manned by American crews.[14] Thirdly, a considerable number of Bomber Command squadrons were withdrawn and lent or permanently assigned to other Commands during the year. Some went to Coastal Command and others to the Middle East and India.

The fourth explanation of the failure to expand, was the introduction of new types of machines. During the year the Hampden, Whitley, Blenheim and Manchester went out of operational service. The Lancaster, the Mosquito and increasing numbers of Halifaxes came in. While these changes were taking place, squadrons had to be withdrawn from the line to be re-equipped and to allow time for the crews to be introduced to their new machines.

The introduction of these new types of bomber caused a complete transformation in the composition of the force. Of the forty-nine squadrons which had been operational on 1 January 1942, ten had been heavy, thirty-five medium and four light.[15] Twelve months later, of the forty-nine operational squadrons, thirty-two were heavy, eleven medium and six light. Thus, even if Sir Arthur Harris could not muster more operational aircraft in December than his predecessor had been able to do in January, those which he could call upon were machines much superior in speed and bomb lift to the earlier types. In particular the Lancaster had, by the end of the year, began to assert its position as the 'ideal' bomber.[16] These changes already began to have an effect upon the capacity of the command in 1942, and in that year Bomber Command dropped about 14,000 tons of bombs more than it had done in 1941, despite the fact that in 1941 about five hundred more sorties were flown on bombing trips than in 1942.[17]

Nevertheless, Bomber Command in 1942 was still incapable of carrying the very great weights which had been envisaged as necessary to achieve the aim of destroying German morale. It was also still far short of the activities which became possible for it in 1943 and the following years. When it is realised that Bomber Command flew nearly twice as many sorties in 1943 as it had done in 1942, and that in 1944 the Command flew about five times as many sorties as in 1942, then it becomes clear that 1942 was indeed, as Mr. Justice Singleton had suggested, an introductory year. The limitation in the size of the force was still a salient limitation on the achievement.

Of even greater significance than the introduction of these more powerful aircraft into Bomber Command was the development of a radar aid, which for the first time in the war offered the bombers a chance of finding their targets at night. On the night of 8 March 1942, Gee was used operationally for the first time in an attack on Essen. Two nights after this, the Lancaster bomber made its first bombing attack. Thus, within forty-eight hours Bomber Command showed its new colours.

Though Gee proved to be highly effective as a navigational aid, it did not realise the high hopes which had been entertained of it as a blind bombing device. Two more radar aids were, however, being developed which offered prospects of overcoming this problem as well. H2S and Oboe as they were called were later to have a marked effect upon the accuracy of the force, but in the meantime Sir Arthur Harris' squadrons had to go into action without the problem of blind bombing having been solved.

This, broadly speaking,[18] was the weapon which the new C-in-C had with which to carry out the February directive. This was the weapon with which he had either to vindicate or destroy the idea that the independent bomber force was an effective weapon of war.

Sir Arthur Harris' principal task was the destruction of town centres in Germany, and particularly in the Ruhr. It would have been unreasonable to suppose that Bomber Command, with its still limited resources, could achieve victory in 1942, but if it was to survive as an independent weapon, it had in 1942 to cause sufficient damage to provide convincing evidence that in 1943 or 1944 it would succeed in achieving decisive results. The Government, as Sir Stafford Cripps had said, were aware of the other uses to which British resources could be put. If therefore the attacks of 1942 alone were not expected to be decisive in Germany, they would be decisive for the future of Bomber Command. For the advocates of the strategic bombing offensive, this was therefore the supreme test. They strained every nerve to overcome the tactical difficulties which had thitherto denied Bomber Command any outstanding success.

The most important of these tactical difficulties were, firstly, the achievement of a good concentration over the target area in time and space, secondly, the sighting of the target, and thirdly the delivery of the most devastating blow possible. If the first of these difficulties could be overcome, there was the prospect of saturating the defences of the towns which were being attacked, and so of causing much greater damage. There was also the hope that the bombers would in these circumstances enjoy a greater immunity from attack. Gee would be a great contribution to the solution of this problem. The more accurate navigation which would become possible would enable the bombers to keep on track, which would result in a concentration in space, and on schedule, which would result in a concentration in time. The second problem, that of sighting the target, remained unsolved, for Gee was found to be inadequate for the final recognition of the target. It could not be used as an accurate blind bombing device.

The real solution of the problem lay in the introduction of further radar aids. This problem was, however, too urgent to await the satisfactory completion of H2S and Oboe, and there did seem to be a way in which the difficulty might be lessened in the meantime, and which, in itself, would be the best medium for the use of these radar aids of the future. This was the creation of a specially trained and, so far as possible, specially equipped target finding force. If a few machines could, with their superior crews and superior devices, find and mark the target, the main force would be able to bomb it.

At the Air Ministry this idea commanded considerable support. In his report, Mr. Justice Singleton had recognised the need for something on these lines, and the idea also appealed to Lord Cherwell. Sir Arthur Harris was more doubtful. He did not welcome the idea of creating a corps d'élite nor was he convinced of the need for this revolution. He could, however, do no more than delay the introduction of an idea which commanded such powerful support, and on 11 August 1942 the A.C.A.S. (Ops.), Air Vice-Marshal Bottomley, informed Sir Arthur Harris that the Path Finder Force would be established in Bomber Command. The real success of the famous P.F.F. was to depend upon radar aids which were not available at its inception, but the decision to create this force was vindicated in time to come.[19]

The third problem, that of delivering the most effective blow, was one which had commanded much attention in 1941, when the suspicion that German attacks were more effective than R.A.F. raids grew to a certainty. Thus in 1941 the idea of concentrating on fire raising as the most effective means of destruction had received the approval of the Air Staff. Sir Richard Peirse's doubts about the plan combined with the diversions against Brest and the winter lull had, however, prevented the practice of this theory in 1941. The February directive had reaffirmed confidence in the idea that the incendiary bomb was the most destructive bomb, and the criticisms of Bomber Command which were levelled in Parliament at the beginning of the year suggested to Lord Cherwell that the time had come to use it.

The C.A.S. agreed and on 21 March the D.C.A.S. told the C-in-C that the incendiary plan, which had been worked out in October 1941, was to be put into practice as soon as possible. Seven days later Sir Arthur Harris, despite his lingering doubts about the incendiary bomb, directed 234 bombers to attack Lübeck, so that the theory could be tested. This attack proved to be the most outstanding success which Bomber Command had ever achieved, and it must still be ranked as one of its greatest victories.

This attack on Lübeck, though it was the most successful achievement of Bomber Command in 1942, was not the most remarkable. Though the town was beyond Gee range, the weather was excellent, and the defences slight. According to the C-in-C, Lübeck was "built more like a fire-lighter than a human habitation". He did not think it could be compared to any other German town.

If, therefore, as Sir Arthur Harris claimed, it was not a fair basis on which to draw the assumption that the incendiary was a superior bomb to the high explosive, it was also not a fair indication of the level of efficiency to which Bomber Command had reached. Very much greater difficulty was encountered when the attempt to "Lübeck" Rostock was made. The towns of the Ruhr and particularly Essen, which was repeatedly attacked, were with their much stronger defences and ever-present industrial haze an even more striking illustration of the continuing difficulties and hazards of night bombing. It was to these stiffer tasks that the C-in-C addressed himself with vigour.

By calling upon aircraft of the O.T.Us to strengthen his first line, Sir Arthur Harris twice succeeded in getting more than a thousand bombers off the ground on a single raid. The first of these gigantic operations was directed at Cologne on the night of 30 May. The casualties were not unduly heavy, and the results were impressive. The photographs taken after the raid showed that a third of the town had been grievously damaged.[20] A second thousand bomber raid was aimed at Essen on the night of 1 June, but this time the weather, as always over Essen, was unfavourable and the town escaped "relatively lightly". There was another raid of almost equal dimensions on Bremen at the end of June, but once again the results were rather disappointing.

Nevertheless, after these attacks, Bomber Command could claim with justice that the offensive against Germany had "achieved a new degree of intensity, typified by the 'thousand raids' which far surpassed all previous standards of aerial warfare". These massive attacks were, of course, in conformity with the lines of the February directive, but they were also designed to impress the Government, and particularly the critics of strategic bombing, with what could be done if Bomber Command was expanded to a much greater size. For the time being they could not be sustained, for training had to be continued at the O.T.U's, and there were no more 'thousand raids' after June. Nevertheless, Bomber Command could still claim in September that it had maintained "an unbroken series of concentrated raids on the German Reich such as the enemy had never previously experienced".

Bomber Command was not, however, concentrated entirely on Germany, nor did it follow exclusively the area bombing technique. An increasing number of mines were laid in enemy waters, several precise attacks were made on industrial targets in France, and notably on the Renault factory on the night of 3 March. There was even a precision attack on the M.A.N. factory at Augsburg carried out in daylight on 17 April by a small force of Lancasters.

Thus in 1942 Bomber Command, though it still had to admit its failures, achieved its first real tactical successes both by area bombing and precise attack. It had, in fact, successfully negotiated the "introductory" phase.[21]

These achievements changed the whole outlook. Bomber Command had now drawn the attention of the world. Whatever misgivings there were, there could be no doubt that the bombers had inflicted severe damage on Lübeck and Rostock, on Bremen and Emden, on Cologne and Essen. There could be no doubt that the Command had achieved the almost miraculous feat of operating a thousand bombers on a single night. "What shouts of victory would arise", Sir Arthur Harris enquired, "if a Commando wrecked the entire Renault factory in a night, with the loss of seven men! What credible assumptions of an early end to the war would follow upon the destruction of a third of Cologne in an hour and a half by some swift moving mechanised force which, with but 200 casualties, withdrew and was ready to repeat the operation 24 hours later! What acclaim would greet the virtual destruction of Rostock and the Heinkel main and subsidiary factories by a Naval bombardment!" Yet these and other feats were the achievements of Bomber Command whose first line strength on 15 June 1942 was no more than 584 aircraft, or 11% of the total first line strength of the R.A.F. and the Fleet Air Arm. Even this small force was still the jack of all trades. Half its effort was still devoted to the naval war, and its strategic aims were widely dispersed over Europe from Germany to France to Italy.[22] Sir Arthur Harris claimed that it was the master of all trades but, he added, "Bomber Command provides our only offensive action yet pressed home directly against Germany. All our efforts are defensive in their nature, and are not intended to do more, and can never do more, than enable us to exist in the face of the enemy. Bomber Command provides the only means of physically weakening and nervously exhausting Germany to an extent which will make subsequent invasion a possible proposition, and is therefore the only force which can, in fact, hurt our enemy in the present or in the future secure our victory".

This argument, which would have been impossible in February 1942, was circulated to the Cabinet by the Prime Minister in August 1942.[23] That was what the bombing offensive under the direction of Sir Arthur Harris had achieved in four months. This was the moment for Lord Trenchard to speak again. "As the enemy conquered Poland and France by their 'tank blitz', so we can smash the German machine by the 'bomber blitz'", he declared. But this could not be achieved if Bomber Command was to remain the "Cinderella" of the armed forces as the result of a policy which, to Lord Trenchard, seemed "half-hearted and feeble".

Lord Trenchard had, of course, always believed in the strategic bomber as a decisive weapon of war, and now under the vigorous leadership of

Sir Arthur Harris, he discerned the first real evidence that he had been right. "Can anyone", he asked, "foretell the results of even three months' ruthless bombing of Germany on the Cologne scale?" However this may have been, and it seems doubtful if anyone could, either in Britain or Germany, it was certain that Bomber Command, with the resources at its disposal, could not mount an attack on that scale, even for only three months. Before the offensive could reach decisive proportions, there would have to be a great expansion of the Command.

The issue which now had to be decided was therefore not only whether the successes of 1942 compensated for the failures of 1940 and 1941, but whether they promised results in 1943 and 1944 which would justify the further expenditure of manpower, materials and shipping space which an expansion on the scale demanded would consume. Important as the promising achievements of Bomber Command were, there were other factors which weighed heavily on those who had to decide.

In October the three Chiefs of Staff reported, "Sufficient experience[24] has already been gained to show that it will not be tactically possible to establish and maintain a large Allied army in France until German military power has been undermined." Despite the fact that the Second Front would obviously be the greatest contribution that the Western Allies could make to Russian success and so to victory, the Chiefs of Staff were "forced to the conclusion" that German military power must be undermined by the destruction of the industrial and economic war machine, before invasion could be attempted. "For this process", they agreed, "apart from the impact of the Russian land forces, the heavy bomber will be the main weapon…"

America and Britain, they urged, should aim at the creation of a force of four to six thousand heavy bombers by April 1944. This target, they thought, could be achieved if adequate priority was accorded to bomber construction. They also believed, on the evidence of 1942, that a force of these dimensions would succeed in its aim, which they now defined as "the progressive destruction and dislocation of the enemy's war industrial and economic system, and the undermining of his morale to a point where his capacity for armed resistance is fatally weakened".

The immediate aim was to expand Bomber Command from the thirty-two operational squadrons which it had in September 1942 to fifty operational squadrons by the end of the year. The Prime Minister suggested to Sir Archibald Sinclair that two squadrons should be obtained from Coastal Command, one from the Airborne Division, two by restricting the flow of aircraft to Middle East and India,[25] two more by improving 'working up' in Bomber Command, nine by scheduled increases from the Ministry of Aircraft Production and two by further exertions by the Ministry of Aircraft Production. He promised Cabinet support for the expansion, and assured the Secretary of State that it would enjoy priority over all competing claims.

Bomber Command was no longer in danger of disintegration. It was now the turn of the other services to worry about their future. The Chief of the Imperial General Staff, for instance, found the prospect of four to six thousand bombers alarming. How could the army be supplied as well? Air Force requirements would, he feared, compete with army needs from wireless equipment to "tent pegs". Whether this would be so or not remained to be seen. The important point was that Bomber Command had re-established its prestige and was once more regarded as an integral part of the offensive against Germany, as the essential weapon with which to prepare the way for invasion.

The paper, which the Chief of Air Staff submitted to his colleagues on 3 November 1942 entitled "An estimate of the Effects of an Anglo-American Bomber Offensive against Germany", did not therefore seek to convince them that a bombing offensive was essential, this was already decided. It was merely an exposition of the reasons for believing that the offensive, provided that it was mounted in sufficient strength, would succeed in paving the way to final victory.

Like Lord Cherwell before him, the Chief of the Air Staff thought that the best yardstick against which to judge the probable result of a bombing offensive was the German attack on England. He claimed that a good deal was known about the results of the R.A.F. attacks on Germany, but the evidence was obviously much less complete than that about the Luftwaffe attacks on England. In the year ending 30 June 1941 the Luftwaffe had dropped 55,000 tons of bombs on Britain, and 36,000 tons of these had been aimed at industrial areas.

About a quarter of these 36,000 tons were thought to have fallen in built up areas. 41,000 people had been killed and 45,000 seriously

A classic portrait of Air Chief Marshal Sir Arthur Harris, Commander in Chief of Royal Air Force Bomber Command, seated at his desk at Bomber Command HQ, High Wycombe, 24 April 1944. (*Historic Military Press*)

An early Bomber Command attack underway. The original caption to this image states that it shows 'AA fire during raid on Mannheim' on 16 December 1940. It is one of series belonging to an Allied prisoner of war. (*Historic Military Press*)

The burnt-out wreckage of a 37 Squadron Vickers Wellington, Mk.Ia P2515 (LF-H), after it was shot-down by flak during a leaflet-dropping, or *Nickel*, raid on the night of 23/24 March 1940. Having taken off from RAF Feltwell, the bomber crashed in flames in a wooded area of the Eifel Mountains in Western Germany. One member of the crew was killed in the crash – the Second Pilot, Sergeant D.W. Wilson – whilst the remainder were taken prisoner. However, the pilot, Flying Officer Paul F. Templeman, had sustained serious burns injuries from which he died on 31 March 1940. (*Historic Military Press*)

Aircrew of 75 (New Zealand) Squadron parading in front of one of their Vickers Wellington Mk.IC aircraft at RAF Feltwell, 1941. (*Historic Military Press*)

Avro Manchester L7515, 'EM-S', of 207 Squadron pictured during 1941 or 1942. First flying on 25 July 1939, and entering service in November 1940, the Manchester was an operational failure due to its underdeveloped, underpowered, and unreliable engines. However, the aircraft was the forerunner to the successful Avro Lancaster, which would become one of the more capable and famous bombers of the war. (*Mark Hillier Collection*)

A low-level oblique aerial photograph showing the damage caused to Frankfurt during the Second World War. By the time of the German surrender, the once famous medieval city centre (seen here with the Cathedral in the foreground) had been destroyed. After the war, the official assessment of the damage caused to this city by the RAF and USAAF stated that between one and two thousand acres had been devastated. (*NARA*)

US servicemen of the 105th Combat Engineers study three partially completed tanks at the badly damaged Krupp Grusonwerk armament factory at Buckau, eighty-five miles south-west of Berlin, in May 1945. (*NARA*)

The ruins of an I.G. Farbenindustrie factory at Ludwigshafen, pictured after the German surrender in 1945. The equipment seen here was part of a synthetic oil section. (*NARA*)

Pictured on 11 April 1945, RAF officers inspect an unfinished siege gun in a wrecked building of the Krupps armaments works at Essen, Germany, a principal target for Bomber Command throughout the war. The Krupps AG works at Essen, Germany, was seriously damaged by Bomber Command in 1943, and further wrecked in the daylight raid of 11 March 1945. (*Historic Military Press*)

US troops inspect a Focke-Wulf Fw 190 that lies uncompleted and undelivered among the ruins of th Oschersleben factory, May 1945. (*NARA*)

A group of civilians gather in the bomb-damaged and rubble-strewn square by the damaged statue of the artist Albrecht Duerer in Nuremberg in May 1945. Repaired, the statue can still be seen today at the junction of Albrecht Duerer Platz and Bergstrasse. (*NARA*)

injured. Nearly 350,000 houses were made uninhabitable for the duration of the war, and 1,000,000 people were "displaced" from their homes. There were two and a half million incidents of damage to house property which required repair. In addition to this, destruction of factories, power stations, shipping and harbour facilities and public utilities had caused a reaction on the war effort which the Chief of the Air Staff wisely refrained from expressing in statistical terms.

If the Anglo-American bomber force could be expanded to five thousand by June 1944 and six thousand by the end of the year, it would, during its period of expansion, be capable of dropping 25,000 tons of bombs per month by June 1943, 50,000 tons in December 1943 and 65,000 tons per month by June 1944. Finally, in December 1944 it would at its peak drop no less than 90,000 tons of bombs. Under such a plan, one and a quarter million tons would fall on Germany in 1943 and 1944. Thus, six million houses would be damaged, 900,000 civilians would be killed and about one million seriously injured. Twenty-five million Germans would have been made homeless.

These estimates were conservative, the Chief of Air Staff claimed, because R.A.F. bombing in 1943 and 1944 in the light of experience and with the aid of scientific devices would almost certainly prove to be much more efficient than German bombing had been in 1940 and 1941, but he made no mention of a point which was causing the Prime Minister considerable concern. Assuming that the bomber force could be expanded to these dimensions, then obviously a large element of it would consist of American bombers, manned by their own crews.

The Americans were, according to the Prime Minister, "obstinately" persisting with daylight bombing. They had not yet succeeded in penetrating the German defences, and Mr. Churchill was inclined to doubt if they ever would. If they could not switch to night bombing, it was possible that they would be able play only a small part in the combined bomber offensive. The decision about American bomber tactics was, however, beyond the control of the British Air Staff, and also, as he found, beyond that of Mr. Churchill.

Nor did the Chief of the Air Staff mention a point which was causing the Chief of the Imperial General Staff anxiety. Even assuming that the Americans solved their problem or adopted British tactics, it would still be impossible, and to his mind undesirable to concentrate all these bombers on the strategic offensive against Germany. There would still be the Battle of the Atlantic to fight. There would also be the war against Italy, targets in Occupied Territory would have to be bombed, and the Airborne Army would need aircraft.

There were therefore loopholes in the Chief of the Air Staff's argument as far as he had proceeded, and these were to be the cause of much difficulty and dispute in the years of war which remained. But there was another possibility which was to cause controversy not only between the services, but within the R.A.F. The Chief of the Air Staff clearly intended that these four to six thousand bombers should be employed on area bombing, but he did not actually say so. There was renewed belief that precision attacks might still prove themselves to be the more efficient medium for the bombers. Throughout 1942 there was continued interest in the possibility of a second offensive against German oil resources.[26] There was growing interest in the idea of attacking German ball bearing production.[27]

Both these ideas could only be carried out by precision bombing. There had already been a successful precision attack on Renault in France. Might this not in time be repeated against the ball bearing factories in Schweinfurt or the oil installations at Pölitz? Area bombing was after all only one of the many ways by which Bomber Command might contribute to the reduction of German armed strength to that point where invasion would become possible. Here was the germination of ideas which were to develop into major arguments of the first importance when, in 1943, the American bomber force finally did break through into Germany.

Whatever might be the eventual solution of all these problems, it is necessary now to return to the Chief of the Air Staff's argument of November 1942. He calculated that an attack on the lines he had indicated would destroy one third of German industry. He was informed that Germany was already fully mobilised, and had reduced her standard of living to the minimum bearable. He therefore concluded that any loss which could be inflicted on any branch of industry would inevitably fall on war production. He therefore believed that Germany must have been seriously shaken by the 1942 raids, and that she would certainly be broken by those of 1943 and 1944. Here then the strategic misconception, which had its origins in 1941, was repeated, and applied to one of the most gigantic operations of war ever planned.

Some of the flaws in the Chief of the Air Staff's argument had been pointed out, for instance by the Prime Minister and the Chief of the Imperial General Staff, but no one had detected the great reserves of economic and industrial strength which Germany was now beginning to bring into action.

Chapter 6

The First Effects of Strategic Bombing

The bombing offensive of 1942 was not in itself expected to produce decisive results. Nevertheless, the success which it was deemed to have achieved was accepted as evidence that the heavier attacks planned for 1943 and 1944 would succeed in disrupting the German war economy and the nation's morale. The first significant result of the offensive was therefore the restoration of confidence in the principle of strategic bombing, which had been so seriously shaken by the experiences of 1940 and 1941. It now remains to consider how far this restoration of confidence was justified by the actual effects of the 1942 campaign upon the structure of Germany.

The effects of strategic bombing are complex, and it is advisable here to indicate the lines along which this investigation will be conducted, and to expound the methods of assessment which will be used. The important effects of strategic bombing are the national effects which have to be distinguished from the purely local effects. It is possible, for instance, to devastate a single city with disastrous local effects, both on industrial production and morale, and yet to find that national production was unimpaired and national morale imperceptibly affected.

There are three types of national effect which may be usefully distinguished; the effects on national industrial production, the effect on national morale and the effect on national policy. The first two of these are direct in so far as they result from damage inflicted upon factories, resources and communications, upon houses, public transport and the amenities of civilised life. They are of course intimately connected, for production may fall owing to poor morale and morale may fall owing to reduced production. If they are severe enough, both will contribute to the disruption of the national economy. The third, that is the effect upon the national policy, is indirect in so far as it is a by-product of bombing, but it is none the less important for this reason. Bombing may intentionally or inadvertently drive the country which is being attacked to revise its air policy. Severe enough effects in any of these fields could produce results which would have a decisive influence upon the outcome of the war.

All these types of national effect have it in common that they must obviously ensue from the local damage which was inflicted by the bombing attacks. These local effects must therefore be the focal point from which any study of the national effects of bombing must proceed. The problem is therefore to find a means of expressing local effects in national terms.

While there is obviously no mathematical method of calculating the indirect effects of bombing, the ideal way of finding economic effects might seem to be by statistical calculations. If, in the case of industry for instance, the loss of production which was caused by the bombing at the local points which were attacked could be computed, and if sufficient statistical evidence could be assembled to indicate the role of these points in the national economy, then it would be possible to find the precise amount by which national production was reduced by bombing.

A serious attempt to achieve this has been made,[1] but the figures which have been reached, though they shed light on the problem, are of limited competence. An estimate of this kind cannot be kept as a pure calculation. It is impossible to arrive at any result without a considerable measure of speculation. As a calculation, the whole process breaks down at the beginning owing to the difficulty of discerning the influence of bombing among the many other factors which affect production, even at the local points, and also the impossibility of finding a really satisfactory index by which to express production levels. Quite apart therefore from the immense difficulties of attempting to translate local production losses into terms of national loss, which are very great, especially when the subject is an expanding economy, it is impossible even to arrive at conclusive figures about local production losses. A statistical examination, though it can be helpful if the relevance and competence of the figures is closely defined, is liable to create a misleading, and is certain to produce a partial, solution of the problem.

A better way of seeking this solution is to examine the local effects with a view to assessing the destructive power of the bombers, and then to analyse the behaviour of the national target. By a comparison of the two findings it is then possible, by a reasoned argument, to determine whether the destructive power of the bombers was approaching or overtaking the ability of Germany to withstand them, or, in other words, the extent to which the bombing offensive was succeeding.

Thus, the problem reduces itself to an examination of, firstly, the extent to which the destructive power of Bomber Command was approaching or overtaking the replacement rate of which German industry was capable. In this case the German production curve is the decisive argument. Secondly, it must be determined whether the effect of bombing on morale was sufficiently marked to produce economic or political effects. Finally, it has to be decided whether the local damage which was caused by the bombing made a sufficiently serious impression upon responsible Germans and led them to take decisions which had any significant effect upon policy which would be reflected in war production and military strategy.

The principal disadvantage of this method of proceeding is that it leaves a certain ambiguity about the effects of bombing which fall between the two extremes of success and failure. This is particularly unfortunate in the case of the 1942 offensive which cannot rank with those of 1940 and 1941 as a virtual failure, and yet which does not approximate to the final offensive as a virtual success. Clearly the effects of bombing are most difficult to assess when they are least obvious. This is, however, a difficulty which confronts any method of assessment, and, since the evidence does not permit a precise statement, it is one which has to be faced with resignation.

In this chapter we shall therefore examine the local effects of the 1942 bombing offensive from which all national effects must have ensued. This will be our means of gauging the destructive power of Bomber Command. Then we shall consider the behaviour of the German economy, that is the performance of industry and the activity of the workers. We shall then be in a position to judge the economic effectiveness, or in other words, the direct achievement of the campaign. Finally, we shall analyse the fluctuations of German policy, and in particular the policy which governed the Luftwaffe, to see if the offensive produced any indirect consequences of note.

For Germany the local effects of the 1942 raids were the most severe which she had yet experienced. Before March 1942 German towns had been scarcely touched by bombing, but by September an area of 2,280 acres had been torn from their centres.[2] In the process great numbers of Germans had been bombed out of house and home, considerable damage had been done to industrial plant, to communications and to the public utilities upon which modern life depends. Nevertheless, surprisingly few people had been killed.

In Lübeck, for instance, the number of dead only just exceeded three hundred and the four raids on Rostock killed no more than about one hundred and sixty people. The Thousand Bomber attack on Cologne killed about four hundred and seventy of the population. More surprising than this, however, was the speed at which conditions in the stricken cities were brought under control, and the persistence with which essential activities were carried on. The German government excelled at the exercise of authority and the provision of relief, and these, as the British had themselves recognised, were the keys to sustained morale.

Obviously, the greater part of the attack fell on the civilian population, for most of the bombs were intended for the centres of the cities. In most cases the industrial areas of the towns attacked did not lie in or near these centres. In the case of Düsseldorf, for instance, the chief industrial plants were widely scattered in the suburbs of the town. Thus, on the whole, these plants were only hit by stray bombs, or those few which were precisely aimed at them.

Therefore, as far as industrial results were concerned, the effect of the bombing depended more upon dislocation than upon direct destruction. This did not mean that industrial undertakings escaped altogether. From a total of one hundred and fifty major industrial establishments at Lübeck, the March attack caused the complete destruction of nine, heavy damage to eleven and some damage to a further thirty-five. In Rostock Gauleiter Hildebrandt reported that the raid had been a "catastrophe" and he said that the Heinkel works had been hit most severely of all. Generalfeldmarschall Milch was told that aircraft production there had been "seriously affected". The situation suggested that the production quota for June could not "possibly be achieved". During the Thousand Bomber raid on Cologne a much larger number of industrial works were destroyed or damaged, and in several, production was brought to a standstill.

Nevertheless, the direct industrial damage, which these examples illustrate, was insignificant by comparison to what happened to the centres of the towns. At Lübeck, the centre of the town, the Altstadt, was densely built up and populated. More than thirty thousand people lived in this central area of no more than 2.3 square kilometres as compared with the ninety thousand who lived in the much larger suburban area of some forty-four square kilometres. The Altstadt was largely of mediaeval construction, so that the buildings were inflammable and the streets narrow and tortuous. A more promising target for a fire attack could scarcely be imagined.

It is not therefore surprising to find that the whole area of the Altstadt became a sea of flames in the Bomber Command attack. These were only brought under "some semblance of control" on the following afternoon. Meanwhile rubble blocked the streets and the trams could not run. Help had to be called in from outside, and the soup kitchens which arrived had to care for no fewer than twelve thousand people. Out of a total of 19,125 buildings in the city, 1,425 were destroyed, 1,976 were heavily damaged, and a further 8,411 were more slightly damaged. Electricity and gas plants suffered heavily, telephone connections were reduced to a chaotic condition, and somewhere in the region of three thousand people appear to have fled the city.

Goebbels recognised that the situation was "far from pleasant" and this was, in fact, the occasion of his investiture by Hitler with "sweeping powers" to organise relief. This was, however, an isolated attack, and Lübeck only suffered one further serious raid and this did not take place until 1944. The people who had left the city gradually returned, the rubble was cleared up, and in a surprisingly short time more or less normal activity was resumed.

The same thing happened in Rostock after the four Bomber Command attacks on successive nights in April. Immediately after the attacks Goebbels was informed that no less than 70% of the city's dwelling houses were destroyed.[3] Signs of exhaustion began to appear. 150,000 people had to be evacuated.

The works managers had to give the workers a day's holiday so that they could evacuate their families, and, presumably at the same time, recover their own strength. In a further report about the state of Rostock, made on 2 May 1942, the Gauleiter spoke of the necessity for the strictest discipline in handling the refugees in this and "other such blows". They should not be allowed, he thought, to slip through the fingers of the party and travel across the Reich spreading stories. Nevertheless, the Gauleiter, in the same report, was able to advertise his own success by reporting that full production would be resumed in a few days, and that people who had left the city were gradually returning with restored confidence. They were clearing up their homes, in some cases they were bringing back their children, and perhaps above all, they were displaying no signs of hostility to the Party. Allowing for the fact that the Gauleiter would naturally desire to make a favourable impression upon Goebbels, the general tendency was, as at Lübeck, towards rapid recovery, not towards mounting panic. All the same Goebbels was not pleased that Edda Ciano was allowed to see Lübeck and Rostock. Other 'bombed' towns would, he thought, have been more suitable for her eyes.

The Thousand Bomber attack on Cologne rendered more than forty thousand people homeless. These attacks on Lübeck, Rostock and Cologne were, of course, among the most spectacular achievements of Bomber Command in 1942, and they were the exception not the rule. Nevertheless, persistent attacks on Essen and Bremen and several other towns were productive of some results.

If the effects of the air raids on these towns could be shown statistically, if, for instance, the economic effects of the attack on Cologne could be expressed in terms of industrial production lost, it would then be possible to draw detailed conclusions about the local effectiveness of the 1942 campaign. This is not, however, possible and it is therefore only feasible to draw more general conclusions. The most obvious deduction is that in no instance did Bomber Command succeed in delivering a knock out blow against any city. The nearest approach to this was probably achieved at Lübeck and Rostock, but in both cases, recovery was possible and, in fact, took place quickly.

It proved impossible to reduce morale enough, and above all for long enough, to produce a disintegration of community life in the cities which were bombed. Still less was it possible to cause sufficiently heavy damage to make the continuance of community life a physical impossibility. Thus, the towns revealed powers of recovery which were afforded by a vigorous administration and a stout-hearted people. Such panic as was engendered by the attacks was in every case local and temporary.

The fact therefore emerges that in 1942 Bomber Command's destructive power was inadequate to throw a city into disorder for more than a strictly limited period. While it attacked Rostock, Lübeck recovered, while it attacked Cologne, Rostock recovered and while it attacked Essen, Cologne was recovering. The critical point at which recovery would be impossible was certainly never reached in 1942, and in view of subsequent events, it may be suspected that it was never approached.

The local effects of the 1942 campaign therefore appear to have been relatively small. Nevertheless, there were effects. Much destruction had been done, and though it is impossible to say what this cost in loss of production and so on, it is safe to assume that it was costing something. The only question of importance is whether the cost was sufficiently great to affect the national economy, or to divert the policy of the German leaders from its intended course. In other words, were these local effects sufficiently serious to become national effects?

Taking first the economic effects of the bombing, the test is to examine the behaviour of the German economy, to discover whether or not it exhibited any signs of embarrassment as a result of the damage inflicted by Bomber Command.

By the end of 1942 German armaments production had increased by nearly 80% since the beginning of the year,[4] while the volume of consumer goods production was slightly greater by the end of the year than it had been at the beginning. These two facts alone suggest that the bombing offensive of 1942 failed to achieve any significant effect upon the German economy. The damage which was inflicted did not prevent armaments production from rising steeply and the rise in armaments production was not achieved at the expense of consumer goods production. In other words, the German economy, so far from displaying symptoms of exhaustion, was showing itself to be vigorous and resourceful. The explanation of this state of affairs lies in the great reserves which still lay behind the war economy of 1942. The fact which had eluded, and continued to elude, British intelligence experts, was that in 1942 the German war economy, so far from being strained to the limit of its capacity, was only just embarking upon a period of remarkable expansion which was only to reach its peak in July 1944.

Some examination of how the German economy came to possess these reserves is clearly called for, because the resilience with which these reserves endowered Germany was, in general, the major factor in her buoyancy under the mounting air attack, and, in particular, the principal explanation of how so much local damage resulted in so little effect. The German war economy of 1942 was in a relatively relaxed condition, partly because of an intentional policy pursued by Hitler, and partly because of an unintentional inefficiency which was either tolerated by, or unknown to, the German Government.

The cardinal element of Hitler's policy was the display, and if necessary, the use, of overwhelming military strength at the decisive moment. This was the key to his political conduct before the war, and his military strategy was the purest extension of that policy. Hitler intended that the series of diplomatic coups d'état should culminate in a series of Blitzkriegs. The last coup d'état was the non-aggression pact with Russia, and the first Blitzkrieg was the campaign in Poland.

The armed preponderance which enabled Germany to defeat Poland and France, and offered the prospect of annihilating Russia was, however, only relative to the armed strength of her opponents. It by no means represented the greatest armed strength which the economic capacity of Germany could have established. In fact, Germany had in the years before the war armed herself with relative ease. Her standard of living had increased and she had in fact produced guns and butter. The backwardness of Russia, the political decadence of France, the pacifism of Britain and the isolationism of the U.S.A. had suggested to Hitler that his opponents could be dealt with swiftly and singly.

Time, he knew, would fight against Germany. Time might draw Russia into the war from the East and America from the West. Time would allow Britain to build up her armed strength. If these possibilities were realised, Germany would find herself involved in a long war, a war which she could not win. "Time", Hitler told his Commanders-in-Chief after the Polish campaign, was "more likely to be an ally of the western powers than of us."[5]

For Germany everything depended on speed. Hitler's hopes could only be realised if Germany could strike down her enemies before they could get to their feet. By 1939/40 Germany did possess an overwhelming preponderance of armed strength. Everything was staked on the assumption that that moment was decisive. This was the policy to which the German economy had been geared. It therefore seemed unnecessary to intensify the war economy after the outbreak of war. The goods had already been delivered; they had only to be used. Economically the war seemed to have been won before it began.

On the contrary it seemed desirable to reduce the intensity of the war economy step by step with each victorious campaign, so that German industry should be ready to assert itself in the post war world market. Hitler, in fact, ordered reductions in armaments production after the defeat of France and again after the initial victory in Russia.[6] For German industry the order of the day was "business as usual" and an extraordinary degree of private enterprise not only managed, but was intended, to survive. Indeed, the speed and ease with which the first German victories were won took the administration by surprise. "The plans which were previously laid", Reichsminister Funk declared early in the war, "must therefore in many cases now be changed, economic life not having to be changed over to the full extent as the mobilisation plans foresaw". Thus, with a relatively high standard of living and a relatively low intensity of war effort, the German economy possessed a great reserve of power. This reserve was the by-product of the policy which Hitler had consciously pursued.

In addition to this, there was another source of reserve power in the German economy produced by the inefficient methods of production and allocation which were allowed to survive. Control of the war economy lay in the hands of those who did not understand it, the military bureaucracy. As an example of the state of affairs which prevailed, the system of steel allocation may be quoted. Each of the claimants, the Wehrmacht, the Reichsbahn and the various industries, demanded more steel than it wanted, was allocated less than it demanded but more than it could use. Then the Wehrmacht issued priorities to its suppliers which were based on exaggerated requirements.

In this way the firms were able to waste steel and meet civilian orders, for which they could not have obtained a regular allocation. This was typical. Firms were allowed to retain their trade secrets, which are the enemy of organised national production, and were ordered to produce such a variety of armament types that long runs were often impossible, and in many cases the products became obsolete before they were delivered. Here then was a second great reserve in the German war economy.

These were the products of Hitler's belief in a short war, and these reserves were left unexploited for as long as Hitler continued to believe that victory was just around the corner. This he continued to believe for an unnaturally long time. The failure to invade Britain in 1940 did not seem vastly important. British troops had been driven from the Continent, and her military forces could be contained and ultimately annihilated in the Middle East. The failure to smash Russia in 1941 was a serious setback, and a certain amount of re-armament was called for, but there did not seem to be any reason to lose confidence that the decisive blow could be struck in the spring of 1942.

It was only the disaster at Stalingrad and, to a lesser extent, the defeat at El Alamein, and the increasing activities of American industry together with the mounting scale of the strategic bombing offensive which, by the end of 1942 and the beginning of 1943, forced Hitler into a radical change of policy. A long war was then inevitable. Reichsminister Albert Speer, who had been put in charge of the limited re-armament required for a second Russian campaign at the beginning of 1942, was, from that time forward, to receive ever increasing powers to improvise an economy of total war from the material designed for a Blitzkrieg.

These increasing activities had only an imperceptible effect upon the extent of economic mobilisation in 1942, for, as we have seen, the increase in armaments production was achieved without a corresponding reduction in the output of consumer goods, and without a significant reduction in the manpower working in the consumer goods industries. Increased efficiency rather than greater mobilisation was the source of Speer's achievement in 1942. The main reserve within the German economy remained substantially intact.

This meant that the local damage inflicted by Bomber Command could not affect the war economy. Such losses of production as did occur could be substantially absorbed by the reserve of strength. In fact, while the British Air Staff believed they were striking a telling blow at the heart of the German war economy, they were only pounding a capacious cushion of reserve.

However resilient the German war economy may have been, a collapse of morale would still have paralysed it, but this could occur only if the collapse was severe and widespread. The offensive of 1942, as we have seen, produced only local and temporary morale effects. Even these effects did not prove to be infectious. In so far as national morale was concerned, the R.A.F.'s more effective attacks did little or nothing to compensate for the less successful ones. In the last resort the maintenance of morale depended on the quality of the people being attacked, but just as a veteran army, accustomed to discipline and danger, proves to be the most effective in battle, so the civilian morale of Germany tended to stiffen under the discipline which was imposed upon it by the Government, and after it had survived the initial shock of bombing.

The Bomber Command attack on Lübeck had exposed certain weaknesses in the organisation of the people under air attack. As a result, Hitler placed Goebbels in charge of this task. The Reichspropagandaminister understood the essentials of his job, the provision of relief and the exercise of authority. The resources of the Reich were thrown into the rescue of Lübeck. If the people did not respond to the provision of relief, the police state had many other means of keeping them under control. The difficulties which arose in Lübeck, Rostock, Cologne and other bombed towns were kept local and made temporary. For this Germany had to thank the stoic qualities of her people and the vigorous nature of her administration.

Thus in 1942 it seems probable that the bombing stiffened rather than weakened the determination of the people. To this extent Speer's task was somewhat eased. Göring's idea that no bombers would ever reach the Reich had exploded but when the people began to feel the weight of war, they began to apply themselves to war.

How far the point of collapse lay beyond the stage of stiffening determination, and whether that point could be reached by the bombing which was still to come, none could say in 1942. As will duly emerge, the optimism of the British about this was at times to be almost paralleled by the pessimism of the German leaders. Even if the question did remain open at the end of the year, the conclusion does emerge that the bombing offensive in 1942 failed to achieve its direct aims. The German war economy did not suffer either from physical damage it sustained, nor did it suffer as a result of declining morale among the industrial workers.

The people had, in fact, reacted not in the sense which Lord Trenchard had believed likely, but more in that which Mr. Churchill had suggested in 1917. Nor did the evidence of 1942, limited as it was, offer a good prospect of the bombing achieving decisive results in 1943. The whole condition of Germany indicated that a war of attrition against her economy and morale would be much larger and longer task than the British Air Staff, basing their attitude on faulty intelligence, believed. To this extent, but to this extent only, the restoration of British confidence in the principle of strategic bombing which was created by the 1942 offensive was unjustified.

In war there is always a clash of illusions, and the direct consequences of strategic bombing are not by any means always the only consequences. In searching for the indirect effects of the 1942 offensive it is natural to fix attention upon the Luftwaffe, for it was the Luftwaffe which had to deal with the attacks. Even though the German Air Force was one of the acknowledged targets of Bomber Command in 1942, it was not really susceptible to direct effects from bombing, for aircraft production was protected by the reserves and recuperative power[7] common to the whole war economy at the time, and the night bombers could not, and never intended to engage German fighters in combat.

Such effects as the offensive had upon the Luftwaffe were therefore inevitably indirect. Bomber Command was principally interested in damaging the Luftwaffe in the service of Russia and other projected land operations, for, from its own point of view, air superiority did not appear to be essential. Nevertheless, any damage to the Luftwaffe was of great importance, for, ultimately the battle for air superiority became one of the decisive battles of the war, with effects of the utmost importance for all the battle fronts, and not the least for the strategic bombing offensive.

In 1942 two significant tendencies began to appear, which had important consequences for the future of the Luftwaffe. The first was its increasing deployment long the Western Front as a defence against bombing, and the other was the growth of its defensive, by comparison with the decline of its offensive, arm.

During 1942 the Luftwaffe had many duties to perform, and its activities were spread over three fronts. In Russia the German army was struggling against menacing opposition and it needed air support. In the Middle East Rommel's offensive failed, and again the German army needed air support. At the same time a third front had been created in the air by Bomber Command: the western air front, and this too the Luftwaffe had to hold. The most solid achievement of the bombing offensive in 1942 was that it contributed significantly to the burden which was imposed upon the Luftwaffe at the vital moments when the Russians and the British were turning to the offensive in the East and in North Africa.

This was a burden which the Luftwaffe was inadequate to sustain. It was no longer possible for the High Command to concentrate the German Air Force at one decisive point. It was now dispersed on three fronts and whatever the importance of the Russian and Middle East campaigns, Germany could not leave her towns and cities undefended.[8] "We must have day and night fighters", Göring said in September 1942, "which will inflict such punishment that the enemy's losses in aircrew personnel will be so high that he will no longer be able to go ahead with his plan to burn the cities of Germany one after another."[9] Göring had recognised that Germany would soon have to deal not only with a British bombing offensive, but an American as well.

Göring had also recognised by September 1942 that the Luftwaffe was wholly inadequate for the tasks which confronted it. He wanted fighters, both day and night, for the defence of the Reich. He wanted long range heavy bombers, speed bombers, dive bombers, transport aircraft and army co-operation machines. He wanted an air force capable of checking the bomber offensive from Britain by close defence and retaliation, capable of launching strategic attacks on Russia. He wanted his air force to be able to destroy Russian tanks and British aircraft carriers, but when he surveyed the scene, he found little to please him.

Only in the Ju. 87 dive bomber, the Ju. 88 all-purpose machine and the Ju. 52 transport could he take real satisfaction. He envied the British their Spitfire, their four engine bombers and their wooden Mosquito, because nothing comparable was coming along in Germany. When he thought about the German four engine bomber, the He. 177, he wanted to "scream". Its two pairs of engines each welded together, which tended to burn, and could only be serviced by unscrewing "nearly everything", he found so "entirely stupid" that he said he could not express himself.[10]

Göring wanted a balanced and powerful air force, but he and Germany now had to pay the price of neglect and complacency. The Luftwaffe, like Hitler himself, had not prepared for a long war. It had consequently failed to expand in size, and it had failed to keep abreast of modern developments. A comparison between the Lancaster and the He. 177 was sufficient to indicate this. The German aircraft industry was capable of an enormously expanded production, the first signs of which began to appear in 1942, for it had been working at very low pressure,[11] but it was not capable of balanced expansion. The offensive arm of the Luftwaffe which had once fathered the conception of the 'knock out blow' was crippled by the lack of a promising heavy bomber prototype.[12]

The initial swing of the Luftwaffe from being an offensive weapon to becoming a predominantly defensive one was therefore due principally to German neglect and failure, rather than to the pressure of the British bombing offensive. Nevertheless, the increasing reliance which Germany placed on close defence rather than counter offence was ultimately to have the most serious consequences. It will be necessary to return to this theme in subsequent chapters to see what these consequences were, and how far they were due to the combined bomber offensive. Meanwhile it is sufficient to say that the initial unbalancing of the Luftwaffe was basically due to German neglect, and that the bombing offensive in 1942 did little more than drive home the logic of a policy which other circumstances had already imposed on Germany.

Why then, it may be asked, should the campaign of 1942 belong to the 'years of achievement' when so little was accomplished in the form of direct or indirect national effects? The reason is that in 1942 Bomber Command became for the first time technically efficient. It is true that its destructive power did not yet approach the standard later acquired by a much larger force with better equipment, but its destructive power had already far exceeded anything possible to the 1941 force.

Part IV

The Climax of Area Bombing and the Return to Selective Bombing, 1943–1944

Chapter 7

The Year of Conflict, 1943

By the end of 1942, Hitler's Blitzkrieg theory had collapsed. The German invasion of Russia, which had begun with a series of crushing victories, was now developing into the greatest disaster ever sustained by German arms. The Russian victory at Stalingrad was one of the decisive battles of the war. In the Middle East General Montgomery's Eighth Army had driven Rommel back from the approaches to Cairo and then had given pursuit in the last great chase across the desert. Allied forces under the command of Lt. General Eisenhower had invaded North Africa from the West and it was only a matter of time until the last German troops were driven from Africa into the sea or the prisoner of war cages. German offensive air operations had practically ceased and though Germany was still to win successes in the Battle of the Atlantic, the defeat of the U-boat was approaching. Germany had lost the initiative and henceforth her best energies were devoted to the unwholesome task of defence. It was now the turn of the Allies to determine the course of the war.

The enormous and relentless manpower of Russia, the unparalleled productive power of the United States of America and the geographical position of Great Britain, a fighting ally, ensured the ultimate defeat of Germany. The object of the Casablanca Conference, where the President of the U.S.A. and the Prime Minister of Great Britain met with their Chiefs of Staff in January 1943, was to find the formula for German defeat.

The outposts of Hitler's Empire had already been breached. It remained to decide how and when to break into its heart. At the beginning of 1943 Hitler still commanded a powerful nation at arms which was to prove as resolute in defence as it had been ruthless in attack. Inevitable as the ultimate defeat of Germany was, the task was neither easy nor obvious.

Ever since Dunkirk the British Chiefs of Staff had been reflecting about the possibility of re-entering the Continent in force, but while Britain had no allies and while the German army remained intact there was little more that could be done. This indeed had been one of the reasons for so much hope resting on the performance of the independent strategic bombing force.

The entry of Russia and America into the war changed this. There was now no valid reason why the German army should not ultimately be defeated in the field. General Marshall, the United States Chief of Staff, was insistent that there should be an invasion of France and the Russians repeatedly urged the opening of a second front. At the highest level the doctrine that air power alone could produce victory was no longer proclaimed, simply because it was no longer necessary that it should do so. At Casablanca Sir Charles Portal, the British C.A.S., admitted that the "maximum pressure" must be exerted against Germany "by land operations". "Air bombardment alone", he said, "was not sufficient."

Nevertheless, the problem of conducting these land operations was formidable. At the Casablanca Conference the debate fluctuated between General Marshall's conviction that an invasion of France should be attempted in 1943 and General Sir Alan Brook's that such an enterprise would only be possible if visible cracks began to appear in the German structure. The British won this argument and the upshot of the Casablanca Conference was that an Allied invasion of France in 1943 became extremely unlikely. Surface operations were to be conducted against German's southern flank from the Mediterranean. The main assault against the German army in France was to be delayed until the various agencies of attrition, the Russian army, the Allied army in Africa and the strategic bombing forces had had more time to work on Germany. The principle of strategic bombing had suffered a loss of prestige as a result of invasion possibilities, but it regained much of this because of delays and difficulties in mounting the invasion. The Casablanca Conference designated strategic bombing not as an independent means of winning the war, but as the essential pre-requisite to a successful invasion.

If, however, support for the principle of strategic bombing was strengthened, there was still a conflict of opinion between the American and British Staffs as to how it should be conducted. The R.A.F. had already embarked upon an offensive against German cities aimed at the destruction of morale and economy. To bring this strategy to fruition the British Air Staff had called for a force of four to six thousand heavy bombers by 1944. In other words, the British plan seemed to depend upon the participation of American bombers. The Americans had, however, never been convinced of the wisdom of the area bombing offensive and their own bombers and aircrews had been built and trained for precision attacks by day upon key points in the enemy war economy.

Despite British dismay and indeed scepticism, the American bombers had been rehearsing this form of attack over France during 1942 and in 1943 they were determined to carry out precision attacks on Germany. In other words, they were not prepared to join the R.A.F. in the general assault upon German cities by night. When Sir Charles Portal suggested that one of the most important problems before the Casablanca Conference was to decide what kind of bombing offensive should be aimed at Germany in 1943, he therefore spoke of a crucial issue upon which agreement was not going to be easy.

The divergence of opinion between the R.A.F. and the U.S.A.A.F. was recognised at the Casablanca Conference, but it could not be bridged. In addition to this, a third opinion had to be taken into account. This was the belief, voiced by British and American Admirals alike, that the independent role of bombers was of doubtful value. All battles turned on the Battle of the Atlantic and as many bombers as possible should join in this struggle by attacking submarine bases and so on.

The title deed of the Combined Bomber Offensive, the directive to the "appropriate British and United States Air Force commanders to govern the operations of the British and United States Bomber commands in the United Kingdom", which was issued by the Combined Chiefs of Staff on 21 January 1943, was therefore the product of divergent views all of which had to be incorporated in the document. "Your primary object," the Casablanca Directive began, "will be the progressive destruction and dislocation of the German military, industrial and economic system and the undermining of the morale of the German people to a point where their capacity for armed resistance is fatally weakened". Within this "general concept" the primary targets, "subject to the exigencies of weather and tactical feasibility", were to be in the following order:

(1) Submarine construction yards.
(2) The Aircraft industry.
(3) Transportation.
(4) Oil plants.
(5) Other targets in "enemy war industry".

This order of priority was of course only temporary and, the directive pointed out, could be varied from time to time "according to developments in the strategical situation". The directive also indicated that precision targets were to be attacked by day, while "continuous pressure" on German morale was to be maintained by night. Finally, the directive said "when Allied Armies re-enter the Continent" ... "all possible support in the manner most effective" was to be afforded.

At this moment the Combined Chiefs of Staff resembled a conductor trying to pick up the time from his orchestra in which all the instruments were playing different tunes. Concessions had been offered to all schools of thought. The R.A.F. Bomber Command was assured that its 1942 offensive could be continued. The American Air Force was offered the chance of testing its theory in practice. The naval and military exponents of auxiliary bombing were not neglected. No indication as to which of these various possibilities would become the central theme was given. Instead, therefore, of initiating a combined bomber offensive, the Casablanca Directive began a bombing competition. The commanders of the two bomber forces, Sir Arthur Harris and Lt. General Ira Eaker, were left to interpret this extremely wide directive in their own different ways.

The Casablanca Directive was sent to Bomber Command on 4 February 1943, at a time when Sir Arthur Harris was becoming exasperated by the frequent requests being made to him for Bomber Command attacks upon naval targets in Italy and France, as well as upon specially selected targets of key importance in Germany. The C-in-C thought that the directives which he had received since November 1942 made a depressing study.

During those winter months he had been asked to bomb submarine installations at Lorient, St. Nazaire, Brest and La Pallice. He had been told that a successful attack on the ball bearings plants at Schweinfurt would warrant the cessation of night bombing for two months. He had been asked to attack the Italian fleet at Spezia and the molybdenum mines at Knaben. All these targets, even if they were "attractive in themselves", were from the C-in-C's point of view diversions from and could contribute nothing to, his "primary object" of destroying German cities.

The fact, which was now becoming obvious, that the Americans were not going to join in the massive attack upon German cities which had been suggested in the C.A.S. paper of November 1942, had clearly shaken Air Staff confidence in the whole strategy. If the American Air Force could not be persuaded to act as the supplement to Bomber Command, then perhaps Bomber Command ought to act as the supplement to the American Air Force. Sir Arthur Harris, on the other hand, was determined to carry on the area attack against German cities at all costs. He was prepared to resist all 'diversionary' influences and in the Casablanca Directive he found a mandate for doing so. The first paragraph of this directive, he told the Air Ministry, "categorically" stated that the "primary objective of Bomber Command will be the progressive destruction and dislocation of the German military, industrial and economic system aimed at undermining the morale of the German people to a point where their capacity for armed resistance is fatally weakened".

The misquotation was slight, but nevertheless significant. The opening paragraph of the directive had actually read "Your (meaning the C-in-C Bomber Command and the Commanding General Eighth Air Force) primary object will be the progressive destruction and dislocation of the German military industrial and economic system and the undermining of the morale of the German people to a point where their capacity for armed resistance is fatally weakened."

Thus, the Combined Chiefs of Staff intention was that the attack on morale should be a part and the second part, of the plan. Sir Arthur Harris' interpretation suggested that the attack on morale was the whole plan. Also, by substituting the word "Bomber Command" in place of "your" he made it clear that this first paragraph was, in his view, the special preserve of the R.A.F. By making no mention at all of the remainder of the directive, which ran contrary to the strategy and tactics upon which he had long since resolved, he tacitly suggested that this was the preserve of the American Air Force.

This interpretation by Sir Arthur Harris of the Casablanca Directive is the key to the whole of his conduct in 1943 and all his other actions in that year follow from it in logical sequence. The state of affairs which now existed was highly significant and in order to grasp the meaning of the conflict which followed, some further elucidation is necessary. The failure of the British Chiefs of Staff to persuade the American Air Staff to join in the British attack on German cities, left the British Air Staff without a policy. The four to six thousand heavy bombers which they had counted on as the minimum force necessary to carry out the destruction of German morale would not now materialise for that purpose. On the other hand, Bomber Command did not possess machines suitable for day flying in the face of the German fighter force. The Lancaster could not approach the altitude at which the Fortress was accustomed to fly and the Lancaster pilots had not been trained to fly in the tight formations which were becoming a characteristic of the Eighth Bomber Command. The role of Bomber Command in the Casablanca programme therefore seemed extremely obscure to the Air Staff. For this reason alone, they fell an easy prey to the many pressures applied to them by the Ministry of Economic Warfare, the Admiralty and the American Air Force itself, while it was a long time before they felt confident enough to take a really strong line with the C-in-C Bomber Command.

Sir Arthur Harris was not shaken by the American attitude. He remained confident that the force which he commanded could determine the course of the war and he remained hopeful that eventually the American Bomber Command could be absorbed into his own system either because of its failure to pursue an independent policy or because of the striking success of his own. The conflict in 1943 had the appearance of being between Sir Arthur Harris and the British Air Staff, but it was really a conflict between the R.A.F. Bomber Command and the U.S. Eighth Bomber Command. In 1943 two wars were being waged against Germany in the air. There was no combined bomber offensive until 1944.

While Sir Arthur Harris prepared and launched the Battle of the Ruhr using the Casablanca directive as his authority, Lt. General Eaker, Commanding General of the Eighth Air Force, used the same authority for a different conception. General Eaker's plan started with the assumption that "it is better to cause a high degree of destruction in a few really essential industries than to cause a small degree of destruction in many industries". American intelligence experts, working in close co-operation with the British, found six target systems[1] consisting of seventy-six targets whose destruction, it was believed, would "fatally weaken the capacity of the German people for armed resistance".

These systems were the submarine construction yards and bases, the aircraft industry, and ball bearings industry, oil, synthetic rubber production and production of military transport vehicles. The destruction of these targets could only be achieved in precision attacks by a force of considerable size and this the Eighth Bomber Command did not yet possess. General Eaker pointed out that he would attempt the task in four phases and that he would need 944 heavy bombers in Britain by 1 July 1943, 1,192 by October 1943, 1,746 by January 1944 and 2,700 by 1 April 1944.

A lesser number of bombers would not achieve a proportion of the plan. It was a matter of all or nothing. Penetrations could not be deep unless they were made in strength. The German Air Force could be expected to react in strength with its growing defensive fighter force and the plan emphasised that "if the growth of the German fighter strength is not arrested quickly it may become literally impossible to carry out the destruction planned".

The successful prosecution of the plan was recognised to depend upon a prior or simultaneous attack upon the German fighter force. If the American bombers could gain an adequate command of the daylight air over Germany and if they arrived in England in large enough numbers, General Eaker felt quite confident that the plan could be carried out. The estimate of the destructive power of American bombers, given such circumstances, was not, in General Eaker's view, in doubt. They were, he said, based upon actual experience of raids in January, February and March 1943. With the forces he demanded he could reduce submarine construction by 89%, he could destroy 43% of fighter production and

65% of bomber. German oil supplies could be disrupted,[2] 76% of ball bearing production could be eliminated and 50% of synthetic rubber production could be destroyed. The R.A.F. could co-operate in the plan by attacking cities by night which were related to the target system being bombed by the Eighth Bomber Command.

Sir Arthur Harris welcomed this plan. He believed that the air war must be fought out before the invasion of the Continent was undertaken and the sooner American bombers began to visit Germany in strength the better he would be pleased. He obviously welcomed the division of responsibilities between the Bomber Commands which the plan envisaged and so long as his own Bomber Command was allowed to continue with the area attacks on German cities, now already in full swing again, he was quite prepared to see what the Americans could achieve by daylight precision attacks. He did, however, make it clear that he was not anxious to resume bombing submarine pens, a duty from which he had only recently been released. Whatever other doubts the C-in-C Bomber Command may have had about the prospects of General Eaker's plan he kept to himself for the time being. The plan would mean more bombers over Germany. Events would demonstrate whether the British or the American strategy and tactics were superior.

The C.A.S., possibly for rather different reasons, also found the plan convincing and he wrote to General Arnold, Commanding General U.S. Army Air Forces, urging that the necessary number of heavy bombers should be sent to General Eaker. General Arnold was, however, looking for something more than mere lip service to the American conception of a combined bomber offensive and in his rely to Sir Charles Portal he suggested that "the time has arrived for the establishment of somewhat more formalized machinery for the closest possible co-ordination, or rather, integration, of the two bomber efforts". This suggestion was a shrewd test of the sincerity of Sir Arthur Harris' apparent support for the Eaker plan. The Combined Operational Planning Committee, which was set up as a result of this suggestion, was more or less boycotted by both Commanders. This gave a fair indication of their attitude to an "integrated" bomber offensive.

The most important feature of the Eaker plan, as Lt. General McNarney explained to the Combined Chiefs of Staff in Washington, was the need to reduce the German fighter force. The Combined Chiefs of Staff, who, acting under the President of the U.S.A. and the Prime Minister of Great Britain, were the supreme military authority, accepted this point and signified their approval of the Eaker plan. The defeat of the German Air Force now became mandatory, the achievement of air superiority was accepted as the indispensable prelude to successful strategic bombing operations. No decision of greater importance was taken in the whole course of the war in the air. A revision, or rather an interpretation, of the Casablanca Directive was now called for. Nevertheless, the task of the Air Ministry in preparing the new directive and in getting it accepted was at least as formidable as it was urgent. The Air Staff still had to reckon with the views of Sir Arthur Harris.

The R.A.F. night bombers were now engaged in the Battle of the Ruhr and they were succeeding in delivering the most destructive attacks ever seen in war. These attacks were not the product of air superiority and the German fighter force was, in fact, increasing rapidly in size and efficiency. The success of the night bomber's flight depended not upon the destruction of the enemy's air defences, but upon evasion of them. The R.A.F. night bombers flew unescorted and they were not armed strongly enough, or capable of sufficient altitudes and speeds to meet the night fighter on anything approaching equal terms. They did not fly in formation. The whole object of the tactics adopted was to avoid meeting an enemy fighter at all. Evasion was the key to survival. As General Eaker's plan had made clear, evasion of fighters in daylight was not a feasible proposition. For precision bombing by day the key to success was air superiority and this meant the destruction of the Luftwaffe.

It was to gain this air superiority, which he himself did not think he needed, that Sir Arthur Harris was now required to join with the American bombers in an attack upon the Luftwaffe and the industry which supported it. It was against this change of strategy, as distinct from mere diversionary calls, that Sir Arthur Harris sustained a long and, as far as 1943 was concerned, successful opposition. Against his determination the Air Staff did not prevail with the views of the Combined Chiefs of Staff.

The plan for the destruction of the German Air Force, known as the 'Pointblank' plan, was officially made known to the C-in-C Bomber

Command and the Commanding General Eighth Air Force on 10 June 1943, when a new directive was issued to them by the Air Ministry.[3] "The increasing scale of destruction which is being inflicted by our night bomber forces and the development of the day bombing offensive by the Eighth Air Force have," the directive said, "forced the enemy to deploy day and night fighters in increasing numbers on the Western Front. Unless this increase in fighter strength is checked we may find our bomber forces unable to fulfil the tasks allotted to them by the Combined Chiefs of Staff. For this reason," the directive continued, "the Combined Chiefs of Staff have decided that first priority in the operation of British and American bombers based in the United Kingdom shall be accorded to the attack of German fighter forces and the industry upon which they depend." This seemed quite straightforward.

The only difference between the American and British forces which was essential would be in the tactics to be adopted. The American bombers would attempt the destruction of plants by precision attacks in daylight. The British bombers would disrupt the aircraft industry by area attacks at night. If the directive had said no more, a combined bomber offensive could have begun, for both forces would have been under an obligation to pursue the same principal aim by different means. This was not to be, for the directive did say a great deal more. "The primary object" of the bomber forces still remained "the progressive destruction and dislocation of the German military, industrial and economic system and the undermining of the morale of the German people to a point where their capacity for armed resistance is fatally weakened".[4]

"In view, however," the directive went on, "of the factors referred to … the following priority objectives have been assigned to the Eighth Air Force: intermediate objective: German fighter strength". In a later sentence it said, "While the forces of the British Bomber Command will be employed in accordance with their main aim in the general disorganisation of German industry their action will be designed as far as practicable to be complementary to the operations of the Eighth Air Force". These last sentences left so many loopholes, that, in effect, the C-in-C Bomber Command was virtually excused from taking any significant part in the 'Pointblank' campaign.

When later the Air Staff began to complain that Sir Arthur Harris was not taking part in the attack on the German Air Force, they only had themselves to blame, because they could have issued a much clearer directive on 10 June. Indeed, the draft of this directive, which they had sent to Bomber Command on 3 June, had been very much more in accord with their intentions. "The general responsibilities allocated to the bomber forces in the original directive issued by the Combined Chiefs of Staff,"[5] this draft had said "still hold. The list of objectives, as modified by the Chiefs of Staff is now as follows: intermediate objective: German fighter strength". This left no doubt that both forces were to attack German fighter strength. In the final directive this passage was changed so as to embrace only the Eighth Bomber Command. There was no mention in the draft of the British bombers continuing their "main aim in the general disorganisation of German industry". There was a specific mention of the importance of the bombing of the German ball bearing industry which did not appear in the final directive.

Between the issue of the draft and the issue of the final directive there had intervened a conference,[6] which, from the point of view of Sir Arthur Harris who attended it, had been extremely profitable. The British Air Staff were still either insufficiently attracted to the American view, or insufficiently convinced of the wisdom of that held by Sir Arthur Harris and the conflict was still not brought to a head. A widening divergence of opinion was again concealed by a compromise and by a vague directive. Before, however, proceeding to examine the events which led to the dénouement at the beginning of 1944, it is wise to pause here to consider the size and quality of the weapon whose future direction hung in the balance.

Before the war, in the days when R.A.F. expansion in general had been seriously limited by the prevailing view that national economy came before national defence, there had been a great deal of talk about what the 1941 force would achieve. Events, among them the continuing need for defence, conspired to disappoint most of these hopes. Thus, the hopes which had once been entertained for 1941 were gradually transferred to 1943. Many of these hopes had to wait until 1944 and even 1945 before they were realised, but not all of them were disappointed in 1943. Already in 1942, the appearance of the Lancaster among the ranks of operational aircraft had held out prospects of much larger tonnages of bombs reaching Germany. The introduction of Gee at the beginning of the year, and Oboe at the end, together with the creation of the Path Finder Force in the middle had also offered and to a certain extent realised, the hope that a much larger proportion of the bombs lifted would actually find their targets. The principal limitation on Bomber Command's achievements which remained at the beginning of 1943 was the shortage of aircraft available for operations.

The 'Thousand Bomber' raids had been freaks and in January 1943 there were only 839 aircraft ready for operations. 1943 saw a rapid transformation of this dismal state of affairs and by July the C-in-C could call on 1,153 operational bombers. Nevertheless, as General Arnold once told President Roosevelt, "a lot of airplanes by themselves ... were not air power".[7]

Of even greater significance than the expansion of Bomber Command in 1943 was its new design, which by the end of that year had become stable. Of the 1,226 operational bombers which Sir Arthur Harris deployed in January 1944, 627 were Lancasters, 373 were Halifaxes and 72 were Mosquitoes. The Stirlings and Wellingtons were soon to disappear from the main force and these three remarkable aircraft, the Lancaster built by A.V. Roe, the Halifax by Handley Page and the Mosquito by De Havilland reigned supreme and were never superseded in the R.A.F. during the rest of the European war. The best indication of the development of Bomber Command in 1943 is to be seen in the fact that it discharged 157,457 tons of bombs. In 1942 it had dropped 45,561 tons.

Thus in 1943 Bomber Command became not only a much more formidable weapon than it had ever been before; it also became a much more versatile one. It is only necessary to compare the outstanding achievements of 1943 with those of 1942. As successful area attacks, the raids on Lübeck and Cologne in 1942 seem almost insignificant by comparison with those on Hamburg in 1943. There was no specialist force in 1942 capable of an achievement of the same calibre as the breaching of the Möhne and Eder dams in 1943.

While the arrival of the American Air Force in Europe had stimulated new ideas about strategic bombing, ideas which had received recognition at the Casablanca and Washington Conferences, Sir Arthur Harris was still thinking in terms of the February 1942 Directive. The task of destroying the Ruhr and particularly Essen, which was indicated in that directive, had in 1942 proved to be beyond the capability of Bomber Command. This was largely because, despite the introduction of Gee, the problem of target finding remained unsolved and also because the force had failed to expand enough. Essen had survived under its protective industrial haze.

The expansion of Bomber Command and above all the introduction of Oboe, offered the solution to this problem in 1943. Sir Arthur Harris did not think that the Casablanca Directive made any difference to his 1942 instructions. In the first half of 1943 he therefore applied himself principally to the destruction of the Ruhr in a campaign which came to be known as the Battle of the Ruhr. For the first time in the war really destructive blows were struck at Essen, thanks to the invention of Oboe. The main attack began in March and continued until July. During this period, attacks of increasing weight were delivered against Essen, Dortmund, Duisburg, Bochum, Gelsenkirchen, Oberhausen, Mülheim, Wuppertal, Remschied, München-Gladbach, Krefeld, Münster, Aachen, Düsseldorf and Cologne. Several of these attacks were made by more than seven hundred aircraft and nearly all of them by more than three hundred. Most of the towns were attacked several times. It was also in this period that the Möhne and Eder dams were breached.

In the Battle of the Ruhr, Bomber Command had the guidance of the Oboe aircraft. The concentration and accuracy of the bombing was remarkable. Terrific devastation in the residential areas was achieved and Bomber Command came through the battle without suffering prohibitive casualties. Nevertheless, the tasks ahead of Bomber Command were stiffer. The battle was now to be extended beyond the Ruhr and also beyond the range of Oboe. These attacks would have to be carried out in the face of an increasingly efficient night fighter force. Strategically an immediate onslaught on Berlin might have been desirable, but tactically it was impossible.

The new campaign began with the memorable Battle of Hamburg at the end of July. In a series of very heavy raids a crushing blow was struck at the unfortunate town. The night fighter force was temporarily paralysed by the use of 'Window'[8] and the target was easily located by the use of H2S which, in this instance, proved to be a good substitute for Oboe. In many cases, however, while the attack was fanning out towards Berlin and places like Stuttgart, Leipzig, Nuremburg, Hanover, Frankfurt, Mannheim and Kassel, were attacked, much less successful results were got from H2S, which had a somewhat erratic performance. Blind marking by H2S depended upon extremely skilled operation, which was necessarily rare at the outset, and upon the presence of some water near the target.[9]

The success of most of these raids was not comparable to that achieved in the Ruhr and Hamburg. The prospects for the Battle of Berlin, which began in November, were therefore not nearly so good as they had been for the Battle of the Ruhr.

There were, however, other problems which confronted Sir Arthur Harris in the Battle of Berlin. On 14 October 1943, 291 bombers of the Eighth Air Force were dispatched to attack the ball bearing plants at Schweinfurt. Of these 229 attacked and 60 were destroyed. The news of this was received in America as something approaching a national disaster. A crisis which had long been simmering in the affairs of strategic bombing now burst with full force.

American bombing operations had begun on 17 August 1942 when twelve aircraft of the Eighth Bomber Command had attacked the marshalling yards at Rouen. No bombers were lost. For the remainder of 1942 the Eighth Bomber Command carried out experimental operations over France, which were partly intended to contribute strategically to the Battle of the Atlantic, for most of the targets were submarine bases, but which were primarily designed as a dress rehearsal for the day offensive against Germany. By the end of January, the American Air Force felt emboldened to make its first attack on Germany and on 27 January ninety-one heavy bombers were dispatched to Wilhelmshaven. This, by a curious coincidence, had also been the scene of the R.A.F's first attack on 4 September 1939, but the American Air Force lost no more than three bombers.

Thereafter American bombers gradually began to extend the sphere of their operations. Attacks were presently made on Hamm, another early favourite of the R.A.F., Emden, Vegesack and Bremen. A larger number of attacks on French targets continued. These operations were, however, still essentially experimental and the majority of them continued to be devoted to submarine bases and construction yards. The Eighth Bomber Command was still very small. It was not until March that a force of a hundred bombers could be put up with any consistency. Apart from the attacks on submarines, the efforts of the Eighth Bomber Command were, in the words of an American historian, "tentative, scattered and light". Nevertheless, the casualties which were experienced were also light. Over France, where they could often be escorted, albeit sometimes rather inefficiently, by R.A.F. Spitfires, the American bombers found their job comparatively easy.

Over Germany, which was more important, the small formations of Fortresses, often unescorted, held their own against the German fighters. This success was nevertheless deceptive, for the penetration by the American bombers was still shallow and the German fighters took some time to learn the most advantageous ways of attack. The equality of the bomber with the fighter could not last and on 17 April a force of one hundred and seventeen American bombers suffered more heavily when it attacked the Focke-Wulf plant at Bremen. Sixteen bombers were shot down and forty-six were damaged. It is true that a German reconnaissance aircraft had, by chance, given an early warning of the raid, but the really significant development was the new co-ordinated system of attack which the German fighters were beginning to adopt.

The increasing success of the German fighters pointed imperatively to the need for an American long-range fighter and it also emphasised the necessity of fighting and defeating the Luftwaffe in the air and on the ground. The only long-range fighters available had neither very long range nor adequate fighting power and the Eighth Bomber Command embarked upon the most awkward phase of its history. In order to attack German aircraft production it had to make deep penetrations, but in order to make deep penetrations it needed not only large numbers of bombers (three hundred was regarded as the minimum required for a formation) which it did not yet possess, but also long-range escorts which it also did not possess. It was in largely similar circumstances that the R.A.F. had taken to night bombing and it was these circumstances which led to the American disaster at Schweinfurt in October. The

Luftwaffe had decisively won the first engagement in the Battle for air superiority over Germany.

It was this American dilemma which brought the crisis to a head. On 14 October 1943, the same day as the Schweinfurt attack, General Arnold had written to Sir Charles Portal pressing upon the British C.A.S. the urgency of getting more seriously to grips with the German Air Force. He thought that inadequate forces were being brought to bear not only against the aircraft industry, but against the "German Air Force in being". In a second communication to Sir Charles Portal three days later General Arnold further expressed his uneasiness about the course events were taking. "We must", he said, "bring into the battle against him[10] all of our numerical superiority in aircraft. By this I mean", he continued, "specifically the aircraft of our tactical forces, your home defence forces and the total weight of our combined bomber forces against the installations mutually selected for destruction. Such measures", he concluded, "will require immediate scrapping of some outmoded tactical concepts, closer co-ordination between all elements of our commands and more effective use of our combined resources."

General Arnold was clearly convinced that the battle for air superiority was going to be decisive not only for the future of strategic bombing but also for the land invasion of Normandy, which was to take place in the following summer. He was also convinced that the existing system of air command was inadequate to ensure success in this vital struggle. He was thinking more and more in terms of unified control of larger and more balanced segments of air power. The British system of command with its checks and balances resulting in infinite delays and some bitterness could hardly fail to arouse his displeasure.

However, while the British Air Staff were making a somewhat cumbersome attempt to convince General Arnold that the Spitfire would never make a long-range fighter,[11] Sir Arthur Harris was preparing a campaign utterly different in nature to that envisaged by General Arnold.

For some time, the Air Staff had been uneasy about the way in which Sir Arthur Harris had interpreted the 'Pointblank' directive. In September, for instance, the D.C.A.S. had complained to the C.A.S. that "no town associated with fighter production has been attacked by Bomber Command". Sir Arthur Harris had also ignored or vehemently rejected innumerable hints and requests to attack Schweinfurt, the centre of German ball bearings production, despite the A.C.A.S. (Ops.) belief that the destruction of the ball bearing industry "would contribute more towards a reduction of German fighter strength than any other form of attack".

On the other hand, his own plan for the destruction of German cities with a population of more than 100,000 was now approaching a climax, for the Battle of Berlin was at hand. The American plan of action seemed to have broken down with the Schweinfurt disaster and it seemed reasonable to Sir Arthur Harris that the American Air Force should now join in his campaign, rather than that he should join in theirs.

With this idea in mind Sir Arthur Harris submitted a memorandum to the Prime Minister on 3 November 1943. In this he listed nineteen German towns which he claimed were virtually destroyed, nineteen which were "seriously damaged" and a further nine which were damaged. These lists, he suggested, demonstrated that the Ruhr was largely "out", and that much progress had been made further afield. Nearly all this devastation had been done in 1943 after the introduction of Oboe and H2S.

A number of other areas including Berlin remained to be dealt with and Sir Arthur Harris felt "certain that Germany must collapse before this programme which is more than half completed already, has proceeded much further". "We have not got far to go", he added, "but we must get the U.S.A.A.F. to wade in in greater force. If they will only get going according to plan[12] and avoid such disastrous diversions as Ploesti and getting "nearer" to Germany from the plains of Lombardy[13] ... we can get through with it very quickly. We can wreck Berlin from end to end", the memorandum concluded, "if the U.S.A.A.F. will come in on it. It will cost between us 400–500 aircraft. It will cost Germany the war."

This memorandum was a direct challenge to the fundamental belief which General Arnold had so often expressed and which had been adopted by the Combined Chiefs of Staff. It was a denial of the need for air supremacy. The A.C.A.S. who substantially agreed with Sir Arthur Harris' contentions immediately wrote this significant sentence:

"Embroiled as we are with 'Overlord' and consequently with the necessity of lowering German fighter strength and production we are apt, perhaps, to overlook the possibility that the war can be won in the face of or in spite of an increasing air defence." The C-in-C Bomber Command was outwitting these defences[14] and the Americans should, in the opinion of the A.C.A.S.(I), be capable of the same achievement.

According to his view, the Bomber Command attacks were doing more to win the war than any other offensive, including the Russian. It was, therefore, not at all unreasonable that the Americans should join in the Battle of Berlin. The A.C.A.S. (Ops.) (2) and the D.C.A.S. (3) were, however, agreed that the attack on Berlin was unlikely to end the war, even if damage on the Hamburg scale could be achieved. If the attack failed, then the Luftwaffe would have had time to recover and further bombing might become impossible. The D.C.A.S. thought that a limited and "harassing" attack on Berlin was desirable. This would not "jeopardise" the whole course of the "main" offensive against Germany. Finally, the D.C.A.S. once more emphasised his belief that Bomber Command should attack towns associated with fighter production.

Thus, while Sir Arthur Harris embarked upon the Battle of Berlin single handed, three views of the bombing offensive had come into open conflict. General Arnold believed that everything depended upon attacking and destroying the German Air Force in being, as well as damaging the industry which supported it. Most of the British Air Staff were now convinced that the most urgent task was the reduction of German fighter production and the C-in-C Bomber Command still held to the 1942 plan for destroying German morale. Thus, the British Air Staff were much nearer in thought to General Arnold than they were to their own C-in-C of Bomber Command. This state of affairs was rapidly becoming intolerable to all concerned and as the year of conflict ran out, the Air Staff at last determined to resolve it. Schweinfurt was selected as a test case.

That Schweinfurt was a test case of vital importance is beyond doubt. The population of the place was about 60,000 and it was therefore of limited interest to Sir Arthur Harris. It was also a difficult place to find at night and it could only be reached after a long and hazardous flight into the heart of Germany. On the other hand, it was the most important centre of ball bearing production in Germany.

Investigations by the Ministry of Economic Warfare and the Economic Objectives Unit of the American Embassy had for a long time been enlarging upon the catastrophic effects which would follow the destruction of Schweinfurt not only upon the German Air Force, but upon nearly everything which moved. In mid-November the M.E.W. reported that the three plants at Schweinfurt produced between 40 and 50% of total German supplies of ball bearings. Intelligence reports also indicated that the Germans were displaying all the symptoms of anxiety about these supplies. On 30 November the Director of Bomber Operations told the A.C.A.S. (Ops.) that Schweinfurt was the "outstanding priority target in Germany".

A successful attack on it would, he was convinced, have a far-reaching effect upon Germany's war effort. Bomber Command had so far refused to attack it and had always claimed that the tactical difficulties were insurmountable. However, the A.O.C. Pathfinder Group, A.V.M. Bennett, could, apparently, see "no great difficulty" and the D.B. Ops. felt that the D.C.A.S. should again take the matter up with the C-in-C.

The letter to Bomber Command which followed called forth from the C-in-C one of the strongest of the many strong letters he wrote. Writing personally to A.V.M. Bottomley on 20 December, Sir Arthur Harris said that he did not regard a night attack on Schweinfurt as a "reasonable operation of war". Six or seven attacks would be necessary to ensure the destruction of the town and even then, the factories might escape. Quite apart, however, from his doubts about the operational feasibility of the attack on Schweinfurt, the C-in-C objected strongly to the strategy of which this was to be a part. He felt certain that the importance of Schweinfurt to the German ball bearing industry had been greatly exaggerated and he thought it highly probable that the Germans had already dispersed the industry.

Previous experience of what he called "the 'Panacea' mongers" had made the C-in-C cynical. He thought that the damage already done to the German railway system, would, if envisaged two years earlier, have been regarded as lethal to Germany's entire transport system. The breaching of the Möhne and Eder dams, the destruction of the molybdenum mine at Knaben, the destruction of the marshalling yard at Modane, had all been urged upon him as measures likely to produce vital consequences.

All these attacks had been achieved, but no serious consequences had followed. It would be the same, the C-in-C thought, with Schweinfurt. There was always an alternative factory, marshalling yard or metal to keep things going. The 'panacea' mongers were in his view the unconscious dupes of deliberate German espionage aimed to divert the bombing offensive from more dangerous channels. If Schweinfurt was really as important as the Air Staff believed, then the Americans should bomb it again and, in any case, Sir Arthur Harris concluded, unless the Eighth Air Force first set the town on fire to guide the night bombers, he was "not prepared to take it on".

This last point was a shrewd blow at a tender spot. General Arnold soon found it necessary to declare in public that the American attack in October had been highly successful and that another raid on Schweinfurt would not be necessary "for a very long time, if at all".[15] This had been done to sooth American nerves, but it placed Sir Arthur Harris in a strong position.

The C-in-C's letter, which was shown to the Secretary of State for Air, caused consternation at the Air Ministry. It was the most forthright challenge to Air Staff policy which had yet come from Bomber Command and it placed Sir Arthur Harris in impossible isolation. The C.A.S. now felt convinced that a successful attack upon a key industry was certain to produce much better results than the general attack on all industry, but he wanted to be quite sure that Schweinfurt really was a key point.

A further survey of the position by the M.E.W. and the Economic Warfare Division of the American Embassy convinced the D.C.A.S. that there was no doubt about this and he did not think there was anything to be gained from further arguments with the C-in-C. Either the C-in-C must carry out the directive by the Combined Chiefs of Staff or the Combined Chiefs of Staff must change their policy. A.V.M. Bottomley did not doubt that the first course was the best and he suggested that Sir Arthur Harris should be "specifically" directed to attack Schweinfurt as often as its destruction demanded.

The C.A.S. knew that this might "lead to trouble with Harris" but he was now prepared for trouble. The "prize," he told the Secretary of State for Air, was "worth it". Thus far the British Air Staff moved away from the conceptions which had guided them since 1941. Accordingly, on 14

January 1944 an official directive was addressed to the C-in-C Bomber Command, in which he was ordered to attack Schweinfurt as the first priority until either the place was destroyed, or until other orders were sent. Sir Arthur Harris was told at the same time that the British and American Air Staffs "firmly believed" in the strategy of attacking "selected key industries known to be vulnerable and vital in the enemy's war effort".

In addition, in the attacking of Schweinfurt, the C-in-C was also invited to "adhere to the spirit" of the 'Pointblank' directive sent to him on 10 June 1943. Thus if the Air Staff had taken an unnaturally long time to decide upon a point of view between the American conception and that of the C-in-C Bomber Command, they now made clear in the most uncompromising terms that they would no longer brook strategic separatism or scepticism about the value of the industrial intelligence emanating from the M.E.W.

Sir Arthur Harris remained Commander in Chief, but ceased to be the commanding figure who had dominated the scene for exactly a year and eleven months. The policy, if not the practice, of area bombing was now discarded. The area bombing offensive of 1943 beginning with the Battle of the Ruhr and ending with the Battle of Berlin had not convinced the Air Staff that this was the way to win the war. On the night of 24/25 February 1944, 734 aircraft of Bomber Command were dispatched to Schweinfurt.[16]

On the same day 266 American bombers had also attacked Schweinfurt.[17] The Combined Bomber Offensive had begun. Meanwhile the American Eighth Air Force in the United Kingdom and the Fifteenth Air Force in Italy were now acting under the single command of General Carl Spaatz. More important than this, the long-range fighter which was to prove a decisive weapon in the battle for air supremacy had at last made its appearance. The American Air Forces were now plunging deeply into Germany again and the attack on Schweinfurt was only one among several more aimed at the principle German airframe plants.

The struggle between conflicting views of strategic bombing which had lasted throughout 1943 and into 1944 really ended with the Bomber Command attack upon Schweinfurt. By insisting upon this attack the British Air Staff signified their belief that the future lay with the

American conception rather than with that which had once been their own and was still Sir Arthur Harris'. The American Air Force, under the guidance of General Arnold, had pointed the way back to the strategy with which the R.A.F. had entered the war. But they had done more than this. Their operations, not by comparison with those carried out by the R.A.F. particularly impressive in themselves, had demonstrated not only the importance of air superiority, but they had also shown the way to achieve it.

The impending invasion of Normandy, for which air superiority was so vital, had proved a decisive argument in favour of the American idea and an equally decisive one against Sir Arthur Harris. It was therefore in its contribution to triphibious warfare that the independent American bombing offensive scored its greatest advantage over the independent British bombing offensive. Independent bombing had in 1943 been the Western Allies' principal means of carrying out offensive war against Germany.

In 1944 triphibious war supplanted it. Allied armies began to press in upon Germany from Italy, France and Russia. Strategic bombing became a part of a gigantic offensive which embraced all arms. The heavy bombers were yet to score their most spectacular successes, but they lost once and for all their independent prestige.

It was for this prestige that Sir Arthur Harris had fought so hard and at the moment when he believed his Command was on the point of inheriting it, he found that his ideas were out of date, and he no longer commanded the confidence of his superiors. On 14 April 1944 the combined strategic bomber forces passed under the direction of the Allied Supreme Commander, General Eisenhower. In the offensive against French railways which followed, the R.A.F. gained its education in the technique of precision bombing.

Chapter 8

The Effects of R.A.F. Destruction and the Promise of American Strategy

In 1943 and the opening months of 1944, Germany was confronted with simultaneous assaults upon the morale of her civil population and the existence of her air force. The principal aim of the British Bomber Command was the destruction of the larger German cities. The principle aim of the American Bomber Command was the destruction of the Luftwaffe.

In a sense both these conflicting offensives were involuntary, and they both owed their conceptions to the same cause: the German Air Force. The British attacked cities because, having been forced by the Luftwaffe to fly by night, they could not see smaller targets. The Americans attacked the Luftwaffe because, having resolved to fly by day, they soon learned the necessity of air supremacy. It was thus the Luftwaffe which had dictated British and American strategy.

The British Air Staff had hoped, and Sir Arthur Harris believed, that strategic bombers could, flying at night, evade the forces of German air defence, and cause the disintegration of the German war effort by the massive destruction of German cities. If this could have been achieved, it would have been the most complete vindication of the principle of independent bombing and the most economical of victories. There was, if this could be done, no need for a preliminary engagement with the German Air Force which was certain to be long and expensive.

The American Air Force, on the other hand, preferred the preliminary engagement with the Luftwaffe because it believed that the more economical victory could never be won. It did not believe that the destruction of cities, which admittedly could be achieved at night, would in reasonable time cause the downfall of Germany. It believed that this could only be achieved by a direct, precise and selective attack upon key points in the German war economy. This meant day flying and day flying as had been demonstrated over and over again meant air supremacy.[1]

To General Arnold the effort needed to defeat the German Air Force seemed to be the indispensable prerequisite to successful strategic bombing. To Sir Arthur Harris it seemed only a diversion from the central task. This is the crux of the problem which has to be considered in this chapter.

For a solution events are somewhat disobliging, because the area bombing offensive was never completed, and at no stage did it mount even to the minimum scale which had been deemed essential by those who conceived it. Sir Arthur Harris was only the heir to an inheritance which never reached full maturity. To some extent the potentialities of area bombing must remain an enigma, but speculations about the possibilities of unfulfilled military ventures are endless. Our judgement upon area bombing must be founded upon the evidence of what was achieved by about fifteen hundred bombers, not upon a guess at what might have been achieved by four or ten thousand. It is from the study of actualities, not of possibilities, that the principles of war emerge.

The three great area battles of 1943, the Battle of the Ruhr, the Battle of Hamburg and the Battle of Berlin, shook Germany to her foundations. If it was Sir Arthur Harris who claimed that this was the way to win wars, there were, for a time, among the German leaders few who would have contradicted him, least of all Goebbels, the Minister of Propaganda and Speer, the Minister of Armaments Production, the one responsible for morale and the other for war economy. It was morale and war economy whose destruction was sought in these battles and there were times when both Goebbels and Speer seemed to have doubted whether they could be saved. At the time of the Hamburg raids Speer wondered whether six more battles on the same scale might not finish Germany,[2] and Goebbels had to admit that he was confronted with problems that were "almost impossible of solution".[3]

In 1943 there was no longer the distinction between considerable local devastation and complete national immunity as there had been in 1942. Most of the big raids were at once local and national disasters, the news of which travelled quickly across Germany to Hitler at his headquarters in Russia. "The Fuehrer hears with anxiety," Speer records, "of the losses at Krupps Essen," or again "the Fuehrer is having lots of trouble," Goebbels wrote, "especially with the war in the air."[4]

During the Battle of the Ruhr, Essen, the prime target of 1942, was hit hard and effectively for the first time in the war. The Krupps works, a citadel of German armaments production, no longer escaped and the destruction throughout the whole Ruhr area was prodigious. When Goebbels visited Essen in April, which was only the second month of the great battle then developing, he found the damage "colossal". He thought the city could for the most part be regarded as "written off". Nobody could tell how Krupps was to go on, and it seemed there would be nothing to gain from "transplanting" it, for the moment Essen ceased to be an industrial centre "the English will pounce upon the next city, Bochum, Dortmund or Düsseldorf".

By May the Reichsminister was sunk even further into gloom. "During the past five months the enemy has had the upper hand almost everywhere," he said. "He is defeating us in the air." In consequence Goebbels found that morale was dropping throughout Germany. The battle still continued and speaking of a May attack on Dortmund, Goebbels described the destruction as almost "total". "The fact is," he said, "that the Royal Air Force is taking on one industrial city after another and one does not need to be a great mathematician to prophesy when a large part of the industry of the Ruhr will be out of commission."

The battle of the Ruhr convinced Goebbels that "the air situation should be considered one of the most crucial phases of the war and that it should be conducted quite independently of developments in the East". It was perhaps inevitable that the Luftwaffe now became the target for some recriminations. It was apparently unable to prevent the bombers getting through to the kill night after night. It was incapable of a retaliatory offensive against England about which Hitler was so fond of talking. The situation seemed hopeless.

In the air, Germany seemed to be without the means of defence or attack. People began to complain. Why didn't the Fuehrer explain the situation? And why was Göring nowhere to be seen? "One cannot neglect the people too long", Goebbels thought, "in the last analysis they are the very kernel of our war effort. If the people ever lost their will to resist and their faith in German leadership, the most serious crisis we ever faced would result." British hopes had indeed become German fears.

Presently, however, it began to transpire that the situation was not as hopeless as Goebbels had feared. On 21 June 1943, in an address to Gauleiters in Berlin, Speer was able to declare that the industrial damage in the Ruhr was "not yet considerable". It amounted, he calculated, to no more than one month's delay in the expansion programme. Coal production, he admitted, had been reduced by some 25% and iron production by 24% but expressed in terms of total Reich production these losses amounted to 12% and 11.9%. Owing to the special disaster to Krupps the Luftwaffe lost 18% of its Ruhr produced crank shafts. These losses were serious enough and it was not part of Speer's plan to minimise them.

On the contrary he was at pains to emphasise the gravity of the situation. There was no question, he explained, of evacuating the Ruhr. The whole armaments programme depended upon preserving "to a certain extent" the armaments production there. Energetic measures were to be taken. The anti-aircraft defences of the Ruhr were to be doubled and 100,000 workers were to be brought into repair first the factories, and then the homes of the workers. Half of these were to be brought from their not unimportant activities on the West Wall.

Hitler was to be asked to make supplies of oil from the "operative reserves of the army" available for the transport of this army of builders, and he had already agreed that the Minister of Transport should have power to requisition trams for use in the Ruhr from the Occupied Territories, over the heads of the military authorities. The younger workers in the Ruhr were to be trained in the repair of gas and water mains, since the loss of industrial production caused by bombing was supposed to have been half due to the destruction of these facilities. These energetic measures, Speer believed, would restore the situation and enable the forward march in armaments production to be resumed. Here was a sovereign remedy for a desperate situation which did not rely upon the non-existent potentialities of the Luftwaffe's offensive arm. There was to be no crying over spilt milk. There was to be only reconstruction and production.

While Speer Ministry was taking these vigorous measures to restore the situation in the Ruhr, the "great catastrophe" occurred. Hamburg was the third largest city in Greater Germany. Its population of about 1,700,000 was exceeded only by those of the two capital cities, Berlin and Vienna. At one time the great terminal of German overseas trade, Hamburg had, after the outbreak of war, become the large centre of armaments production. Here was the greatest shipbuilding centre in Northern Europe, the birthplace of the German battleship *Bismarck*. Here some 45% of all German submarine construction took place. Here also were oil refineries, aircraft construction, machine manufacturing, food processing and a chemical industry.[5]

During the night of 24/25 July 1943 the most concentrated and sustained bombing attack ever launched against a single city began. Between this date and the night of 2/3 August Bomber Command attacked Hamburg four times, and dropped no less than 8,623 tons of bombs upon it. In addition to this the American Air Force made two smaller daylight attacks during the same period.

In the first attack of this battle 791 aircraft were dispatched to Hamburg and only twelve were lost. They caused 'enormous' fires and killed roughly 1,500 people. Stocks of coal and coke stored for the winter caught fire and could not be extinguished for weeks. Gas, water and electric mains suffered "lasting damage". Telephone lines were put out of action. Dockyards and industrial establishments suffered heavy damage. The pall of smoke which still hung over the city on the following afternoon obscured the sun in a cloudless summer sky. Part of the population began to wander away.[6]

Thereafter, a harassing attack against Hamburg was sustained until the night of 27/28 July when another great force of night bombers, 787 strong, set out for Hamburg. A carpet of bombs of "unimaginable density" soon transformed several districts into "one sea of flame". Tens of thousands of individual fires joined each other to form one great conflagration. This caused such intense heat that firestorms of hurricane force began to rage through the streets. "Trees, a metre in diameter, were broken off or uprooted, roofs of houses swept away and human beings hurled to the ground or sucked into the flames." Hundreds of corpses littered the streets, thousands lost their lives in the air raid shelters, either burnt to ashes or poisoned by fumes. A mass evacuation of the city began. Two more great night attacks on

29/30 July, which was physically the most destructive of all, and on 2/3 August.

During these few nights of terror between thirty and forty thousand people had been killed, about the same number injured, and some 900,000 were homeless or missing. 61% of Hamburg's living accommodation had been destroyed. 580 industrial and armaments establishments had been destroyed and 180,000 tons of shipping had been sunk. "Instead", the Police President reported, "of individual houses in streets and districts being hit, on the contrary only isolated houses were not affected."

Seeking to explain the catastrophic damage which had been inflicted on Hamburg, the Police President said that his account of the raids could give no real idea of the destruction and terror. Even the impression given by a "gutted area is colourless compared with the actual fire, the howling of the firestorms, the cries and groans of the dying and the constant crash of bombs". In particular he said that the firestorms, which were a new experience for mankind, were the principal explanation of the exceptionally heavy death roll and widespread destruction. These caused hurricanes of fires, probably never known before, "against which all human resistance seemed vain and was in point of fact, despite all efforts, useless".

The struggle by all the firefighters in the city reached climax in the last raid on 2/3 August in which the "detonation of exploding bombs, the peals of thunder and the cracking of the flames and ceaseless downpour of rain formed a veritable inferno". Nevertheless, the firestorms made "every plan and every prospect of defence by the inhabitants purposeless". Houses, which in previous raids would have been preserved, were now burnt out. Often before the necessity for flight could be realised every path of escape was cut off. Hamburg had become a city "rapidly decaying, without gas, water, light and traffic connections, with stony deserts which had once been flourishing residential districts". During, and as a result of, the Battle of Hamburg the population of the city was reduced by more than 60%. Some 970,000 persons fled, were evacuated or killed.

This looked like the 'knockout blow' which Douhet had expected and on 29 July Goebbels recognised that Germany was now facing problems "of which we had no conception even a few weeks ago". Only the day before he had recorded "the last raid on Essen caused complete stoppage of production in the Krupps works. Speer is much concerned and worried".

It seemed that the capacity for destruction now evidenced by the R.A.F. Bomber Command had at last overtaken the capacity for reconstruction and human endurance in Germany. This was a critical moment, for it was evident that the Luftwaffe could not prevent the raids, nor could it pay the English back in their own coin. As Speer was later to admit, everyone wondered what would happen to war production, and Goebbels, as we have already seen, was anxiously watching for the signs of collapse on the home front which had been the undoing of Germany in 1918.

If, however, this was a critical moment for Germany, it was equally a critical moment for the R.A.F. The Battle of Hamburg had already taken Bomber Command beyond the range of its radar aid, Oboe. The success of the Hamburg attacks owed a great deal to two particular circumstances. In the first place the increasingly dangerous German night fighter had been temporarily thrown into confusion by the use of Window, and secondly, Hamburg gave a marked response on the H2S screens carried in the bombers, owing to the large areas of water near it.

These two advantages offered the R.A.F. the chance of making the sustained attacks without serious casualties and in the sure knowledge that the target could be found and hit with relative ease. In the circumstances Hamburg had been an easy target. The road to Berlin was a stiffer proposition. Beyond the range of Oboe, without the salient H2S pictures and in the face of recovering opposition, the old problems of night bombing, navigation and target sighting began to reassert themselves. Several more crushing blows were struck, culminating in the Battle of Berlin at the turn of the year, but the 'catastrophe' in Hamburg was not again repeated, let alone repeated six times. This was the time of Speer's greatness, this was the time when, in the battle of destruction against production that production triumphed. This was what Speer was later to call "the armaments miracle". Nevertheless, this achievement, as the term "armaments miracle" implies, was not easily gained. As before, it was the reserves in the German economy, now in the hands of a brilliant and powerful organiser, which came to the rescue of Germany.

Speer had promised Hitler a substantial increase in armament production by the spring of 1944, and if this promise was to be fulfilled he had to find the means to cause an increase in production amounting to no less than 15–20% per month per weapon.[7] Standing in the way of success, Speer told his audience of Gauleiters at Posen on 6 October 1943, he had to reckon with the effects of air raids which had confined the planned expansion of production to some 3–5% per month, and the need to find from the armaments labour force enough men to supply Hitler with a further twenty divisions on the Eastern Front. The task was indeed formidable, but Speer proclaimed his belief that it could be achieved if the Gauleiters and the people of Germany stood behind him in the measures which he proposed to take.

The bases of the armaments industry, Speer went on to explain to the Gauleiters, were coal, iron, the component industry and power. Coal production could be increased by the employment of more labour, and iron production could be increased with more coal and more labour. The first necessity therefore appeared to be the increased efficiency of labour. To this end one thousand malingerers had already been arrested and sent to concentration camps.

Speer urged the necessity for avoiding changes of labour which resulted in training and loss of productive man hours. He particularly emphasised the need for a quicker resumption of productive work after air raids. He said that even eight days after a raid some firms found that they could mobilise only 20–30% of their labour force. This would have to stop. It was natural that a worker must look after his family but all the same he must return to work after one or two days. The way to ensure that he did, Speer pointed out, was to arrange that the issue of food coupons and war damage certificates was in the hands of the works managers. The workers would thus soon be compelled to call at their factories and could then be told when work was to be resumed.

Increased efficiency alone would not suffice. An increased labour force was also needed. Speer calculated that the basic industries (coal, iron, chemicals, power etc.) employed some 1.8 million workers, the armaments industry, including components, some 5.2 million, and the remainder, which was mainly producing consumer goods and included cottage industry, (Handwerke) some six million. He proposed to secure between one and one and a half million of these six million and transfer them to armaments production. This in turn would make it possible to employ more foreign labour in armaments production.

Meanwhile the medium and small firms were not producing to capacity because they could not obtain the raw materials upon which to work. This, Speer thought, was due to the stupid ordering policy of the Wehrmacht which dealt only in terms of large firms. In future, however, a more enlightened ordering policy and allocation of raw materials would have to absorb this slack. Firms which could not make a valuable contribution to the war effort would have to be closed down and their labour re-employed more profitably.

Germany was still in 1943 producing 120,000 typewriters per annum, 200,000 wireless receivers, 150,000 electric cushions, 300,000 electric counting machines and 3,600 electric refrigerators. There were 512,000 pairs of riding boots, 312,000 pairs of officers' boots, 360,000 service bags for women signal assistants, and 364,000 spur straps being made for the Wehrmacht. The Wehrmacht was also demanding eight hundred tons of piano strings. Here were a few of the nonsensical activities upon which Speer had his eye. He knew all the same that it was not easy to close down firms, and he knew that the Gauleiters often opposed his national measures in their local interests. He frankly warned them that he was told nothing but lies about these firms, but he promised that he would close them all the same. He sternly warned the Gauleiters not to oppose him. "I have spoken," he said.

To show that he meant business Speer mentioned a number of firms which he had already closed down. Nearly all the labour so released had gone over to producing the means of defence against bombing: flak, search-lights, engines and equipment for night fighters. He had even closed two locomotive factories in Berlin and Munich which had been producing 530 railway engines per annum. He had also curtailed the production of signals equipment for the Army. Speer concluded by saying that the three principles upon which the German economy must run were the adjustment of the civilian standard of living to the conditions of the front line, the highest efficiency of labour and extreme economy in the use of materials.

This standard of impossible austerity, efficiency and economy was, of course, never completely attained. Indeed, Speer was still talking about the great unexploited reserves in the German war economy in July 1944.[8] All the same, on the record of what was achieved up to July 1944, Speer was making plans which he had the ability and Germany the resources to realise. The production of armaments did continue to rise and the volume of consumer goods production began to fall. If Germany, even now, was not engaged economically in total war, she was moving decisively in that direction. When Sir Arthur Harris was telling the Prime Minister at the end of 1943 that the Ruhr was largely "out", it was, in fact, going forward to another great expansion of output. Even in Hamburg, where recovery was never complete, a remarkable renaissance took place in the town's armament industries.

Bomber Command had indeed broken through the crust of German economic power, and had produced temporarily paralysing effects on places like Essen and Hamburg. These losses were, however, made good by drawing on the reserves which the national economy possessed, and by the vigorous and rapid way in which repairs and reconstruction were undertaken. A town could be 'knocked out' but not killed. To be fatal the blow would have had to be struck again and again almost without ceasing, and to do this Bomber Command would have required not only a much larger force, but also command of the air.

The success of area bombing was shown to depend too much upon the collapse of a people who would not collapse. The organisation of relief by Goebbels and the organisation of work by Speer proved adequate to give the opportunity for continuing and even accelerating production. The exercise of authority by the Nazi Government proved adequate to make this continuing production an inevitable obligation for the workers.

The undoubted decline in the morale of the people, which had been noted by Goebbels, did not seriously affect their activity. They continued to work because there was nothing else they could do. The man hours which were lost and the declines in efficiency which took place were insignificant among those which were not lost and the standards which were maintained.

Great as Speer's achievement was, it was really the much-maligned Luftwaffe which made his success possible. Without command of the air over Germany the R.A.F. was not only forced to continue bombing in the dark, but it was also prevented from selecting its targets on purely strategic grounds. For these reasons it was not possible for the R.A.F. to follow the Hamburg attacks with six more battles on the same scale and of the same destructive power. Such an enterprise would have carried the night bombers beyond the limits of their technical capabilities, and beyond the casualty rate which they could afford. It was the Luftwaffe which in 1943 still stood between the R.A.F. and the command of the air.

Speer himself was not slow to grasp the significance of air superiority, and he knew that if the Anglo-American Air Forces could gain it, they would be able to "destroy" the "industrial equipment" of Germany at their ease. The American determination to destroy the Luftwaffe was therefore the strategy of victory and the Eighth Air Force attacks on the aircraft industry, carried out in February 1944, produced the gravest crisis for Germany. The damage was so extensive that it seemed "obvious" to Speer, who had been consulted by Milch, that the German fighter force (Jagdwaffe) would have "ceased to exist" within a few months.

It was in the face of this danger that the Fighter Staff (Jaegerstab) was set up within the Speer Ministry on 1 March 1944. A prodigious effort was made not only to ensure that production of fighter aircraft in March equalled that for February, but that a rapid expansion in the fighter force should begin. So successful were these efforts that fighter production in Germany did begin a phenomenal rise. Speer claimed in June 1944 that production in March exceeded the February output by 43% and that by May it had risen by 82%.[9]

These selective attacks on the German aircraft industry caused a crisis which Germany survived, as she survived the general onslaught on her whole economy and morale by area bombing. Obviously, a lot of aircraft which would have been built were not built as a result of the American attacks, which achieved a remarkable degree of destruction. Nevertheless, the crisis which resulted caused more aircraft than ever to be built, for, like the whole German war economy, the aircraft industry had been working at relatively low pressure and was therefore capable of the much more concentrated efforts which were now made for the rest of the war.

In fact, the aircraft industry was an extremely difficult target and its increasing dispersal, often to unknown locations, as well as its reserve capacity made it a singularly unprofitable objective for bombing. In a well-disposed war economy, the most important targets may well by the most inaccessible, and the German aircraft industry had been laid out with a view to war. It was in relatively small and isolated units which readily yielded to further division and isolation.

The German ball bearing industry was a different case for, as British and American Intelligence had correctly diagnosed, it really was concentrated in a relatively few large centres, notable in Schweinfurt. The destruction of this industry would, as Allied Intelligence also correctly diagnosed, have brought not only the Luftwaffe, but practically everything else in Germany to a standstill. When therefore the bombs began to fall in Schweinfurt, it became necessary for Speer to take vigorous counter measures.

At the time of the first American attacks on Schweinfurt, Speer estimated that 70–80% of German ball bearings production was concentrated there, and he believed that if the initial attacks had been quickly followed up by a sustained offensive the industry might have been knocked out.[10] Allied Intelligence experts were therefore not overstating the importance of Schweinfurt, nor were they exaggerating the importance of bombing it. They were, however, neglecting the importance of air superiority as American losses in their two big attacks of 1943 demonstrated. In the event, the attacks could not be followed up and eventually Schweinfurt's contribution to ball bearing production was reduced by dispersal to about 10% of the total.

The Germans had been reluctant to accept the temporary losses which dispersal involved until the necessity became obvious, and they therefore laid themselves open to the danger of a 'knock out blow'. They did, when the emergency arose, succeed in maintaining an adequate flow of bearings to the armament industries. In April 1944 when the Allied attack on ball bearings had been proceeding for some time, Kessler, who was in charge of the counter measures, reported to Speer on production. He said that the average output of bearings in the second quarter of 1943 had been 9,756,694 and that it had subsequently declined as follows:

Oct. 1943	8,818,303
Nov. 1943	9,518,127
Dec. 1943	9,269,509
Jan. 1944	8,661,120
Feb. 1944	7,760,446
Mar 1944	6,811,900

The rather serious decline in the first three months of 1944, was, Kessler reported, due to the bombing of Schweinfurt, Erkner, Cannstatt and Steyr. Towards the end of February production at many important plants had been almost at a standstill but "gigantic" efforts made in the repair of damaged plants, and in production by the undamaged and dispersed plants resulted in March production being equivalent to 70% of the pre-raid level.

These figures, Kessler admitted, were not in themselves decisive. Mere numbers of bearings were not everything. The real danger lay in shortages of special types, but this, he thought, could be dealt with by special reorganisation within the industry. Kessler spoke of the need to press on vigorously with protective measures for the industry including the erection of bomb proof bunkers, the establishment of plant underground and the provision of good air raid shelters in Schweinfurt to create the necessary calm among the workers, who had been streaming "in panic into the open" and not returning "until long after the all clear". Despite these measures, Kessler anticipated production bottlenecks as a result of the shortage of ball bearings.

Speer, on the other hand, did not see the need for this. He believed that great economies could be made in the use of ball bearings and he told the press in a confidential interview that in the case of a four-engined bomber "if you throw out about half the ball bearings, a bit more strength will be needed, but that doesn't matter". In fact, Speer's judgement about this, if it was somewhat exaggerated, proved to be justified and it was not a lack of ball bearings which brought the German war machine to a standstill.

Once again reconstruction, reorganisation and determination had saved the situation. All the same the ball bearings industry was the one example of a primary war product which suffered an absolute loss rather than merely a reduced expansion in the period under review. This loss was not, however, great enough to produce significant effects. Sir Arthur Harris had been quite right when he told the Air Ministry in December 1943 that the ball bearing offensive would not be decisive.

Thus all the attempts by the strategic bombers in the period from January 1943 to March 1944 towards "the progressive destruction and dislocation of the German military, industrial and economic system, and the undermining of the morale of the German people to a point where their capacity for armed resistance is fatally weakened"[11] had been frustrated. After each attack Germany still found the means, materials, manpower and time to reconstruct, to reorganise and to carry on, usually even faster than before.

This was achieved in the face of all the discomfort and terror of the bombing attacks, it was accomplished while the military situation on the Russian front went from bad to worse to calamitous; while the Anglo-American Navies and Air Forces disposed of the German U-boat menace; while the British and Americans made the most ostentatious preparations for an invasion of France; while, in fact, Germany approached ultimate and inevitable defeat. How this example of stoic courage and human endurance was achieved will be the wonder of many succeeding generations, but the explanation of how it was that the strategic bombers failed to break through and smash the German war effort beyond recovery is now obvious. It was above all else the lack of air superiority.

The heavy bombers after years of trial and error had come to an impasse. With air superiority the R.A.F. could have repeated the Battle of Hamburg all over Germany, or they could have turned to a more precise and probably even more damaging attack, for instance, against oil. With air superiority the American Air Force could have followed up their attacks on Schweinfurt and wrecked the whole industry or they could have turned to other "common denominator" target systems.[12] Without air superiority the heavy bombers succeeded in delivering only damaging but not crippling blows.

Yet the need for air superiority was generally recognised, if in some cases only because of its obvious application to the projected invasion of Normandy. The struggle for air superiority had a prominent place in the Casablanca directive and it was the whole object of the 'Pointblank' directive. The difficulty was to find a means of achieving it, for events demonstrated that German aircraft production, like other war production, could not be wiped out, or even decisively reduced by strategic bombers unless they already possessed air superiority.

The solution did not, as Sir Arthur Harris so firmly believed, lie with the bombers alone. On the contrary it lay, as General Arnold had grasped, in the destruction of the German Air Force "in being". This meant that the Luftwaffe had to be engaged in the air and defeated. For this task not only fighters, but long-range fighters, were needed. The contribution of bombing would be to spread the German defences and to force them to give battle.

The introduction of the American long-range fighter was the most significant innovation in air warfare since the construction of the four-engined bomber, and the failure of the R.A.F. to develop a long-range fighter was a grave handicap to the R.A.F. bombers. While it should have been ranging offensively over Germany, the R.A.F. Fighter Command, or as it was most significantly called, the Air Defence of Great Britain, adopted a posture which suggested that the Battle of Britain was still being fought. An earlier provision of the weapons to attain air superiority would have resulted in an earlier fulfilment of the bombing offensive.

Part V

Air Superiority and the Final Offensive, 1944–1945

Chapter 9

The Problem of How to Use Air Power in Triphibious War

The supreme task for Allied arms in 1944 was to be the invasion of Normandy. Whatever had been the conflicts in the past about the wisdom of this operation, they were now over. The political and military situation demanded the presence of American and British troops in France. It was no longer a question of whether or even when to invade Normandy; it was simply a question of how to do it.

All the same the task of getting ashore in Normandy remained formidable. Despite the staggering losses sustained by the German army in Russia, despite the wounds inflicted on the German homeland by the heavy bombers of the R.A.F. and the U.S.A.A.F. and despite the growing predominance which the Allied Air Forces now began to enjoy, the invasion of Normandy was an enterprise which would demand the concentrated, and, as far as possible, the united efforts of all British and American arms on land and sea and in the air as well.

Obviously, air power, in which the Western Allies found their greatest superiority over Germany in 1944, was going to be one of the decisive elements in the triphibious assault upon the fortress of Europe which was now imminent. The way in which this air power could be brought to bear most effectively was, however, less obvious and the various commanders expressed various mutually opposed views as to how air power should be used in triphibious war.

The principal elements of this air power were the Allied Expeditionary Air Force under the command of Sir Trafford Leigh-Mallory, the United States Strategic Air Forces under the command of General Carl Spaatz and the R.A.F. Bomber Command under Sir Arthur Harris.

The Allied Expeditionary Air Force, consisting of British and American elements, had been specifically created for the purpose of rendering support to the ground forces, before, during and after the invasion. The United States Strategic Air Forces consisting of the Eighth Air Force in the United Kingdom and the Fifteenth Air Force in Italy and the R.A.F. Bomber Command, both had independent traditions. All the same, bombing policy, both strategic and tactical, now had to be regarded from the point of view of what would contribute most to the success of the projected land operations, and especially the invasion of Normandy.

It was these land operations which dominated every question and the Combined Chiefs of Staff had ensured that they would, in fact, be the criterion of bombing policy, for they had indicated that control of the strategic bomber forces would for a time be vested in the Supreme Commander of the Allied Expeditionary Force. This meant that in addition to the control which he had over the Allied Expeditionary Forces, General Eisenhower would, at the critical time, also enjoy authority over General Spaatz and Sir Arthur Harris. Since General Eisenhower delegated his authority on air matters to his deputy, Air Chief Marshal Sir Arthur Tedder became the most influential air commander of the day. Even before he gained constitutional control of the Strategic Air Forces which only passed to him on 14 April 1944, Sir Arthur Tedder enjoyed the prestige of an ascendant star, of an heir apparent with fixed prospects of succession.

It was natural that planning for the air campaign in preparation for the invasion should begin under the direction of the commander most intimately concerned, Sir Trafford Leigh-Mallory. The plan which was produced revealed two principal objectives, the attainment of air superiority and the destruction of German lines of communication in France and Western Germany. These aims were to be achieved by two stages, the first strategic, and the second tactical. The strategic aspect of the struggle for air supremacy was a continuation of the heavy bomber attacks upon German aircraft production, which had been the principal aim of the theoretical combined offensive, since the 'Pointblank' directive of June 1943. The tactical phase, coming nearer to the actual time of the invasion, would be the neutralisation of aerodromes in the important areas. In the case of the attack upon communications, the strategic phase would consist of heavy attacks upon railway centres, particularly marshalling yards. This would be followed, again nearer to the time of the invasion, by tactical attacks to cut specific lines and stop specific trains. And in this way, it was hoped to deny air support to the German army, and also to immobilise it in a 'railway desert' at the vital moment when the Allied Armies came ashore.

This was obviously a plan which was far beyond the competence of the Allied Expeditionary Air Force alone. It clearly called for the joint efforts of the American and British heavy bomber forces as well, and, in fact, Sir Trafford Leigh-Mallory was pressing for the co-operation of General Spaatz and Sir Arthur Harris even before his plan had been completed. The C.A.S., who still had direction of the strategic bomber forces, may have hoped that agreement would soon be reached about this between Sir Trafford Leigh-Mallory, Sir Arthur Harris and General Spaatz, but in the event no such amicable arrangement materialised. General Spaatz was unwilling to receive any direction from Sir Trafford Leigh-Mallory, and Sir Arthur Harris' representatives spent much time and produced many statistics to prove that Bomber Command was technically incapable of doing anything other than fire-raising on very large targets.

Both Sir Arthur Harris and General Spaatz were vigorous exponents of the principle of independent strategic bombing. Both personified the tradition started in England by Lord Trenchard and in America by General Mitchell. Both were convinced that heavy bombers could operate only in the independent and strategic sphere. Only by striking directly at Germany herself could they make a contribution to victory, and only in this way could they render effective assistance to the ground forces invading Normandy. The basis of any air plan in support of this invasion, they believed, was to be found in the Casablanca formula, the progressive destruction of Germany herself. Beyond this generality the two commanders did not agree with each other.

Sir Arthur Harris still believed that the area attacks upon German cities of 1942 and 1943 would, if continued in 1944, offer the prospect of outright victory. This was, however, as we have already seen, a largely discredited idea, which had failed to attract the American Air Force or indeed to retain the confidence of the British Air Staff. Nevertheless it had been, and still was, difficult to see an alternative, for if there were now many who disagreed with Sir Arthur Harris' strategic convictions, there were few who could yet deny his tactical and technical deductions which indicated that a German city was still the smallest target which the night bombers could effectively destroy.

The case for area bombing in 1944 was the same as it had been in 1942 and 1943, that is, the apparent inability of Bomber Command to do anything else. Sir Arthur Harris did, however, have other compelling arguments with which to support his case. Whatever view of the economic effects of area bombing in 1943 was adopted, and the Ministry of Home Security estimates placed then much lower than the Bomber Command intelligence reports, it could not be denied that any delay in the campaign would allow time for a German recovery. This Sir Arthur Harris claimed, would not only mean that the prodigious efforts of 1943 would be wasted and come to nought, but that the German recovery would itself be a severe threat to the success of the invasion. Sir Arthur Harris was not at this time claiming that the area bombing offensive alone would win the war, but he was suggesting that unless it was continued the ground forces would be unable to do so.

General Spaatz's conception of the independent offensive was quite different, and while Sir Arthur Harris' prestige had in the last part of 1943 tended to diminish, General Spaatz's had increased. The rapid expansion of the Fifteenth Air Force in South East Europe and of the Eighth Air Force in the United Kingdom meant that the American Bomber forces, so far from being junior partners of the R.A.F., now enjoyed a numerical superiority.

The new bombing policy which General Spaatz hoped to get adopted would have to meet three basic principles.[1] Firstly, it must provide air superiority at the time of the Allied invasion. Secondly, it must offer the prospect of an outright German collapse. Thirdly, and in the event of this not materialising, it must afford maximum assistance to the ground forces invading the Continent. Air superiority was not, in General Spaatz's view, something which could be achieved merely by attacks upon aircraft production. This was only a preliminary step and the assertion of air superiority depended ultimately upon the destruction of the enemy air force in being. Command of the air, essential alike to successful operations in the air and on the ground, was therefore, in General Spaatz's view, the criterion by which the usefulness of any bombing policy had to be judged.

Since it was only by combat with the enemy in the air that the German Air Force in being could be destroyed, General Spaatz felt convinced that the strategic bombers must be directed to targets in Germany which the Luftwaffe would feel compelled to defend. He was not, however, solely concerned with the destruction of the German Air Force. His second and third principles were that the policy adopted must contribute to the outright defeat of Germany and also directly to the success of the land invasion.

A survey of the situation had convinced him that an attack on oil and particularly on petrol production, represented the denominator common to his three principles. The German Air Force would be compelled to defend German oil installations and the desired air combats would therefore be inevitable. The strategic effects of the attack would also be profound, and within six months production was halved. Ultimately Germany might be forced to her knees by lack of oil, but there would be an effect on her armed forces much earlier, which would be a valuable contribution to the success of the invasion. This attack, he thought, should be supplemented by continuing blows against German aircraft and ball bearing production, and also against rubber production. This would in addition be a short tactical campaign against communications in direct support of the invasion.

The test which had to be applied to these proposals was not so much whether they would, in fact, lead ultimately to the defeat of Germany, but whether they would, within the time remaining, now not more than three months, afford sufficient guarantee that the supreme operation, the military invasion of Normandy, would succeed. The choice seemed to lie between reliance on a "clean air victory" within three months with the consequent possibility that the invasion would fail, and the slowing down of the independent air campaign with the consequent increase of direct support for the invasion.

In the view of Sir Arthur Tedder's most influential adviser the prospect of the "clean air victory" within three months was a "long chance" and the prospect of the failure of the invasion, if a clean air victory was attempted, was a "high chance". These differing views produced a virtual deadlock, and it became increasingly obvious that Sir Trafford Leigh-Mallory had neither the prestige nor the constitutional position to do anything about it. The time for an authoritative intervention by the Supreme Command was overdue, for it had now been demonstrated that no system of committees could produce agreement between such widely differing proposals.

Nothing, in fact, except the exercise of unified command over the various air forces would weld them into a single fighting unit. General Eisenhower was prepared to lend full authority to the intervention which Sir Arthur Tedder was now contemplating and he was prepared to resist any separatist tendencies such as the Prime Minister was manifesting on behalf of the R.A.F. Bomber Command.[2] Even if he was to face powerful opposition, the time was ripe for Sir Arthur Tedder to lay the foundations of unified command in the air, and carry through a policy of integrating the activities of the air forces with those which were about to take place on the ground.

The real problem raised by the three proposals made by the three air commanders was to determine whether the transport plan as advocated by Sir Trafford Leigh-Mallory was militarily sound, and whether the oil plan as proposed by General Spaatz was, from the point of view of the invading forces, more advantageous. Arising from this a judgement had to be given upon Sir Arthur Harris' assertion that any policy of precise bombing was still beyond the technical capabilities of the night bombers under his command.

This last problem was already beginning to solve itself, for the Chief of the Air Staff had at the end of February called for experimental attacks against precise targets in France on moonlight nights to find out what could be done. The Air Staff had never completely abandoned the hope of making Bomber Command a weapon of precise attack, and even in the heyday of area bombing they had in the famous directive of February 1942 affirmed this hope, the technical basis of which rested on the introduction of Gee.

The subsequent creation of the Path Finder Force and the introduction of HS2 and Oboe had marked important stages in the advance towards precision bombing at night. The experiment of equipping and training a small part of the Command to indicate the target for the main force had worked well within the limits of the tasks it was set.

On this basis an even more refined and ambitious technique was developed. For the attack on the Möhne Dam in 1943 one pilot

The Background to the Bombing Offensive 155

of exceptional skill and courage was selected to lead a small force of specialist crews. He directed their bombing over the target by R/T control and the result was a complete, if rather costly success.[3] In the following June this "Master Bomber" technique was again tried, and this time on a larger scale. A force of sixty Lancasters was directed and controlled by a master bomber over a precise target in Friedrichshafen. In these and subsequent similar attacks carried out mainly over France, but also over Peenemünde, the system of Oboe controlled marking, developed in the Path Finder Force, merged with the "Master Bomber" technique developed in No.5 Group.

This was the background of the further experiments which were now carried out over France, with a view to gaining "experience of the effects of night attack on airfields, communication centres and ammunition dumps before operation 'Overlord'". The results of these attacks, the first of which was made on the night of 6/7 March against the marshalling yards at Trappes, came as a surprise to Sir Arthur Harris and a justification of Air Staff hopes.

Bomber Command had not of course been uniformly successful in all these raids, but the photographs of the targets after the bombing showed that it had, in fact, despite the expectations of its C-in-C,[4] become a weapon of considerable precision. The technical basis of the counsel which Sir Arthur Harris had tendered about the employment of his Command in support of the invasion had been removed. The French railway campaign was feasible, but it remained to demonstrate that it was also desirable.

Thus, the main problem confronting Sir Arthur Tedder was to decide between the competing claims of Sir Trafford Leigh-Mallory and General Spaatz. This involved an arbitration between the policy of attacking German oil or French railways. The attack upon the German Air Force was not in dispute because there was general agreement upon the importance of air superiority. Indeed, Sir Arthur Tedder suggested that one of the primary roles of the Air Forces was to secure and retain air superiority. This would involve a continued offensive against aircraft production, a continued battle of attrition with the Luftwaffe in the air and also continued deep penetration of Germany to contain the surviving Luftwaffe away from the Normandy area. There was therefore no question of a complete abandonment of the independent and strategic air offensive against Germany and the choice between an independent and an auxiliary offensive was not as clear cut as had been suggested.

On the controversial question of oil or transport, Sir Arthur Tedder had the most unhesitating views, for he had long since made up his mind. The principle which was basic to his entire thought was the principle of concentration. He was determined to be the architect not only of unified air command, but of a policy which could be carried out simultaneously by all air power. He wished to see all the aircraft from General Spaatz's Command, from Sir Trafford Leigh-Mallory's Command and from Sir Arthur Harris's Command, converge upon a single objective. It was a direct contradiction of this principle that any major plan should be accepted unless it was within the scope of all the elements in the three air forces.

The oil plan did, in Sir Arthur Tedder's view, constitute a contradiction of this kind. It might, he thought, be a good independent plan for the American day bombers, but the R.A.F. Bomber Command would be able to play only a limited part at night, and the Allied Expeditionary Air Force, no part at all. In any case Sir Arthur Tedder thought that the effects of an oil attack would be too long delayed to contribute to the success of the invasion. He therefore rejected General Spaatz's advice on the grounds that it did not provide an objective common to all air power, and that it would not contribute to the invasion. The transport plan, which had been proposed by Sir Trafford Leigh-Mallory, would, on the other hand, provide a common employment for all the air forces and it would also, by delaying German troop movements, make a decisive contribution to the invasion.

Sir Arthur Tedder was convinced that the bombing of railway centres had been a powerful factor in the success of the Allied invasions of Sicily and Italy. This view received strong support in the analysis of those campaigns which had been carried out by Professor Zuckerman. Sir Arthur Tedder had no doubt that even more effective results could now be got in France.

If, however, the evidence from Italy and Sicily was a powerful plank in the policy which Sir Arthur Tedder now called for, it was by no means conclusive, and the opponents of his plan found that they could count upon the practically unanimous support of the Intelligence agencies. The Directorate of Intelligence at the Air Ministry, the Ministry of Economic Warfare, the American Economic Objectives Unit and the Directorate of Transportation at the War Office united in their condemnation of the transport plan with the Joint Intelligence Committee.

The principal arguments against the transport plan were ventilated at a crucial meeting held at the end of March. The Chief of Air Staff, still exercising the supreme control of the strategic bomber forces with which he had been charged by the Combined Chiefs of Staff in January 1943, presided. General Eisenhower, the Supreme Allied Commander and Sir Arthur Tedder his deputy, General Spaatz, Sir Arthur Harris and Sir Trafford Leigh-Mallory attended with representatives of the Joint Intelligence Staff, the Ministry of Economic Warfare and the War Office.

In the debate which he initiated Sir Arthur Tedder found himself in isolation. The War Office representative suggested that an attack on the French railways would be unlikely to have any marked effect upon German military movements, largely because, as Sir Andrew Noble of the Joint Intelligence Staff emphasized, the Germans would allow French industry to starve before they allowed the dislocation of transport to affect their own armed forces. Thus, French economic traffic would act as an expendable reserve protecting the real objective of the Allied attack.

If, however, the transport plan was to be condemned, someone would have to present a superior alternative, and this General Spaatz failed to do. Mr. Lawrence of the Ministry of Economic Warfare indicated that the Germans possessed considerable oil reserves in the west, and that an attack on oil would therefore have no significant effect upon military activity until four or even five months after it had begun. Since it was already 25 March and the invasion was planned for the first week of June, the Chief of Air Staff intervened to point out that this showed "conclusively" that the oil plan would not help the invasion in the first few critical weeks. No one else had any other suggestions to make.

When, therefore, General Eisenhower said of the transport plan that "it was only necessary to show that there would be some reduction, however small, (in military traffic) to justify adopting the plan, provided there was no alternative", the decisive word had been spoken. No one could dispute that there would be "some" effect and no one could suggest a convincing alternative. Nevertheless, the decision to adopt the transport plan was a minority decision forced through on the demerits of the oil plan rather than on its own merits.

This was no more than a temporary solution to the problem of how to use air power in triphibious war. The control of the strategic bomber forces, which passed to the Supreme Commander on 14 April, was only a temporary control, and the bombing policy was only an expedient to meet a particular and temporary situation. The two main prongs of the policy which had been adopted, the neutralisation of German air power and the neutralisation of German lines of communication in France, were concomitants of the military operations about to be carried out there.

Despite the vigorous protests of the Prime Minister, who deplored the French casualties which were certain to be caused, and who doubted the military value of the railway plan, these attacks were carried out in the name of military necessity as voiced by General Eisenhower. The auxiliary offensive was a diversion from the independent strategic bombing attack, which can be justified or condemned only upon a military judgement of its effects upon the fighting performance of German arms in France.

Nevertheless, the auxiliary offensive has a significance for the student of strategic bombing. On the negative side, an influence which can be mentioned, but not measured, has to be noticed. This was the slowing down of the independent attack on Germany at a moment when the power of the strategic bomber forces was mounting to its zenith. During April, May and June less than one fifth of the weight of bombs dropped by Bomber Command fell on Germany. During the same period the Eighth Air Force also devoted most of its effort to the auxiliary attack, and its offensive against German industry diminished rapidly. The destruction of German cities was interrupted, and perhaps even more important, the destruction of German oil resources was delayed.

On the positive side there are more measurable influences to be seen. The exercise of control over the strategic bomber forces by Sir Arthur Tedder in the name of General Eisenhower, was the nearest approach to unified air command which the war produced. The common air policy which this made possible had a significance which extended far beyond the auxiliary campaign itself. It was in this auxiliary campaign that the term Combined Bomber Offensive assumed a new significance. While the Eighth Air Force concentrated primarily upon the neutralisation of French and German aerodromes, Bomber Command made the greater attack on the French railways.

Thus, at last the two bomber commands really were pursuing two aspects of the same policy. In addition to this they met on common ground in the joint attacks which they made in great strength upon coastal batteries, the flying bomb sites,[5] troop concentrations and many other tactical targets associated with the land campaign. The Eighth Air Force also made heavy attacks on French railways, the primary target of Bomber Command, and Bomber Command made at least some attacks on aerodromes, the primary target of the Eighth Air Force. Meanwhile the Allied Expeditionary Air Force was playing its part, and the Fifteenth Air Force in Italy was drawn into the struggle. The auxiliary offensive therefore provided not only a common task for Bomber Command and the Eighth Air Force, but a common task for all air power.

The rigid distinction between independent and auxiliary roles for strategic bombers was beginning to fade, and it remained only to find a system of attack which was common not only to all air power, but which was also common to the independent and auxiliary functions which strategic bombers would have to perform in the future. This was the kernel of the whole problem of bombing policy which had been created by the launching of a triphibious assault in Western Europe.

If the heavy bomber forces were to remain, as they had been at the time of the invasion and for some time after it, primarily a weapon of army support, then all the advantages of the strategic assault which they could direct behind the lines and at the enemy's heart would be lost. They could not, on the other hand, abandon the armies which they had helped to establish on the Continent. The army campaign must go on, and no bombing policy could reckon without it.

The French railway attack itself was no solution to this problem, for it could contribute little or nothing to the economic disruption of Germany, however embarrassing it might be to the German army in France or indeed to French industry. It did all the same suggest, as we shall presently see, a principle of attack upon Germany herself which offered a solution of the conflict between the advocates of independent and the advocates of auxiliary bombing. On the other hand, the association with military necessity which railway bombing had acquired during the French campaign was lasting, and this delayed and to a certain extent prevented recognition of its wider implications. Even while the auxiliary offensive was mounting to a climax, the strategic bombers preserved a connection with their independent traditions. Bomber Command continued when it could to attack German cities, and the Eighth Air Force initiated a small-scale attack on German oil resources in May. In June, after discussion with the Air Staff, Bomber Command joined in the little oil offensive.

Thus, while the auxiliary offensive had demonstrated the merits of unified command in the air and had pointed the way to a new conception of the role of air power, the old conception still survived. Here were the ingredients either for a common policy of concentrated attack upon Germany in the final offensive, or for a bitter dispute and a spreading offensive.

Preparations for the final offensive began immediately after General Eisenhower made it known on 6 September that the general destruction of French railways was to cease. The end of the battle in France was in sight, and the auxiliary offensive was virtually over. The Luftwaffe appeared to have been defeated, and the French railway campaign had served its purpose. There was no longer any reason why the Supreme Commander should retain control of the Strategic Air Forces.

The developments of the next few weeks were crucial, for they determined the shape of the final offensive. The forces about to be thrown into this attack were now gigantic, and in July there had been available for operations 5,246 Allied bombers.[6] The miracles of design, production and transport, the gigantic achievements of aircrew training and the enormous task of servicing which this figure conceals can only be suggested here, but the probability that this force might now prove decisive could be overlooked by no one, least of all by the Combined Chiefs of Staff who were now deliberating in Quebec.

The British Chiefs of Staff came out strongly in favour of a resumption of the independent offensive. In particular they were convinced that the time had come to intensify the oil campaign. They were also impressed with the possibilities of a renewed attack upon German morale. So that this policy could be carried out, they proposed that control of the strategic air forces should now pass from the Supreme Commander and be vested jointly in the Chief of the British Air Staff, Sir Charles Portal, and the Commanding General of the United States Army Air Forces, General Arnold. At the same time, they suggested that the strategic air forces should continue to render support to the army when asked by the Supreme Commander.

In the circumstances of September 1944 this proposal, if adopted, was certain to produce confusion and dispersal. The advantages of unified command would be lost, and in place of one sovereign mind three would be substituted. The revival of the independent principle of bombing would inevitably lead to functional, if not a physical, division of the strategic forces.[7]

The attack on oil and morale, the independent part of the plan, would certainly conflict with operations in support of the army. No attempt was made to find a common policy to meet both needs, and it is hardly surprising that General Arnold was disconcerted. He doubted whether this diversified system of command could "obtain the maximum use" from the bomber forces, and he could not understand why no attention had been paid to the possibility of an attack on German communications. Sir Charles Portal showed in his reply that the idea of a 'common' policy had no appeal to him. He said that communications offered good tactical targets for fighter and medium bombers, but not for strategic bombers. He ignored completely the strategic implications of such an attack, though it was by now abundantly clear, on the evidence of the French campaign, that transport bombing produced economic effects before military effects.

However much the British plan had failed to grasp the lessons of the auxiliary offensive, the proposals of the British Chiefs of Staff were at least positive. The contribution of the American Chiefs of Staff was, on the other hand, purely negative. They adopted a critical but not a constructive attitude. If they were impressed with the merits of a common policy, they did not expound its principles, and if they were dissatisfied with the possibility of diversified command, they made no proposals to secure unified command. What was worse than the American failure to make positive proposals was the fact that the British suggestions had to be toned down to meet their objections.

Any hope which may have survived the earlier Allied Conferences of a clear statement of bombing policy by the Combined Chiefs of Staff therefore came to nothing. It was agreed that control of the strategic bomber forces should now be assumed by Sir Charles Portal and General Arnold, and that they should be represented by Sir Norman Bottomley and General Spaatz, but as to policy the Combined Chiefs of Staff could say no more than "the overall mission of the strategic air forces is the progressive destruction and dislocation of the German military, industrial and economic systems and the direct support of land and naval forces".

The use of this well-worn and by now completely platitudinous phrase left the air forces with even less overall direction than they had received from Casablanca. The problem of making policy now had to be faced at a lower level without any new light having been cast upon it, or any authoritative word having been spoken about it from Quebec. The three powers concerned with this problem were the joint executors of the Combined Chiefs of Staff "policy", Sir Norman Bottomley and General Spaatz, and also, by virtue of the need to render "direct support" to the land forces, Sir Arthur Tedder. These three quickly agreed upon the wording of a directive which can be described as no more than a temporary compromise. This directive which was sent out to Bomber Command, the Eighth Air Force and the Mediterranean Air Forces on 25 September, indicated that oil was to be the primary target for the bombers, and, as a second priority, transport, tank production, ordnance depots and motor transport production and depots ranked equally. The German Air Force was no longer regarded as a primary target, but direct support of land and naval operations was said to remain a commitment. Area bombing would continue when the weather was unsuitable for precise attacks.

This was not so much a proclamation of bombing policy as a commentary upon the operations already being carried out. It did little to establish the emphasis which was to be placed upon the various elements of the offensive, and nothing to prevent the spread of the attack. Naturally the offensive immediately began to run out of control. Bomber Command, now beginning to use a radar device known as Gee-H which made precise blind bombing possible, dropped a smaller tonnage of bombs on oil plants in October than it had done in June, the month of invasion.

At the same time Bomber Command did show a remarkable concentration upon area bombing and about two-thirds of its total effort for the month was devoted to this renewed attack on German morale. The Eighth Air Force showed no concentration at all, and attacked a large variety of targets with relatively small weights of bombs. The best concentration which it did achieve was against marshalling yards, one of the second priority targets, and these only claimed about two fifths of the total tonnage for October. The 'combined' bomber offensive was, in fact, beginning to display the characteristics of that which had followed the Casablanca Directive, this time without the excuse provided by the lack of air superiority and the inaccuracy of night attack.

The creation in October of the Combined Strategic Targets Committee (C.S.T.C.) was designed to mitigate the evil consequences of this unsatisfactory state of affairs. Here representatives of the three powers, the British Air Staff, the U.S.S.T.A.F. and S.H.A.E.F. were to meet representatives of the principal intelligence agencies, the Ministry of Economic Warfare and the Economic Objectives Unit of the American Embassy. The intention was that the Committee should adjust the priority of particular targets within the system laid down in the directive, that they should advise a change of direction when they thought necessary, and that they should receive and advise on the suggestions made by S.H.A.E.F., the War Office and the Admiralty. Thus the C.S.T.C. was to be an inter-command, inter-service and international clearing house into which would flow the raw materials of bombing policy, and from which would come, in a refined state, advice for the D.C.A.S. and General Spaatz who had to write the directives.

An international committee, which is not itself sovereign and which has difficulty in recognising a sovereign, can at best produce a compromise and at worst it can degenerate into a propaganda platform. Most of the members of the C.S.T.C. were convinced advocates of the oil plan. The committee, which was jealous of protocol, rigidly upheld the distinction between independent and auxiliary bombing. So long as the transport plan remained tactical and auxiliary to military operations, the case for it was unimpeachable. As soon as it threatened to extend to the strategic sphere, the C.S.T.C. saw a threat to the oil plan, and they saw Sir Arthur Tedder exceeding his constitutional powers.

The forces of contention were too evenly balanced to produce an incisive and concentrated bombing policy. The conviction that the oil attack was a war-winning plan was too strong to ignore. The counter claim that a transport attack was essential to the advance of Allied armies could not be rejected by an Air Staff. The debates of the C.S.T.C., the wording of the directive and the operations which were carried out all bore witness to the deadlock which existed. The final offensive was taking the form not of a "really comprehensive pattern" but what Sir Arthur Tedder could only describe as a "patchwork quilt".[8] To the Deputy Supreme Commander, with his abiding conviction that air power could only be effective if concentrated, this was anathema.

There were, Sir Arthur Tedder said, apparently two ways of winning the war. One was by a land invasion of Germany, and the other was by a strategic bombing offensive. These he did not, however, think were alternatives, nor did he believe that they need conflict with each other. It would be wrong to throw the whole bombing effort into an independent offensive, and similarly it would be wrong to devote it all to army support. This was not an argument for a functional division of the bomber forces.

On the contrary it was an invitation to find one system of attack which would fulfil both needs. The object of an independent attack was to destroy the German war economy. The object of an auxiliary attack was to harass and help with the destruction of the German armies. There were several ways in which either of these tasks might be achieved, but there was, Sir Arthur Tedder argued, only one in which both could be accomplished by a single policy. The one "common factor in the whole German war effort" was, he asserted, the rail, road and water communication system. This denominator was common to the German army, the objective of the auxiliary offensive, and to the German economy, the objective of the independent offensive.

This 'common denominator' theory was the climax of Sir Arthur Tedder's unrivalled experience of triphibious war, both around the

Mediterranean and in North West Europe. In its light it was possible to see that the distinction between independent and auxiliary bombing had become purely academic. It was free from the 'independent' prejudice of the Air Force mind and it was also free from the constricting and even absorbent tendencies which had so often dominated the military and naval argument. It was infinitely the most significant contribution made to the endless debate on bombing policy; it was the nearest approach ever made to the ideal solution of the problem of how to use air power in triphibious war. All the same, as with most ideals, there were several ways in which the 'common denominator' theory could be interpreted. Sir Arthur Tedder's interpretation was not necessarily right. There were also severe practical difficulties which could not be overlooked.

Even if the principle was accepted, it did not follow that transport was the best system against which to direct the common attack. After all, oil was also basic to the needs of the German army and the German economy alike. It was also basic to the needs of the German Air Force, and indeed to a great deal of German transport. By the end of October, it was believed that Germany's reserves of oil were virtually exhausted, and that her production had been reduced to a critical level.

The defection of Rumania had already cut her off from that hitherto fruitful source. If this was accurate intelligence, then it obviously followed that the fighting efficiency of the German army and the Luftwaffe as well as the level of war production which could be maintained in Germany, depended directly upon the amount of oil which the synthetic plants could turn out. Intelligence also suggested that the Germans were still capable of carrying out rapid repairs to damaged oil plants. From this it was reasonable to infer that a reduction in the intensity of the oil offensive would soon be reflected in increased German war production and increased activity by the German army and air force.

Sir Arthur Tedder was evidently not entirely satisfied with this kind of evidence. He had pointed out that communications were the only targets which could not be dispersed or deployed underground. Dispersal of industry made transport no less vulnerable, but it did make it a good deal more vital. The results in France had shown what could be done, and he believed that in Germany the effects would be even more striking. Whereas the Germans had been able to face the paralysis of

French industry with comparative equanimity, the paralysis of German industry would be decisive. In Germany there would be no need to avoid causing civilian casualties as there had been in France, and in Germany, Sir Arthur Tedder believed, there would not be the reserves of labour waiting to repair the damage as there had been in France.

Even if intelligence about oil did tend to exert the greater influence because alone among the target system it was handled by a Cabinet Committee, it was obvious that an arbitration between the transport and the oil plans was likely to be extremely difficult on the basis of the facts which were known. There was too much to be said on both sides. Further thought would show that there was no need to make this arbitration. Both systems were 'common denominators' and they could be regarded, as the attack on the railways and aerodromes in the auxiliary offensive had been, as two aspects of the same policy: the neutralisation of the German armed forces and the destruction of the German war economy.

The forces available were strong enough to undertake both attacks. What was needed was therefore not a decision in the oil and transport conflict, but a concentration of all efforts against both, and the elimination of diversionary tendencies. Whether this could be done or not depended upon the ability of the commanders in the 'field' to overcome the tactical and technical difficulties inherent in a policy of concentration, and upon the strength of the makers of policy to enforce their decisions.

Sir Arthur Harris, one of the commanders in the 'field', was optimistic about neither possibility. He suggested that bombing policy was still not purely a matter of strategy. It also had to reckon with the tactical considerations of weather and enemy opposition. Heavy bombers, he said, had to attack what they could, which, even at the end of 1944, was not always the same as what they ought. As an example of what he meant, Sir Arthur Harris took the case of the attack on German canals. After the breaching of the Dortmund-Ems canal, the next logical target would be the Rothensee ship lift. It would, however, the C-in-C claimed, not be possible to make this attack unless very heavy 'cover' was provided.

To an American Air General 'cover' would have meant a fleet of long-range fighters, but to Sir Arthur Harris it still meant evasion. He therefore suggested that if the Rothensee ship lift was to be bombed there would have to be simultaneous area attacks on one or both of the neighbouring towns of Magdeburg and Halle. Then, he predicted, the advocates of concentration would promptly ask him why he had bombed Halle and Magdeburg. In 1942 or 1943 this argument would have been infallible, for obviously a lack of superiority makes nonsense of the principle of concentration, particularly of geographical concentration. In November 1944 it was largely out of date. Air superiority was turning to air supremacy. Bomber Command casualties had been reduced to a fraction of their previous level and from 47,903 sorties dispatched in the last three months of 1944 only 395 bombers or 8% had failed to return.

In addition to this the obstacle of weather, though never defeated, was being reduced, especially by Gee-H the new blind bombing radar aid, and a device known as Fido for dispersing fog at aerodromes. Sir Arthur Harris was, of course, not unaware of these developments, and it may be suspected that his continued advocacy of the guerre de course was basically due to his surviving conviction that the area attack on German towns was still intrinsically the most damaging blow which could be struck at Germany.

The other obstacle which Sir Arthur Harris saw standing in the way of a concentrated policy was what he described as the number of cooks engaged in stirring the broth. The Admiralty, he said, had "resuscitated a U-Boat threat", the ball bearings experts were again vocal and the "nearly defunct" S.O.E.[9] had again "raised its bloody head" to produce what he hoped would be its "final death rattle". After more than two and half years of too much advice and too few orders, Sir Arthur Harris may be excused this outburst, but the malady which he had diagnosed proceeded from the same cause which was now exercising Sir Arthur Tedder and had in the past worried General Arnold: the absence of a supreme and unified air command. The system of committees and sub-committees, of advisory bodies and technical experts aggravated rather than smoothed, and complicated rather than clarified the development of bombing policy. The air forces lacked a supreme authority; they lacked a commander of the international prestige and military stature which were the qualities of General Eisenhower.

Nevertheless, Sir Arthur Tedder's exposition of the 'common denominator' principle had made its mark. On 29 October the D.C.A.S. told him of the Air Staff decision to widen the scope of the transport attacks, and to appoint a working committee to advise the C.S.T C. on transport targets. Inherent in this decision was the recognition that the transport plan had something more than a purely tactical and auxiliary value.

A new declaration of policy now became possible, and on 1 November the second directive of the final offensive was issued. There were now only two primary objectives, oil and transport. Such area bombing as the "weather or tactical conditions" made inevitable was to be directed at towns associated with oil production or transport centres. Oil remained the first priority and transport second, as was emphasised in a covering letter to Sir Arthur Harris, but the real significance of the directive was, as the covering letter also showed, not the relative positions of oil and transport, but the pruning away of the other tasks which had appeared in the directive of 25 September. Every possible effort was to be concentrated against oil and transport and there was to be the "minimum diversion of effort from these target systems". The 'common denominator' theory had now become a principle of bombing policy. It only remained to see it carried out in practice.

There was an immediate intensification of the combined bomber offensive against oil and transport targets. In November the Eighth Air Force dropped nearly 16,000 American tons of bombs on oil targets, which was more than twice the weight it had dropped on them in any previous month. Bomber Command dropped a further 14,000 British tons on these targets, which was more than 3,000 tons more than it had devoted to oil in any previous month, and nearly five times the weight it had dropped on them in October. The Fifteenth Air Force sustained a lesser attack upon oil targets in South East Europe. The Eighth Air Force also showed an impressive concentration against transport targets on which it dropped about 15,000 American tons in November, but the Bomber Command participation in this aspect of the policy was on a much smaller scale, and under 5,000 British tons were added to the American attack. Thus, the Eighth Air Force, by dropping more than 75% of its tonnage for the month on oil and transport targets, faithfully reflected in its operations the policy which had been adopted for the final offensive.

Bomber Command, on the other hand, reflected this policy more dimly, and though the area bombing offensive was reduced, it did in November claim more than half the total weight of bombs dropped in that month. It took an emergency to raise the oil and transport offensive to terms of equality with, and at times of superiority over, the area bombing attack in Bomber Command. The emergency came in December when Rundstedt launched the German army on its last offensive in the Ardennes. This had a bad effect on the oil campaign, but it produced a tremendous concentration by both forces against transport targets.

The fear that the German Air Force might revive with the introduction of jet fighters, and that the German U-boat fleet, with the introduction of Schnorkel,[10] would again become a danger, threatened to disturb the course of the final offensive. Both fears did, in the event, prove to be false alarms, and despite the distinctly defensive tone of a directive issued in January 1945 the bombing offensive suffered no significant check. Time was, however, beginning to work against the oil plan. The view was beginning to appear, particularly in the American Air Force, that the oil plan must be practically completed, and already in December 1944, General Spaatz had begun to talk of concentrating every element of Allied air power in a massive assault upon transport all over Germany. Also, as the end of the war came in sight, even the reasonably short-term strategic plans began to lose much of their value.

Another factor militating against the oil plan in these last months, was the increasing support for massive area attacks designed to break the last strongholds of German administration. While, however, the Eighth Air Force, following the logic of these arguments, showed an ever increasing, and finally an almost total concentration against transport targets, and Bomber Command carried out a steadily increasing assault against German cities,[11] the British Air Staff remained by no means convinced that the oil offensive could be abandoned. Despite the growing area offensive, Bomber Command sustained an intense attack against oil in 1945, and as much as 26% of its total weight of bombs dropped in the last four months of the war went down on oil plants.

Eventually, however, it became increasingly obvious that transport was the only target worth pursuing to the end, or at least as long as the army had to advance. A massive Bomber Command attack against Dresden carried out on the night of 13/14 February called forth a sharp rebuke from the Prime Minister in March. Mr. Churchill was beginning to worry about coming into control of an "utterly ruined land". Sir Arthur Tedder therefore had little more than formal difficulty in devising the last great bombing operation of the war in March: the isolation of the Ruhr. When the Allies became preoccupied more with the occupation than the destruction of Germany, the strategic bombing offensive was over.

Chapter 10

The Vindication of Strategic Bombing and the Collapse of Germany

During the first half of 1944 the German war economy was still expanding. Despite new big mobilisations for the Wehrmacht, and despite all the damage which the heavy bombers had done, the production of all kinds of armaments continued to go up. At the same time the needs of the civilian population were still, if on a somewhat more austere scale, being met. When the Allied armies went ashore in Normandy on 6 June 1944, the strategic bombers had not carried out the Casablanca mission. They had not destroyed the German economy, nor had they "fatally weakened" the morale of the German people.

Air power had shown itself to be a decisive force in the conduct of military and naval warfare, but as an independent conception it seemed bankrupt of success. In July 1944 Germany reached the highest level of war production since the expansion began in 1942.

Six months later at the turn of the year, Germany was in chaos and the total collapse of her power to wage war was imminent. Her basic industries, coal, steel, gas and electric power, oil and transport were all faced with ruin, and this was primarily the achievement of strategic bombing. Even when Speer was proclaiming the great industrial victory of July, the first decisive blows from the air had been struck, and Germany, who was giving ground before the Allied advance on land from the East, the West and the South, was already facing defeat at the centre. After four and a half years of sustained endeavour without proportionate success, the strategic bomber did, in the final offensive, vindicate itself as a third means of waging war. Our task in this chapter is to examine the changes which made these devastating blows possible, and the extent to which they were responsible for the downfall of Germany.

The conduct of bombing in the final offensive was different not only in degree, but different in kind to any earlier attacks. There were a number of influences which contributed to this change, the increased size of the bomber forces, the greater destructive power of the bombs and the further development of technical aids to navigation and bomb aiming, but the greatest change of all was the growing state of air superiority which began to prevail in 1944, and which by the autumn was growing to air supremacy.

In previous chapters we have seen a great deal of evidence about the value of air superiority, but this has been negative evidence to suggest the penalties of its absence rather than the advantages of its achievement. We have seen how the absence of air superiority promoted on the one hand the guerre de course of the R.A.F. Bomber Command, and, on the other hand, the strategically unprofitable attack on aircraft production by the American Eighth Air Force. We have seen how the absence of air superiority placed a premium upon tactical feasibility, often at the expense of strategic desirability. We have seen, in fact, how the German Air Force prevented the R.A.F. and the U.S.A.A.F. from inflicting decisive damage upon the German war economy. Now, in 1944, it is possible to begin an examination of the positive evidence about air superiority.

Air superiority is not easily defined in theory. It has been said to consist in that state of affairs when it is possible for an attacking air force to carry out its operations without effective interference from the defending air force. This definition is true as far as it goes, but it is necessary to distinguish between limited or local and general air superiority. The guerre de course may provide a limited and local ability to carry out offensive operations without effective opposition. Indeed, Sir Arthur Harris' tactics of 1943 had provided this kind of immunity, but it varied from place to place, from night to night and from scientific invention to scientific invention. The attacks on Hamburg in 1943 seemed to demonstrate a kind of air superiority; the attack on Nuremburg[1] in 1944 seemed to demonstrate its loss. In any case the selection of targets always had to reckon with the German fighter force, and the gulf between what ought to be bombed and what could be bombed was always there and was sometimes great. Strategic intelligence was powerless to dictate the course of the bombing offensive.

This gulf between strategic desirability and tactical feasibility is really the measure of air superiority. When the two are separated only by the weather, then air supremacy exists. According to the extent to which they are separated by the enemy fighter force, so the degree of air superiority fluctuates. Thus, it appears that air superiority is not a static condition which can be precisely defined or dated. It is not something which can be achieved suddenly and then forgotten. On the contrary the battle for air superiority is continuous, and though significant landmarks can be discerned in the struggle, it is not possible to examine it in the light of isolated events, but only as the product of many contributory influences.

The Allied air superiority of 1944, which was to revolutionise the effects of strategic bombing, was the product of four cardinal developments each of which followed one another with unpremeditated logic. At the beginning of the war Germany possessed the most powerful air force in the world, but it was nevertheless in her own conduct that she began to lose the war in the air. German neglect of the Luftwaffe was the first stage in the development of Allied air superiority.

However powerful the Luftwaffe may have been, the Battle of Britain demonstrated that it was neither powerful enough, nor well enough directed to overcome the forces of British 'close defence'. If, however, the British were elated by the victory of the R.A.F. fighters, the Germans were not unduly depressed by the defeat of their bombers.

Hitler believed that the war could be won on the Continent and that Britain would have to recognise a German Europe whether she was invaded or not. Long term plans for the Luftwaffe were no more necessary than any other long-term military plans. The war could be won by a new series of lightning blows with the existing equipment. Thus, while the R.A.F. was struggling to bring the Stirlings, Halifaxes and Manchesters into production, no corresponding effort was being made in Germany. The Luftwaffe thus tended to become obsolete and defensive.

The British Air Staff, on the other hand, maintained a burning and almost blind faith in the principle of an independent air force and the ultimate efficacy of a strategic bombing offensive. Despite the urgent needs of defence, which had consumed so much energy since 1938, and despite the weighty evidence which had accumulated in 1940 and 1941 against the validity of their theories, the Air Staff never abandoned their plans for a bombing offensive against Germany.

It was thus that the R.A.F. won the initiative in the war in the air and this was the second stage in the struggle for air superiority. The battle was transferred from Britain to Germany and the inherent tendency of the Luftwaffe to become defensive was gradually developed into a preoccupation. The decisive extent of the British initiative which had been gained, even by 1942, can be measured by comparing the damage inflicted on Lübeck by the R.A.F. with that done to Exeter by the Luftwaffe. A "Lübeck attack" now replaced the term a "Coventry attack" in the phraseology of the war in the air.

Hitler seems to have recognised that the only solution to this problem was a heavy counter-attack against Britain. He called for A.A. guns as a means of defence, and bombers and secret weapons as a means of retaliation. The bombers, however, were not forthcoming and, as Göring had to be told, there was only the distant prospect of anything comparable to the Lancaster. Thus, the Luftwaffe had no alternative other than to rely on 'close defence' and build the fighters which the German designers did seem capable of producing. The constantly increasing severity of the bombing offensive from England further accentuated the gradient of this vicious spiral. The arrival over Germany of the American day bombers and the new threat which they offered, brought final realisation in Germany that the initiative in the air was utterly lost. Hitler continued to talk about bombers, and some of his plans actually interfered with the production of fighters, but, in effect, all real hope of an offensive air force was abandoned. This was the third stage. The creation of the Fighter Staff in March 1944 was the swansong of the German bomber force. The struggle for the initiative in the air was not, all the same, in itself a decisive battle.

The German fighter force of 1942 and 1943 had kept pace with the expanding British and American bomber forces. The serious consequences for Germany of having to devote so much effort to holding the bombing offensive were already apparent in Russia and Italy, but at least the bombing offensive was held. The final and decisive stage of the struggle for air superiority was reached with the introduction of the American long-range fighter.

The Americans had obviously half hoped that their heavily armed Flying Fortresses would, if packed in tight formations, be capable of such concentrated fire power that they alone could triumph over the fighter defences. This idea proved to be an illusion and the long-range fighter had to be called in to arrest the slaughter of American bombers.

The Americans sought to increase the range of their fighters by fitting external petrol tanks and despite their failure to persuade the British to do the same thing with the Spitfire, the ever-increasing range of the

P.38 and P.47 resulted in mounting German losses in the air during the autumn of 1943. The bombing offensive was developing teeth and for the first time in the war the security of the defensive arm of the Luftwaffe was seriously threatened. In the middle of December, the famous Mustang long range fighter made its appearance in Europe. This formidable machine scored immediate and spectacular successes. For the Luftwaffe it was the beginning of the end.

In January 1944 the mounting strength of the American escort fighter force made possible a tactical development of the first importance. Hitherto the function of the fighters had been to protect the bombers. The Luftwaffe could always choose the moment for attack. Now, however, large numbers of American fighters were sent to Germany charged with the duty of "pursuing and destroying the enemy". No German aircraft, whether on operations or not, was any longer safe. The American fighters roamed far and wide over Germany demoralising and destroying the Luftwaffe in being wherever it appeared. Now the German air force, having already lost the strategic initiative, lost the tactical initiative as well.

The battle for air superiority was rapidly being won by the bomber-fighter offensive. On 6 June 1944 General Eisenhower was able to tell his troops, "if you see fighter aircraft over you, they will be ours".

How the air superiority, won by the American bombers which brought the German fighters up, and the long-range fighters which shot them down, ultimately developed into an Allied air supremacy is one of the effects of the final bombing offensive itself. It was nevertheless the degree of air superiority which had been attained by the late spring of 1944 which offered the British and American bomber forces, for the first time in history, the prospect of decisive strategic operations. The achievement towards which the R.A.F. had contributed so much at the beginning and so little at the end was nevertheless of equal advantage to the R.A.F. and the U.S.A.A.F.

War is a relatively inefficient art and many victories are to be explained more in the blunders of the vanquished than in the genius of the victors. The struggle for air superiority might have been shorter if the allies had grasped its full meaning earlier, but the outcome might have been different if the Germans had not turned a blind eye upon the greatest potentiality of air power, the long-range bomber.

Yet it was inevitable that Germany with her limited oil resources should deny herself what once seemed the relative luxury of a big bomber force. In any case both her traditions and her position as a first-class Continental power made a concentration upon land fighting inevitable. She was, in the event, able to stave off defeat until her armies had been decisively beaten in the field on three fronts, until her capital city had been occupied by invading armies. Certainly, the occasion of German surrender was the product of a long series of hard-fought battles on land, ranging from Stalingrad in the East, El Alamein in the South to Caen in the West.

The extent to which the strategic bombers hastened these advances from the perimeter by their battle at the centre is a question which can only be answered by military historians. The extent to which Germany was defeated at the centre before the allied armies crossed her frontiers is, however, obviously a problem which confronts the air historian. The fact that the final German collapse was simultaneous at the perimeter and the centre makes any distinction between armies and air forces as absolute war winners invidious. This difficulty need not concern us in our search for the effects of strategic bombing in the final phases of the war. The disintegration of the German war economy is a process which can be reconstructed temporally and causally.

Though it was not until September that the combined bomber forces were released from S.H.A.E.F. control, it was nevertheless some months earlier that the first crucial strategic attacks were launched against Germany. In effect, the final offensive began in May when the Eighth Air Force turned its 'marginal' effort against oil plants of Germany. In the following months this became a combined attack when the R.A.F. Bomber Command also began to devote a 'marginal' effort to the oil offensive.

These initial attacks were aimed principally at the production of aviation fuel, and despite the limited weight of bombs devoted to them, it soon became evident that a crippling blow had been struck at the Luftwaffe. In April, before the bombing began, German production of aviation fuel had been 175,000 tons and the Luftwaffe had consumed 165,000 tons. In May, as a result of the American attacks, production fell to 156,000 tons, and in June, after the combined attacks had begun, it was reduced to 53,000 tons In July production fell to 29,000 tons. Thus, within three months the strategic bombers had, with relative ease, converted a small credit balance into an alarming deficit. Nevertheless, it was not only the Luftwaffe which suffered. Production of carburettor fuel had been reduced to less than half of its April level by the end of July and the output of diesel oil had gone down by about one third.

Already at the beginning of June Speer had realised the gravity of the situation, and he knew that the functioning of the hydrogenation plants would be "practically decisive for the war".[2] He had faced and overcome this kind of crisis before, in the ball bearing industry, the aircraft industry, and, more generally, in the Ruhr and Hamburg. Once again, he was confident that vigorous reconstruction could soon restore the situation. He had visited some of the hydrogenation plants damaged by the American May attacks and he believed that they could soon be got working again.

The task was, however, beyond the plant managers who might be very good at turning knobs, but who could not deal with catastrophes. Accordingly, Hitler had agreed to the appointment of Geilenberg as Commissioner General for Immediate Measures. Vast allocations of building labour and material were to be placed at his disposal, and Speer reminded the building industry that they had to count with every day of production which could possibly be achieved.

The situation at the end of May was already serious, but it was very far from hopeless. Speer told the building industry that the "unhindered" flight of bombers across Germany need not become a ground for despair. Photographic reconnaissance was deceptive, and plants which looked as if they had been put out of action for several months could, as they knew from experience, actually be repaired in two or three weeks. The Luftwaffe, he said, had made "catastrophic" mistakes in this connection during their attacks on Britain, and now the Anglo-American Air Staffs would make the same mistake. If, however, the attacks were insufficiently sustained, it also seemed that they were not heavy enough and Speer estimated that between 60 and 70% of the damage could be averted by improved splinter protection at the oil plants.

In view of the fact that the Eighth Air Force attacked oil plants on only three days in May, that the total weight of its attack was no more than 2,883 short tons, and that the heaviest individual attack weighed only 547 short tons,[3] these comments by Speer were amply justified, but as a basis for future hope they were due to be gravely disappointing to the Minister. In June and July, the attack, now augmented by the R.A.F., became heavier and more persistent. Though the oil offensive represented only a minute fraction of the potential of the combined bomber forces, it was already taking a different course to anything previously known. It was being sustained.

In June most of the plants being repaired after the May attacks were again destroyed and a lot more damage was done. Daily output of aviation fuel in June never exceeded two thousand tons after the twelfth day of the month, and on two days it was below one thousand tons. In April, prior to the raids, average daily production had been nearly six thousand tons. Reconstruction was again undertaken and despite several small attacks, aviation fuel production was restored to 2,307 tons on 17 July. In the next four days, however, all this work was again destroyed and on 21 July only one hundred and twenty tons could be turned out.

Speer had already taken all measures to speed up the repairs to damaged plants, he had done what he could to provide protection against bombs, he had started a drive to produce generators for the Wehrmacht so that carburettor fuel might be economised, and through the Planungsamt he had reduced the ration of petrol for home use. He had also suggested to Hitler that Wehrmacht consumption of carburettor and diesel oil should be cut down, that flying should be curtailed to the minimum as further measures of economy, and that, as measures of defence, more smoke screens and dummy plants should be established and a greater concentration of A.A. guns placed round the oil plants, even if this did mean weaker defences for German towns. Above all he called for an increase in the fighter defence. Unless an adequate system of defence for the synthetic plants could be devised, there would be little point in repairing them, and, he told Hitler, "an impossible situation will arise which must have tragic consequences".

These "tragic consequences" were certain to ensue unless the operations of the strategic bombers could be effectively halted. Yet the only way to do this was to challenge the air superiority which they and the long-range fighters had now achieved. The German fighter force alone was capable of attempting this. Neither fog nor flack seemed to hinder the bombers. The fighters alone could stop them. The different suggestion which Speer made to Hitler at the end of July that fighters should be withdrawn from the front and devoted to the defence of the Reich became a positive demand by the end of August.

In that month only twelve thousand tons of aviation fuel had been produced, the equivalent of two days production before the bombing, and the supply of carburettor and diesel oil was falling off so seriously that Speer thought it impossible to contemplate any further offensive operations on land. In addition to this, only "abnormal changes" in the situation could offer any hope of retaining the bases of chemical production for explosives and agriculture.

If the Luftwaffe could not protect the synthetic oil industry, the basis not only of its own activity, but of all military activity, and the chemical industry as well, everything would be lost. Speer was claiming all the time that fighter production was increasing at a phenomenal rate,[4] but the value of this claim, even if it was true, was doubtful when the fuel situation was becoming so desperate.

There was, in fact, Speer told Hitler, only one hope, and this was that the bombers would break off the engagement for a short time. This would enable the synthetic plants to get back into production. When the bombers returned, the Luftwaffe might then be able to inflict very heavy losses upon them. For this effort he demanded that everything must be thrown in. Fighters must not be sent to the front and flying instructors must be mobilised for the battle. This final throw would mark the rise of a new German Air Force, or else its final downfall.

There was only one solid foundation for this naive but desperate optimism and that was the season. If the weather turned bad in the autumn, the heavy bombers might be unable to operate for a time, and that time might offer the chance of German recovery. The weather was the only serious threat to the allied bombing offensive, and the only serious hope for Germany. The stage of allied air supremacy had been reached, and even the weather proved to be a fickle ally to Germany.

The decisive success which the strategic bombers had achieved by the end of August was casting down the first line of German defence, the fighter force, it was threatening the second line, the army, and its influence was already extending to the economic sphere via the chemical industry. All the same the wheels of German industry were not ceasing to turn because of a shortage of oil. Transport was mainly by rail and canal, and industry relied principally upon diesel oil, which, in proportion, had suffered the least. Even if the success of the oil offensive did open the whole German structure to a 'knock out blow' from the air, that blow had not yet been delivered, and there seemed reason to believe that, in the meantime, a further expansion of armaments production might take place in the second half of 1944.

In an address to a conference of Gauleiters at Posen on 3 August, Speer outlined the methods by which this second 'armaments miracle' was to be achieved. Hitler had already decreed that no new type of weapon was to be introduced without Speer's permission, and by this measure it was hoped to increase the production of existing types by 20%. Hitler had also ordered a further simplification of weapon types, and what Speer described as "ballast" for the soldiers at the front was to be eliminated. A further increase in production of between five and ten per cent was expected as a result of the concentration of all production planning in the Speer Ministry and the consequent abolition of competition between the three services. Further reserves could be mobilised by a more systematic exploitation of the occupied territories. In Germany herself there were three million 'hand workers', and Speer believed that the armaments firms could find activities for them.

A more ruthless attitude to illness and idleness in the factories themselves could also be adopted. Then there were army dumps, about which apparently little was known. As an example of what might be found in them, Speer quoted the case of several dumps which had been examined. Among these was one in Vienna which was found by accident to contain one thousand lorries and a number of passenger vehicles. In another place a stock of 180,000 petrol canisters, which were urgently needed, was found. These were labelled as water canisters for use in North Africa.

In addition to these further measures of rationalisation, more intense mobilisation and drawing upon stocks, there were yet other ways in which armaments production might be increased, and their movement to the front speeded up. Hitler had agreed to Speer's proposal that all long-term capital development in the basic industries should be suspended for nine months. Thus, by sacrificing the long-term needs of power stations, agricultural machinery and so on, a further immediate increase in armaments production could be achieved. Hitler had also consented to more stringent measures being taken towards the throttling of the

German export trade. Methods of speeding up the flow of armaments from the factory to the front would have to be devised, and all army repair services behind the front placed under the Speer Ministry.

Speer must, however, have realised that the achievement of these ambitious schemes depended ultimately upon the efficacy of the German fighter force, and he was at pains to point out to the Armaments Staff that fighter production must be kept up. The absorption of the Fighter Staff by the Armaments Staff did not, he emphasised, mean a lower priority for fighter production. This of course brought him straight back, face to face with the oil crisis. All he could say was that the destruction of the oil plants must not influence aircraft production policy. It was only to be hoped that the weather would call a halt to the bombing, and then, within five weeks, he assured his audience, Geilenberg would nurse production of aviation fuel back to 75% of its normal level.

In September the continuing oil offensive produced an even more desperate situation. Production of aviation fuel in that month sank to the critical level of 9,400 tons, and for eight days after 11 September oil production had been at a complete standstill. Nevertheless, the bombers continued to allow short breathing spaces between their attacks, and Geilenberg's efforts were rewarded each time with a few days production before destruction again overtook the repairs.

Even so, repair work was becoming more difficult each time, and no underground plants were yet in production. All the same hope died hard and Speer continued to pin his faith upon winter weather and a revival of the German fighter force. Vigorous repair measures would go on, despite the criticisms of some people who thought it a waste of time to build targets for bombers. Germany now had a jet fighter in prospect which would fly on J.2 fuel, a mixture of carburettor and diesel oil, and a deterioration in the weather during the last three months of the year might be expected to allow a revival of all kinds of oil production. Once again, however, Speer felt it necessary to emphasise to Hitler the importance of getting the fighters up to tackle the bombers. He demanded that at least a thousand of them should stand by to protect the oil plants, which he hoped to get back into production during October and November.

Already, there was talk of curtailing the production of aircraft in the interests of an intensified drive to produce flak. If, however, the diminishing supply of petrol and the acknowledged failure of the Luftwaffe were reasons for these suggestions, the increasing embarrassment of the chemical industry, dependent as it was upon the production of synthetic oil, endangered the production of explosives. A gun without ammunition would be no better than an aircraft without petrol, and in any case the performance of flak was no more satisfactory than the performance of the fighters.

In two attacks on Leuna, each said to have been made by eight hundred aircraft, only three bombers on the first, and eight on the second, had been shot down by flak.[5] In either case the weather was still the only serious threat to the bombers.

The much-discussed weather did, in October, do something to help the production of oil in Germany and the output of aviation fuel showed some slight signs of recovery, but the winter weather proved to be no match for the bombers, with their new radar aid, Gee-H, and the repair organisation was increasingly powerless to deal with the heavy destruction, especially that dealt out by the large bombs of the R.A.F. Speer commented to Hitler upon the quality of these heavy bombs, and he spoke of their "extraordinary accuracy in attaining the target", (Eine ausserordentliche Zielsicherheit festzustellen ist), even though they were often dropped at night. Speer's last ally, the weather, had deserted him and he began to recognise that a collapse of the armed forces was imminent and inevitable.

The small reserves of aviation fuel which still remained in January 1945 would soon be exhausted. All stocks of carburettor and diesel oil had already been exhausted. Even a small amount of oil production would in future only be possible if the plants could be repaired and worked free from further attacks, and this was all that the Wehrmacht and the Luftwaffe would receive. As we have already seen, British Intelligence had diagnosed just this situation. To crown a decisive victory in the oil offensive the strategic bombers had only to keep up the attack through the winter weather and prevent any recovery. This they did not fail to do.

Even before he admitted to Hitler that the battle for oil was lost, Speer had to report the first consequences of this defeat. The virtual elimination of the Luftwaffe as an effective, or at least a constant, weapon of war, left the whole German war economy open to the strategic bombers. In

September the systematic transport offensive began. Almost immediately the situation in the Ruhr became alarming.

Before this bombing began, it had been usual to shift about 20,000 wagons of coal daily in the Ruhr area. Already by the beginning of October the disruption of transport had become so severe that it was only possible to move between 7,700 and 8,700 waggon loads a day. If the attacks continued, Speer had to warn Hitler, dumps of coal would mount up in the Ruhr and during the winter "an exceptionally serious coal and consequent production crisis" would arise.

At the beginning of November, seeing that these attacks were being continued and realising that Germany was now heading for "complete disaster and general catastrophe", Speer proclaimed a second Battle of the Ruhr, a battle for the existence of the Reich. "Transport", he told the Zentrale Planung, "governs us all", but the most urgent problem was the coal crisis which its disruption had already caused. Winter supplies of coal for the railways had sunk by practically half and they were continuing to diminish at the rate of 40,000 tons a day. Many important power stations were already struggling with inadequate supplies of coal and a few had even closed down. Gas works were in a similar plight. Most metal producing works were nearing the end of their coal stocks. A large number of vital armaments works had run out of coal and were no longer producing.

An immediate decline in munitions output of between 25 and 30% was to be expected. For six weeks the Ruhr had been in danger of isolation and this danger was now becoming a reality. The transport offensive by the destruction of the equally important railways and canals was rapidly reducing the bases of the German war economy to a state of chaos.

There seemed to be two ways in which this desperate situation might be tackled. The first, as usual, was by a tremendous effort to repair and repair again the damage to the railways and canals. For this purpose, Bormann had drafted 50,000 foreign workers, formerly employed upon the construction of fortifications, into the Ruhr, and Speer was proposing to release another 30,000 from the armaments industry for the same task. He was even going to employ ten per cent of the miners on this work, for it was not much use producing coal if it could not be moved to the consumers.

These efforts could, and did, produce temporary improvements. On one occasion when the bombing slacked off for three days, loading of coal had increased from six to twelve thousand waggons a day, but, since there was no longer any effective means of defence, the only hope of a permanent and substantial recovery was a change of allied bombing policy. Like the weather, the British and American Air Staffs, whom Speer had once regarded as his allies, had now deserted him, and the change of bombing policy for which he had hoped did not take place.

The other way of mitigating, or at least delaying, the worst consequences of the crisis was to start using up all the stocks of semi-finished components in an attempt to maintain for a time the existing level of armaments production. Thus, by mortgaging the future to the present, Speer hoped to keep the output of armaments up to 100% with only 20% of the long-term quotas available. By these means, and by drawing on the reserves which had been intended for the further expansion of production, which of course did not materialise, the output of finished armaments was kept up for longer than might have been expected. Even this achievement was, however, of doubtful value for the transport offensive often made it impossible to move the weapons to the front.

At the turn of the year the whole German war economy, long since denied its proper basic production, began to founder in the coal famine. The loss of territory before the advancing armies was also becoming a serious problem, but the strategic bombers had dammed German production at source before this became a decisive factor. Even before the coal bearing lands of Upper Silesia had been overrun by the Russian armies, the transport blockage was already preventing Germany from working all the coal mines which she did possess.[6]

The gigantic dislocation of rail and canal transport, supported by the continuing offensive against oil and other forms of attack,[7] resulted in a spreading paralysis of the entire German economy. Steel production, for instance, which in the first quarter of 1944 had been running at the average rate of 3.06 million tons per month, fell to the average rate of 1.32 million tons per month during the last quarter.[8] It was no more possible to run industry without coal than to fly in the air force without petrol. Where there was electric power, gas was lacking, where coal was to hand and weapons could be produced it was often impossible to transport them away. When this catastrophic and total defeat behind the lines, inflicted by the heavy bombers, merged with an equally total defeat on the perimeter, inflicted by the land forces, Speer became finally convinced that the war had been irretrievably lost.

A study of the final offensive is a study in the consequences of air superiority and the crucial importance of strategic intelligence. The indecisiveness of the bombing offensive before 1944 was due not to the failure to inflict damage, but to the inability of the bombers to inflict the right kind of damage, and above all their inability to sustain it. The area attacks on German towns, which was the only way in which large scale devastation could be achieved by a force which did not possess air superiority, was ultimately a barren strategy. Decisive results could not be secured unless all the most important towns could be destroyed and destroyed again simultaneously.

As a target, German industrial towns resembled the many-headed hydra. As one was struck down another grew up, and before the second had been demolished the first had recovered. Area bombing could only have succeeded against a people less resolute than the Germans, and British Intelligence grossly underestimated the qualities of the German people. The shock tactics of the first 'thousand' bomber raid on Cologne, of the Battle of Hamburg and finally the double attack on Dresden, were the most effective, but the panic which followed was in each case temporary.

Against a resolute enemy the only way to achieve decisive results by bombing is first to destroy something materially vital to his war effort and then to prevent its repair. Thus, decisive results could never have been achieved by area attack against German towns, if only because there were too many of them.

Yet selective attacks against vital segments of the German war economy, though more economical in effort expended and more humane in the destruction of human life, were no more effective than area bombing in destroying the German war potential, until they could be ceaselessly concentrated and sustained.

The initial American attacks on the ball bearing plants of Schweinfurt did, like the R.A.F. destruction of Hamburg, produce a seemingly desperate crisis in Germany. It was the failure to follow up these attacks immediately and again and again which gave the Speer Ministry the opportunity to reconstruct and disperse the industry. Even if on occasions it does call for the utmost gallantry by the aircrews and a preparedness to face heavy losses by the Air Staff, it is relatively easy to inflict heavy initial damage upon any industry which can be got under the bomb sight, or within the scan of radar, but it is a much more formidable task to extend and sustain this initial damage.

Yet it is only if the attack can be sustained and extended that decisive results can be expected. The resourcefulness of a resolute and powerful industrial nation is astounding. The speed at which tangled girders were straightened, the debris of masonry was cleared aside and improvised buildings erected again and again is a tribute to German industry and a caution to air force commanders. It is therefore only when air superiority has been gained that strategic bombing will become decisive.

Once the bombers are able not only to find and attack really vital targets of basic importance to the war economy, but to return again and again to them, regardless of what photographic reconnaissance suggests, then and then only does the battle of concrete against bombs swing decisively in favour of the bombs. Passive defence alone against bombing is useless. The bomber can choose its target at will, and there is always something which cannot or has not been protected. When air superiority has been attained, the effectiveness of a bombing offensive is simply a matter of strategic intelligence. Thus, the cardinal difference between the final bombing offensive and all the earlier attacks was the ability of the bombers to select a target and continue attacking it, not until it appeared to have been destroyed, but until Germany surrendered. In a sentence, it was the difference between air superiority and the lack of it.

Despite this salient distinction it would nevertheless be a mistake to consider the final bombing offensive in isolation either from the earlier phases of the attack, or from the land campaigns which developed simultaneously. As we have already seen, the bombing offensive before 1944 had been the means of attaining the air superiority which was exploited in 1944, and it must also have taxed German economic reserves to some indefinable extent.[9]

The years 1940 to 1943 were the breeding ground for the sweeping victories of 1944 and 1945, not only in Britain and America, but in Germany herself. The final offensive was also part of a triphibious assault upon the fortress of Europe. It was by no means wholly an application of the principle of independent air power. The advance of the allied armies contributed to the success of strategic bombing, notably by over-running the outposts of the German early warning system, by dispersing and dissipating the German fighter force, and finally by occupying territory of economic significance. Similarly, the bombing offensive contributed to the success of the campaign on land, both directly and indirectly.

The shortage of oil in December 1944 was one of the principal causes of the Russian break through from the Baranovo bridgehead. The German army had 1,500 tanks in that area, but most of them had no fuel. The dislocation of transport was one of the principal explanations of the collapse of the Ardennes offensive in January 1945, and the shortage of anti-tank guns seriously weakened the German army in all these crucial battles.[10]

These were a few of the many points at which the two principal elements in the triphibious assault overlapped. Nevertheless, it is wise to recall Speer's opinion that the final air offensive alone could have ended the war. Apart from all other factors, the oil offensive left Germany without the means of defence, and the transport offensive without the means of production.

The war of 1939–1945 has demonstrated that air power is the core of modern warfare, but it has also demonstrated that the conquest of the air has not introduced a revolution to the art of war. The Second World War has, in fact, shown that the principles of air warfare are similar to those of naval warfare.

The crux of naval air power was the command of the sea. The destruction or neutralisation of the enemy fleet should be the first object of naval policy. Only when this had been achieved could the Navy proceed to the ulterior task of blockading the enemy nation and securing an independent and strategic victory. Only when this had been achieved could the Navy render effective auxiliary service to the Army by transporting troops across the seas, and preventing the enemy from doing the same. In the First World War the naval blockade of Germany depended upon the command of the sea exercised by the Grand Fleet. Similarly, the movement of British and Allied troops across the seas, and even across the English Channel, depended upon the command of the sea exercised by the Grand Fleet. If Germany had won the Battle of Jutland, Britain would have lost the war.

In the case of air power, the same principles can now be seen to apply. The basic element of air power is air supremacy and the first objective of war in the air should be the destruction or neutralisation of the enemy air force. Only when this has been achieved can the heavy bomber seek its ulterior and independent object which is the destruction of the enemy war economy. Only when this has been achieved can an air force render effective support to land and sea operations by attacking communications, concentrations of troops and so on, or by destroying naval forces.

There are however, two important respects in which air power differs from naval power. The first is in the greater versatility of air power. Some great nations, by virtue of their self-sufficient economies, are not vulnerable to the weapon of blockade. Others which themselves would be vulnerable may break out and conquer new territory by means which naval power cannot prevent. This indeed was what Germany achieved in 1940. No measure of self-sufficiency or foreign conquest can, on the other hand, render a nation secure from the effects of a well-directed strategic bombing offensive.

The second point at which air power differs from naval power is the extent to which the first supersedes the second. A navy can no longer exercise command of the sea unless its sister service also enjoys command of the air. Further, no army can advance to victory unless its sister service also exercises command of the air. As Lord Tedder has said, "air superiority is the pre-requisite to all war-winning operations whether at sea, on land or in the air".

Naval history has established that there is no variant to the principle that naval power depends upon the command of the sea. Neither the 'guerre de course' waged in many wars by French cruisers, nor the 'guerre de course' waged in two world wars by the German submarine have shaken the rock-like strength of the Royal Navy. Nor have they determined the outcome of wars.

Air history is shorter, but again no variant has yet appeared to the principle that air power depends upon air supremacy. In the air as at sea the 'guerre de course' has failed. Nor does it seem probable that in the foreseeable future any innovation can shake the truth of this central principle. The methods of war are ever changing but the principles seem to remain from century to century.

Appendices

Appendix I

Note on Statistical Methods of Measuring Bombing Effect

Note on statistical methods of measuring bombing effect with special reference to the work of the U.S.S.B.S. and B.B.S.U.

Strategic bombing is normally an attack upon production, and certainly measuring the influence which it has on production is one of the most desirable ways of attempting to assess its effects. Both the U.S.S.B.S. and the B.B.S.U. were therefore striking at the roots of the problem when they attempted to make a statistical analysis of the effect of bombing upon the trends of German production. When in particular they attempted to discover the effect of area bombing in this way, they were also attempting one of their most difficult problems, for area bombing is the most complicated in its effects of all kinds of bombing. When considering the question of the statistical expression of bombing effect, it is therefore of particular interest to examine the ways in which the calculations about the effects of area bombing were conducted.

The U.S.S.B.S. produced the following figures as an indication of the loss of production as a percentage of total annual German production attributable to area bombing.

Year	%
1942	2.5
1943	9.0
1944	17.0
1945	6.5 (January to April only)

The B.B.S.U. reached the following rather different conclusions.

Type of Production	1942	1943		1944		1945
	Jan.–Dec.	1st Half.	2nd	1st Half.	2nd.	1st Half
War	0.25	1.8	3.8	1.0	0.9	1.2
All	0.56	2.7	8.2	4.4	7.2	9.7

The U.S.S.B.S. pointed out clearly that the "number of variables involved" made these "estimates very rough, especially towards the end of the period". In any case, the report went on to point out, these figures did not give a good indication of the extent to which war production had suffered, because it had generally been possible to divert production losses from the essential industries.

The B.B.S.U., who also indicated some of the uncertainties of their figures, were nevertheless much more confident about the results which they obtained. They were also more ambitious than the U.S.S.B.S., for they sought to show the effect not only on total production, but, within that, the effect on war production as well. On the evidence the B.B.S.U. concluded that "area attacks against German cities could not have been responsible for more than a very small part of the fall which actually occurred in production by the spring of 1945, and .... in terms of bombing effort, they were also a very costly way of achieving what they did achieve".

Area attacks accounted for nearly half of the entire effort put forth by the R.A.F. Bomber Command during the whole of the war. During this great offensive no less than 478,000 tons of bombs were dropped and some 300,000 Germans were killed in addition to a further 780,000 wounded. 82,000 acres of built up areas in Germany were devastated. It is therefore not only a matter of academic interest that any assessment of the usefulness of this campaign should be based on the most careful reasoning; it is also a matter of the greatest military importance. It is natural that there should exist the desire to find some precise statement of what this effort achieved.

Figures like those produced by the U.S.S.B.S. and the B.B.S.U. as the solution to this problem do, however, present serious dangers. Even if the points at which the calculation becomes a speculation, and if the methods of the calculation as well as the sources on which it is based are advertised, there is still a tendency for the figures themselves to gain the mastery which they may not deserve. Even as the broadest indication of the effect of the area bombing offensive these figures can only be of value if these points are carefully exposed.

The investigations of the U.S.S.B.S. and the B.B.S.U. were both based upon statistical analyses and these analyses in turn were principally based upon the answers to questionnaires submitted by the U.S.S.B.S. to a very large number of industrial firms in Germany, the interrogation of the heads of some of those firms, and the examination of German statistical records.

In addition to the many and obvious disadvantages of the questionnaires as a historical source, there were two which in this case are worthy of special mention. The firms which had been bombed out of existence did not return questionnaires for obvious reasons. This threw the sample out of balance and tended to produce an understatement of the effect of bombing. The U.S.S.B.S. came to the conclusion that the loss of production towards the end of the war, which was attributable to the general collapse of the German economy, and not specifically to the area bombing attacks which would tend to exaggerate the effects of area bombing, would compensate for this error. This was of course quite true, but whether these two compensating factors would, in fact, cancel each other out, or indeed whether they were even remotely comparable was a problem far beyond the realm of calculation. The B.B.S.U. decided that the same error would be compensated for by the fact that workers from the totally destroyed factories would have been absorbed by others which were continuing and increasing production. It is unnecessary to comment upon the speculative nature of this assumption.

The second principal disadvantage from which the questionnaires suffered was the unreliability of the answers. There is a strong supposition that many of the firms did not possess the necessary records to make detailed answers to the questions which were put to them. Indeed, during the war, the Statistische Reichsamt had found it impossible to collect complete information for this and other reasons.

German statistical records which might have provided a useful check upon these questionnaires also suffered from severe disadvantages. The files of the Reichsgruppe Industrie, which were one of the main sources, fell into a disordered state owing to the repeated evacuation of the offices in which they were maintained. In some cases, there was no assurance that the figures which were being studied represented actual or merely estimated production levels. Figures from the Statistische Reichsamt appear to have been liable to errors resulting from mistaken classification of the industrial groups and double reporting. After the war Speer commented upon the unsatisfactory way in which industrial statistics were collected in Germany during the war, and he also referred to incompetent processing of the figures which sometimes produced "appalling inaccuracies". Thus the U.S.S.B.S. and the B.S.S.U. were presented with material which concealed more than the usual statistical hazards. These were likely to introduce an element or error into any calculation. Moreover, since it was impossible to extract much of the most desired information from the questionnaires, another source of error was introduced by the complicated and roundabout methods which both surveys were compelled to adopt.

Finding that it was impossible to collect production statistics in terms of units produced, the U.S.S.B.S. had to establish production levels by reference to receipts from sales. This did not, of course, establish the production level directly, because the receipts would not indicate whether the goods sold had come from direct production or from stocks. Similarly, they would not show the amount of stock piling which was going on. In order to correct this error, the U.S.S.B.S. also consulted the statistics of electricity consumption by the firms. In this way the best index of production which could be devised was devised.

The production level in a sample of towns was then calculated and related to total German production at various times. In this way it became possible to calculate that 15,000 tons of bombs destroyed one per cent of national production. By a rule of three method it was then a simple matter to calculate the effect on national production of any given tonnage of bombs. In this way the overall estimates, which have already been quoted, were reached. In this connection it is important to note that any inherent errors in the calculation were multiplied by the number of times 15,000 would go into the tonnage which was actually dropped, in other words by about two in 1942, about nine in 1943 and about seventeen in 1944.[1] In addition to this, however, there was another serious source of error in this calculation. The calculation was based upon figures which were collected for 1943 and the first half of 1944, but the results were computed for 1942 and 1945 as well as the second half of 1944.

As the U.S.S.B.S. Report pointed out, bombing accuracy improved as the war went on, and this meant that the figures for the second half of 1944 and the first part of 1945 would tend to be an understatement of the actual effect of the bombing. On the other hand, the fact that an ever-increasing number of bombs would fall into craters made by the old ones and the effects would therefore become subject to the law of diminishing returns would tend to compensate for this error. Even so this was another speculation, which could not be checked, and may have produced a larger or a smaller error.

The B.B.S.U. devised a different employment for substantially the same basic material. They endeavoured to find what the trend of production in the bombed towns would have been if they had not been bombed, and then, by a comparison with the actual production, to find what the bombing effect had been. They were presented with the same problems as the U.S.S.B.S. in finding a satisfactory index of production, and like the U.S.S.B.S. they used the receipts of the firms as the indication of their production. By this means they calculated the production levels in a number of representative towns which had not been bombed. These "controls" they considered represented the trend of production in Germany. They then repeated the process in a sample of twenty-one towns which had been subjected to typical area bombing. The effect of the bombing was deduced from a comparison of the two results.

This investigation was not, however, designed to show the effects on the towns, but upon various groups of industry. By considering the figures for the groups of industry the B.B.S.U. found it possible to calculate figures of the extent to which area bombing depressed not only national production, but within that, national war production. This was more ambitious than the calculation which had already been made by U.S.S.B.S. The B.B.S.U. calculation produced the following figures for the iron and metal processing industry:

	1942	1943		1944		1945
		1st Half.	2nd	1st Half.	2nd.	Jan.–April
War	3.0	14.5	46.5	24.2	39	54.2
All	2.1	10.3	31.9	16.8	26.4	37.1

The interesting thing about these figures is not only that they show a very high rate of loss attributable to area bombing, but they also show a higher rate of loss in the sector of war production than in that of total production. Both of the conclusions which these figures suggested cut across the evidence which other information suggested, and, in fact, the B.B.S.U. found that these particular figures were "spurious", and they were accordingly excluded from the final reckoning. If, however, these particular figures were "spurious", then it seems strange that the other figures, which incidentally produced results which were more in accordance with the general trend of the evidence, should have been accepted. After all the figures were the product of the same calculation.

It is now possible to consider the validity of these two calculations. On the admission of the U.S.S.B.S. and the B.B.S.U. they cannot be accepted, and are not intended, as exact statements of bombing effect. The real question is whether they can be accepted as approximate guides to the effect of the area bombing offensive, for as such they have been widely accepted. An examination of the sources which were used and the methods of calculation which were adopted suggests that it is extremely unwise to base any firm conclusions upon these figures. The error may be small, but on the other hand it may be very great. There is no way of finding out.

The figures do suggest that the area bombing offensive failed to reduce the German economy to a state of disintegration, but this is already obvious from more simple and reliable evidence. The figures themselves do not give a reliable indication of the extent to which production was reduced, and so they leave the prudent historian with the main problem of how to assess the effects of an offensive, which was neither an obvious failure nor an obvious success, still unsolved.

Probably the greatest value of these statistical investigations has been to demonstrate this very difficulty. The priceless opportunities for an immediate investigation which could alone be enjoyed by these teams of research workers and the ingenious methods which they had at their disposal, neither of which was neglected by the U.S.S.B.S. or the B.B.S.U., and yet the comparatively barren results which were produced must be a caution to all who follow.

The science of statistics is still in its infancy, but it is an infant which wields tremendous power. Statistical calculations are often the springs of historical deductions and the foundations of political, military and economic policy. From time to time there comes a sharp reminder that this faith in figures is often a blind faith,[2] and yet to judge from contemporary literature and the pronouncements of statesmen, it is practically universal. The historian who declined to accept any statistical evidence because much of it is uncertain would, however, be as foolish as the archaeologist who refuses to dig because rats might have disturbed the strata. The historian, like the detective, must seize upon all the evidence he can find, but like the jury he must also weigh the evidence with care.

Just as he will naturally be concerned with the provenance of a document or the date of a photograph, so, in the case of statistical evidence, he must be concerned with the data and the method which has produced the result. Primary statistics are always more likely to be accurate than processed statistics, and the answer to vital questions are more likely to be accurate than those to incidental questions. By primary statistics is meant the measurement of a quantity by counting. By processed statistics is meant the estimation of an amount by indirect methods. By a vital question is meant an enquiry which is likely to produce a simple and accurate answer and by an incidental question an enquiry which cannot or will not be directly or perhaps accurately answered.

Nearly all figures are technically inaccurate. It is, for instance, often possible to find in British documents several different statements of the number of bombers which operated on a particular night. No one will ever know the exact tonnage of bombs dropped in the war, or the exact number of aircraft shot down. This, however, does not matter. The figures are substantially correct. They are primary statistics. In the case of the secondary statistics, however, there is no assurance that the figures are even substantially correct, and it is at these points that it is advisable to lean on the other evidence, and if necessary, to curb the ambition to provide answers at all. Humility is at times a necessary quality in the historian.

There is, of course, always the possibility that statistics may be 'cooked', a possibility which, as we have seen, exists in the case of the German figures for aircraft production, but this is a danger which is neither peculiar to statistics nor new to historians. The forgery is an ever-present danger to the historian, as the comparatively recent case of the Austro-Balkan documents with which Masaryk and Friedjung concerned themselves, reminds us. Like the philatelist, the connoisseur of art and antiques, the historian must defeat this threat by judgement and experience.

Appendix II

Letter by Air Commodore Slessor, Director of Plans, 13 April 1940

13th April, 1940.

S.46368/D. of Plans.

Sir,

I am directed to inform you that in consequence of the new situation created by the German invasion of Scandinavia it has been necessary to review our major air plans. The following decisions have accordingly been made.

2. There are two hypotheses:
   A. The Germans do not invade the Low Countries but authority for unrestricted air action is given.
   B. Germany invades Holland and/or Belgium.

Hypothesis A.
3. Plan W.A.8 will be implemented. In view however of the lack of suitable bases in France for the operation of our heavy bombers, and also of the prosed employment of at least a proportion of No. 5 Group for minelaying operations (Plan W.A.15), the area to be covered by our heavy bombers should be limited in the first instance to a zone north of Lat. 51°N. (i.e. including both the Ruhr and the industrial area around Leipzig).
4. The force at your disposal will be Nos. 3, 4 and a proportion of 5 Groups and, if the situation on the Western Front permits, units of the A.A.S.F. In the latter contingency it is suggested that the A.A.S.F. might patrol part of the southern area as well as undertaking the bombardment operations referred to in para. 10 of Bomber Command Operation Instruction No. 26.

5. The objectives in order of priority are:
   (a) Identifiable oil-plants (List C.1. Plan W.A.6).
   (b) Identifiable electricity plants, coking plants and gas works (List 1, Plan W.A.5(a)).
   (c) Self-illuminating objectives vulnerable to air attack (Lists D.1 and D.2, Plan W.A.8).
6. In addition, if the operation is authorised in the immediate future, harassing action by patrol aircraft should be directed particularly to the main German ports on the Baltic.

Hypothesis B. – If Germany invades Holland and/or Belgium.
7. Under this hypothesis, it is intended to initiate attacks on vital objectives in Germany, directed in the first instance against targets in the Ruhr area in order to cause the maximum dislocation on the lines of communication of a German advance through the Low Countries.

   This plan will be known as Plan W.A.4(c).

   It will be put into effect immediately a German invasion of either Holland or Belgium begins. Aircraft may therefore be routed direct across the Low Countries.
8. The objectives for attack will be:
   (a) Troop concentrations – the co-operation of heavy bombers in this action is already provided for by the allocation of 2 Whitley squadrons under the control of B.A.F.F. (the objectives are detailed in B.A.F.F. signal No. North Ops. 102 dated 12/4).
   (b) Communications in the Ruhr, i.e. the marshalling-yards listed in Annex A to this letter.
   (c) The oil plants in the Ruhr (Vide Annex A, and list C.1. Plan W.A.6).
9. The force at your disposal will be Nos. 3, 4 and 5 Groups, less the two Whitley squadrons allotted to the B.A.F.F.
10. The operations of our heavy bombers are to be confined mainly to night action in order to conserve our force, but dusk or dawn attacks may be carried out at your discretion. (If you consider an attack on oil objectives before nightfall would be advantageous –

the object being to set them alight and thus facilitate subsequent night operations – you will no doubt undertake it.)
11. The principle weight of attack should be directed against the oil plants; the attack of marshalling-yards being confined to harassing action (vide A.M. letter No. S.1338/D. of Plans dated 19.2.40). In the event of it being impossible to identify the oil-plants, or to attack them with sufficient accuracy, any self-illuminating or identifiable targets, such as coke-ovens, may be selected. Some possible targets in this category are listed in Annex A.
12. You should be prepared to undertake this operation as a sustained effort although you will appreciate that, as operations develop, it may be necessary either to divert certain squadrons to deal with closer objectives west of the Rhine or to extend the operations to embrace other night objectives as in Plan W.A.8.
13. Long-delay-action bombs may be used in either of these operations. (vide A.M. letter S.2436 dated 12th April, 1940).

I am Sir,
Your obedient Servant,

(sgd.) J. C. Slessor.
Air Commodore,
Director of Plans.

It should be understood that neither of these operations will be initiated without executive order from the Air Ministry.
(initialled) J.C.S.

Note: The target lists are not here reproduced.

Appendix III

Letter by Air Vice-Marshal Bottomley, Deputy Chief of the Air Staff, 14 February 1942

Air Ministry,
London, S.W.1.
14th February, 1942

S.46368/D.C.A.S.

Sir,

    I am directed to refer to Air Ministry letter CS.8337/II/D.B. Ops. dated 4.2.42, and to say that, in order to enable you to make your offensive fully effective on the introduction of TR.1335 equipment on operations, it has been decided that the principle of conservation of your forces, laid down in Air Ministry letter CS.10488/D.C.A.S. dated 13.11.41, should be modified. You are accordingly authorised to employ your effort without restriction, until further notice, in accordance with the following directions. Clearly this does not warrant pressing your attacks if weather conditions are unfavourable or if your aircraft are likely to be exposed to extreme hazards.

2. In the opinion of the Air Staff, the introduction of TR.1335 will confer upon your forces the ability to concentrate their effort to an extent which has not hitherto been possible under the operational conditions with which you are faced. It is accordingly considered that the introduction of this equipment on operations should be regarded as a revolutionary advance in bombing technique which, during the period of its effective life as a target finding device, will enable results to be obtained of a much more effective nature.

3. The period in which this device can be used as an aid to target location and blind bombing will be governed by the ability of the

enemy to develop counter-measures when the secret of its nature and operation has been disclosed. Much will depend on the security measures observed in its employment and the care taken by air crews to ensure the destruction of the apparatus and to avoid mentioning or discussing it in the event of their aircraft being forced down over enemy territory. It is unlikely, however, that under the best possible conditions this period will exceed six months from the date of its introduction. It is accordingly of first importance to exploit the advantages it confers to the full. The maximum effort possible having due regard to weather and other hazards should be exerted throughout the period it is thus available, and particularly in the first few weeks of your operations.

4. In addition to the foregoing factor, a resumption of your offensive at full effort is considered desirable for the following reasons:
   (i) This is the time of year to get the best effect from concentrated incendiary attacks.
   (ii) It would enhearten and support the Russians if we were to resume our offensive on a heavy scale, while they were maintaining so effectively their own counter-offensive against the German armies.
   (iii) The co-incidence of our offensive with the Russian successes would further depress the enemy morale, which is known already to have been affected by the German armies' reverses on the Eastern Front.

5. In accordance with these principles and conditions, a review has been made of the directions given to you in Air Ministry letter S.46368/D.C.A.S. dated 9.7.41 and it has been decided that the primary object of your operations should now be focused on the morale of the enemy civil population and in particular, of the industrial workers. With this aim in view, a list of selected area targets (taking account of the anticipated range of the TR.1335 equipment) is attached in Annex "A" to this letter. An additional list of targets beyond this range, which can be attacked when conditions are particularly favourable and when a correct assumption of the accuracy and powers of concentration obtainable with the equipment has been made, are also included in Annex "A".

6. You will note that Berlin has been included amongst the latter targets. In this case, your operations should be of a harassing nature, the object being to maintain the fear of attack over the city and to impose A.R.P. measures. The scale of effort and tactics employed should be designed to incur the minimum casualties and for that reason they should be undertaken at high altitude even if this entails carrying reduced bomb-loads. Apart from these particular operations against Berlin, the cardinal principle which should govern your employment of TR.1355 from the outset, should be the complete concentration on one target until the effort estimated to be required for its destruction has been achieved. Estimates of the scales of attack required are given in Annex "C".
7. Essen is the most important of the selected primary targets, and by attacking it first, the maximum benefit should be derived from the element of surprise. I am to suggest, therefore, that this should be selected as your initial target for TR.1335 operations, to be followed by attacks against the remaining priority areas listed in Annex "A".
8. When experience in the employment of TR.1335 has proved that, under favourable conditions, effective attacks on precise targets are possible, I am to request that you will consider the practicability of attacking first, the precise targets within TR.1335 range and, later, those beyond this range listed in Annex "B".
9. During the estimated effective life of TR.1335 as a target finding and blind bombing device, it will not be possible to equip more than a relatively small proportion of your force. It is, therefore, of the first importance that tactical methods to assist the remainder of the force to achieve concentration, both when the target is capable of being illuminated and under blind bombing conditions, should be studied, developed and applied to the maximum possible extent. In this connection I am to remind you of the principles and scales of attack with incendiary weapons laid down in Air Ministry letter S.46368/II/D.C.A.S. dated 25.10.41.
10. Apart from your primary offensive on the above lines, I am to say that the following additional commitments will still have to be met from time to time:

(i) Attacks on factories in France are to be undertaken as notified to you in Air Ministry letter S.46368/D.C.A.S. dated 5.2.42. If a favourable opportunity for the initial attack on the Renault plant has not occurred before you begin operations with the TR.1335 equipment, attacks on the French factories are to be carried out only when weather conditions are favourable and at the same time are unsuitable for the concentrated bombing of targets in Germany within this Directive.

(ii) The operations of No. 2 Group are to continue to be governed by the directions of Air Ministry letter S.46368/II/D.C.A.S. dated 25.11.41 bearing in mind the commitment of army air support as stated in para. 7 of that letter.

(iii) Periodical support for the operations planned by the Adviser of Combined Operations will be required in accordance with the directions issued to you in Air Ministry letter 3164/Plans dated 21st December, 1941.

11. Finally, I am to say that, although every effort will be made to confine your operations to your primary offensive, you should recognise that it will on occasions be necessary to call upon you for diversionary attacks on objectives, the destruction of which is of immediate importance in the light of the current strategical situation. In particular, important naval units and the submarine building yards and bases may have to be attacked periodically, especially when this can be done without missing good opportunities of bombing your primary targets.

I am, Sir,
Your obedient Servant,

(sgd.) N.H. Bottomley.

Air Vice-Marshal,
Deputy Chief of the Air Staff.

Note: *The Annexes to the above letter are not here reproduced.*

Appendix IV

Letter by Air Vice-Marshal Bottomley, Assistant Chief of the Air Staff, 10 June 1943

Air Ministry,
London, S.W.1.

10th June, 1943.

S.46368/A.C.A.S.(Ops.)

Sir,

   I am directed to refer to Directive C.C.S.166/1/D dated 21st January, 1943, issued by the Combined Chiefs of Staff and forwarded to the Commanding General, Eighth Air Force and the Air Officer Commanding-in-Chief, Bomber Command under cover of Air Ministry letter S.46368/A.C.A.S.(Ops.) dated 4th February, 1943. This directive contained instructions for the conduct of the British and American bomber offensive from this country.

2. In paragraph 2 of the directive, the primary objectives were set out in order of priority, subject to the exigencies of weather and tactical feasibility. Since the issue of this directive there have been rapid developments in the strategical situation which have demanded a revision of the priorities originally laid down.
3. The increasing scale of destruction which is being inflicted by our night bomber forces and the development of the day bombing offensive by the Eighth Air Force have forced the enemy to deploy day and night fighters in increasing numbers on the Western Front. Unless this increase in fighter strength is checked we may find our bomber forces unable to fulfil the tasks allotted to them by the Combined Chiefs of Staff.

4. In these circumstances it has become essential to check the growth and to reduce the strength of the day and night fighter forces which the enemy can concentrate against us in this theatre. To this end the Combined Chiefs of Staff have decided that first priority in the operation of British and American bombers based in the United Kingdom shall be accorded to the attack of German fighter forces and the industry upon which they depend.
5. The primary object of the bomber forces remains as set out in the original directive issued by the Combined Chiefs of Staff (C.C.S.166/1/D dated 21st January, 1943) i.e.: "the progressive destruction and dislocation of the German military, industrial and economic system, and the undermining of the morale of the German people to a point where their capacity for armed resistance is fatally weakened".
6. In view however, of the factors referred to in para. 4 the following priority objectives have been assigned to the Eighth Air Force:
Intermediate objective:
German Fighter strength.

Primary objectives:
German submarine yards and bases.
The remainder of the German aircraft industry.
Ball bearings.
Oil (contingent upon attacks against Ploesti from the Mediterranean).

Secondary objectives:
Synthetic rubber and tyres.
Military motor transport vehicles.

The Air Officer Commanding-in-Chief, Bomber Command
The Air Officer Commanding-in-Chief, Fighter Command
The Commanding General, Eighth Air Force.

While the forces of the British Bomber Command will be employed in accordance with their main aim in the general disorganisation of

German industry their action will be designed as far as practicable to be complementary to the operations of the Eighth Air Force.
7. In pursuance of the particular requirements of para. 6 above, I am to request you to direct your forces to the following tasks:
    (i) the destruction of German air-frame, engine and component factories and the ball bearing industry on which the strength of the German fighter force depend
    (ii) the general disorganisation of those industrial areas associated with the above industries
    (iii) the destruction of those aircraft repair depots and storage parks within range, and on which the enemy fighter force is largely dependent
    (iv) the destruction of enemy fighters in the air and on the ground.
    The list of targets appropriate to these special tasks is in Appendix "A" forwarded under cover of Air Ministry letter S.46368/III/D.B. Ops. dated 4th June, 1943. Further copies of this list, which will be amended from time to time as necessary, will be forwarded in due course.
8. Consistent with the needs of the air defence of the United Kingdom the forces of the British Fighter Command will be employed to further this general offensive by:
    (i) the attack of enemy aircraft in the air and on the ground
    (ii) the provision of support necessary to pass bomber forces through the enemy defensive system with the minimum cost.
9. American fighter forces will be employed in accordance with the instructions of the Commanding General, Eighth Air Force in furtherance of the bomber offensive and in co-operation with the forces of Fighter Command.
10. The allocation of targets and the effective co-ordination of the forces involved is to be ensured by frequent consultation between the Commanders concerned. To assist this co-ordination a combined operational planning committee has been set up. The suggested terms of reference under which this Committee is to operate is outlined in Air Ministry letter CS.19364/A.C.A.S. (Ops.) dated 10th June, 1943.

11. It is emphasised that the reduction of the German fighter force is of primary importance; any delay in its prosecution will make the task progressively more difficult. At the same time, it is necessary to direct the maximum effort against the submarine construction yards and operating bases when tactical and weather conditions preclude attacks upon objectives associated with the German Fighter Force. The list of these targets is in Appendix "B" forwarded with the Appendix "A" referred to in paragraph 7 above.

I am, Sir,
Your obedient Servant,

(Sgd.) N.H. Bottomley,
Air Vice-Marshal,
Assistant Chief of the Air Staff.
(Operations)

Appendix V

Letter by General H.H. Arnold, Commanding General, US Army Air Forces

D.C.A.S.

Please give me an answer as "candid" as you like. (Intld.) C.P. 17/10.

War Department
Headquarters of the Army Air Forces Washington

14th October, 1943.

Air Chief Marshal Sir Charles Portal, GCB., DSO., MC.
Chief of the Air Staff,
Air Ministry,
Whitehall,
S.W.1.

Dear Portal,

Overlord hangs directly on the success of our combined aerial offensive and I am sure that our failure to decisively cripple both sources of German air power and the GAF itself is causing you and me real concern.

I am afraid that we are not sufficiently alert to changes in the overall course of the air war.

In particular I refer to the fact that we are not employing our forces in adequate numbers against the German Air Force in being, as well as its facilities and sources. On my part, I am pressing Eaker to get a much higher proportion of his force off the ground and put them where they will hurt the enemy. The apparent deviation from his priority objectives established by the Combined Chiefs of Staff has caused me some concern. I was particularly concerned over substantial forces being directed toward shipbuilding cities while the German fighter forces are at their present strength.

It was my increasing concern that led to my letter to you dated 25 September 1943, urging you to provide P.51 accompanying support or make P.51's available to me.

The general course of the war very clearly requires, to my mind, our bringing more of our overall available airplanes into actual contact with the enemy. As presently employed, it would appear that your thousands of fighters (a number given as anywhere between 1,000 and 3,000 in England) are not making use of their full capabilities. Our transition from the defensive to the offensive should surely carry with it the application of your large fighter force offensively.

In the case of the Regensburg raid, for example, it was known in England that fighters had moved south from Denmark and north from Brest to German and northern French bases to meet the Regensburg bombers and to stop them on their withdrawal. At that time, we apparently had the great majority of the German fighter force on known airdromes refuelling at known periods of time. Nothing was done about it. Why should not all of our medium bombers and vast numbers of your Spits (equipped with belly tanks and bombs) have smashed the Germans while they were pinned to their refuelling airdromes?

We have put long range tanks in our P.47s. Those P.47s are doing some offensive action several hundred miles from England. In their basic design, our P47s were shorter range aircraft than your Spitfires.

Is it not true that we have a staggering air superiority over the Germans and we are not using it?

Should we not make it possible to put all fighters in an effective offensive action against the German Air Force at this critical time?

The above is a candid letter written to get your equally candid reply. Thanks.

Sincerely yours,

(Sgd.) H.H. Arnold,

General U.S. Army,
Commanding General, Army Air Forces.

Appendix VI

Report by Air Chief Marshal A.T. Harris, Commanding-In-Chief, Bomber Command, 3 November 1943

Prime Minister

After the first "1,000" raid last year you suggested prescribing 20 German cities by public pronouncement, and proceeding thereafter with their systematic destruction. On further consideration the idea was dropped because weather and tactical considerations would have made it difficult to tie ourselves down without handicap to so inelastic a procedure, and once the enemy had noted our determination so to proceed, the consequent concentration of defences would have avoidably jeopardised the Force.

You may like a brief picture of what has been accomplished on the more elastic plans adopted.

The cities and towns of outstanding service to the enemy war effort listed hereafter are marked "Virtually Destroyed", "Seriously Damaged", or "Damaged". (N.B. "Virtually Destroyed" expresses devastation to a degree which makes the objective a liability to the total German war effort vastly in excess of any assets remaining. In many cases the devastation approaches complete destruction of the town. "Seriously Damaged" portends percentage destruction greater than anything which we have experienced).

Comparative examples of the extent of devastation are instanced by:

Coventry	(100 out of 1,922 acres devastated)
Hamburg	(6,200 out of 8,383)
Cologne	(1,785 out of 3,320)
Essen	(1,030 out of 2,630)
Elberfeld	(825 ex 1,068)

Berlin has 480 acres devastated. Inner London 600.

"Devastation" in the case of German towns can only be assessed from vertical photography. We claim only what can be seen in the photographs. What actually occurs is much more than can be seen in any photograph.

Virtually Destroyed 19 (excluding French towns)	Seriously Damaged 19 (excluding Italian towns)	Damaged 9
Hamburg	Frankfurt	Brunswick
Cologne	Stuttgart	Darnstadt
Essen	Duisburg	Leverkusen
Dortmund	Bremen	Flensberg
Düsseldorf	Hagen	Jena
Hanover	Munich	Augsberg
Mannheim	Nuremburg	Leipzig
Bochum	Stettin	Friedrichshafen
Mülheim	Kiel	Wismar
Köln Deutz	Karlsruhe	In addition there is vast "casual" damage in certain built-up areas outside the towns named, e.g. throughout the Ruhr, and in some towns accidentally or incidentally hit, e.g. Delmenhorst, Wedel
Barmen	Mainz	
Elberfelt	Wilhelmshaven	
München/Gladbach/ Rheydt	Lübeck	
Krefeld	Osnabrück	
Aachen	Munster	
Rostock	Russelheim	
Remscheid	Berlin	
Kassel	Oberhausen	
Emden		

France	Italy
St. Nazaire	Turin
Lorient	Milan
	Spezia
	Genoa

In addition, many industrial targets in occupied countries, serving the German war effort have been very heavily damaged, e.g. Renault, Gennaviliers, Le Creusot, Montluçon, Montbéliard, etc., etc. The U.S.A.A.F. have made great progress with the destruction of key plants (but not enough, because the minimum number of aircraft for their plan have not materialised in the promised quantity).

From above you will see that the Ruhr is largely "out" and that much progress has been made towards the elimination of the remaining essentials of German war power.

Most of this damage has been done since March this year, when the Heavies came into full production and Oboe, H2S and the Pathfinders served to concentrate the effort.

There remains (in order of priority which can never be strictly observed owing to weather considerations, phases of the moon, tactical circumstances, etc.):

Berlin
Already comparatively worse off than London. (I await promised U.S.A.A.F. help in this the greatest of air battles. But I would not propose to wait for ever, or for long, if opportunity serves).

The Central Complex.
Leipzig, Chemnitz, Dresden and the "Little Ruhr" viz: Eisenach, Gotha, Erfurt, Weimar, Schweinfurt (Seriously Damaged).

The Berlin Road
Bremen (Seriously damaged), Hanover (Virtually Destroyed), Brunswick (Damaged), Magdeburg (Untouched), and Osnabrück (Seriously Damaged).

The "Upper Rhine"
Frankfurt (Seriously Damaged), Ludwigshaven (I.G. Farben Works) (Damaged), Karlsruhe (Seriously Damaged), Darmstadt (Damaged), Stuttgart (Seriously Damaged).

The S.E. Complex
Friedrichshafen (Damaged), Augsburg (Damaged), Munich (Seriously damaged),
Nuremburg (Seriously Damaged).

The East
Pilsen, Posen, Breslau, Vienna, Wiener Neustadt.

The Baltic
Kiel (Seriously damaged), Wismar (Damaged), Stettin city (industrial area already wiped out).

The Saar
Mop up the small coal and steel towns.

The Ruhr
Solingen, Witten, Leverkusen. Tidy up all round when occasion serves.

I feel certain that Germany must collapse before this programme which is more than half completed already, has proceeded much further.

We have not got far to go. But we must get the U.S.A.A.F. to wade in in greater force. If they will only get going according to plan and avoid such disastrous diversions as Ploesti, and getting "nearer" to Germany from the Plains of Lombardy (which are further from 9/10ths of "war-productive" Germany than is Norfolk), we can get through with it very quickly.

We can wreck Berlin from end to end if the U.S.A.A.F. will come in on it. It will cost between us 400–500 aircraft. It will cost Germany the war.

(Sgd.) A.T. Harris.

Air Chief Marshal,
Commanding-in-Chief,
Bomber Command.

3rd November, 1943.

Appendix VII

Letter by Air Marshal Bottomley, Deputy Chief of the Air Staff, 1 November 1944

Air Ministry,
London, S.W.1.
1st November, 1944
CMS/608/DCAS

D. C-in-C. Here we go round the mulberry bush.* ATH.

Sir,

I am directed to refer to Air Ministry letter CMS/608/DCAS dated 25th September, 1944, and to inform you that in view of the great contribution which the Strategic bomber forces are making by their attacks on the enemy petroleum industry and his oil supplies, it has been decided that the maximum effort is to be made to maintain and, if possible, intensify pressure on this target system. The petroleum industry, including storage, therefore, continues to hold the highest priority so as to prevent rapid recovery which would immediately be reflected in the enemy's strength and war economy.

2. In conjunction with, but subordinate to the offensive against oil targets, the maximum possible disorganisation of the enemy's transportation system should be created, particularly in the Ruhr area.
3. In order that there shall be the minimum diversion of effect from these target systems, enemy tank production plants and depots, ordnance depots, M.T. production plants and depots have been deleted from the current directive. When the Supreme Commander considers that the situation is such as to warrant special attacks on these objectives, requests will be made in accordance with the

procedure outlined in paragraph 4 of the letter quoted in paragraph 1 above.

4. With regard to attacks on important industrial areas, your attention is directed to the importance of the industrial, administrative and transportation systems of the Ruhr area, as affecting the enemy's war economy generally and as affecting the major land offensive which is planned by the Supreme Allied Commander, and with the weather out of mind!* The special operation 'Hurricane I' was designed with these factors in mind. (See Air Ministry letter CMS/608/DCAS dated 13th October, 1944).

5. In order to meet the requirements indicated above, the instructions set out in Air Ministry letter CMS/608/DCAS dated 25th September, 1944, still stand except that as regards paragraph 4 you will now consult as necessary the Deputy Supreme Allied Commander who will normally co-ordinate air action in accordance with ground force requirements. The directive issued under cover of that letter is however cancelled, and the attached directive No. 2 substituted. This directive is also being issued to the Commanding General, Mediterranean Allied Air Forces and the Commanding General, Eighth Air Force.

I am, Sir,
Your obedient Servant,

N.H. Bottomley,
Air Marshal,
Deputy Chief of the Air Staff

* *These comments are by Sir Arthur Harris*

Appendix VIII

Directive No.2 for the Strategic Air Forces in Europe

Directive No.2 for the Strategic Air Forces in Europe

General Mission

In accordance with the instructions received from the Combined Chiefs of Staff, the overall mission of the Strategic Air Forces remains the progressive destruction and dislocation of the German military, industrial and economic systems and the direct support of land and naval forces.

Priorities of Objectives
2. Under this general mission you are to direct your strategic attacks, subject to the exigencies of weather and tactical feasibility, against the following systems of objectives:

First priority
(i) Petroleum industry, with special emphasis on petrol (gasoline) including storage.

Second priority
(ii) The German lines of communication
   (a) The operations of the Strategic Air Forces based in the United Kingdom are to be directed against enemy lines of communication, with particular emphasis upon the Ruhr.
   (b) Target lists will be issued from time to time for all Strategic Air Forces.

Important Industrial Areas.
3. When weather or tactical conditions are unsuitable for operations against the systems of objectives mentioned above, attacks are to be delivered on important industrial areas with blind bombing technique as necessary. As far as operational and other conditions

allow, these are to be directed so as to contribute to the maximum destruction of the petroleum industry and the dislocation of the target systems indicated above.

Targets and Target Priorities

4. The list of strategical targets in paragraphs two and three above, best calculated to achieve this aim, and the relative priorities accorded them, will be issued separately. These priorities will be adjusted from time to time in accordance with the situation.

Counter Air Force Action

5. As a result of air action against the production, maintenance and operational facilities of the German Air Force, its fighting effectiveness has been substantially reduced. At the same time, our combined air strength has vastly increased. In these circumstances, we are no longer justified in regarding the German Air Force and its supporting industry as a primary objective for attack. Our major efforts must now be focussed directly on the vital sources of Germany's war economy. To this end, policing attacks against the German Air Force are to be adjusted so as to maintain tactical conditions which will permit of maximum impact upon the enemy. No fixed priority is therefore assigned to policing attacks against the German Air Force. The intensity of such attacks will be regulated by the tactical situation existing.

Direct Support

6. The direct support of land and naval operations remains a continuing commitment.

S.O.E. Operations

7. All S.O.E./S.I.S. operations will be in accordance with existing instructions and procedure.

Co-ordination

8. The procedure as at present established for the co-ordination of operations between the various Air Forces will continue.

Air Ministry.
CMS/608/DCAS
1st November, 1944

Notes

Introduction
1. Mahan, *The Influence of Sea Power Upon History* (Little, Brown and Co. (Sampson Low), Boston, 1928 Edition).
2. Lapeyrouse – Bonfils: *Histoire de la Marine Française*", quoted in Mahan, op.cit., p.133.
3. Campbell, *Lives of the Admirals*, quoted in Mahan, op.cit., pp.133–134.
4. Cp. Prof. Mead Earle's Paper, *The Influence of Air Power upon History*, p.21.
5. Churchill, *The World Crisis 1911–1918* (Odhams Press, London, 1938).
6. In the earlier case of the Zeppelin threat, Mr. Churchill as First Lord of the Admiralty had ordered bombing attacks against Zeppelin sheds in Germany. The R.N.A.S. carried out raids against these targets at Düsseldorf, Cologne, Cuxhaven and Friedrichshafen. See *World Crisis*, op.cit., Vol. I pp. 266–267. This is especially interesting as an early reflection of the 1943 'Pointblank' directive.
7. *The War in the Air*, Vol. VI., Paper by Mr. Churchill, 21 October 1917. It is one of history's cruellest ironies that it fell to Mr. Churchill, while he presided over the nation's finances in later years, to impose disastrous economies on the fighting services.
8. Under the so-called "Ten Year Rule".
9. The following figures were given to illustrate the percentage of total German production (excluding Czechoslovakia) which came from the Ruhr:

Bituminous Coal	73%
Coke	75%
Coal Tar and by-products	70%
Pig Iron	67%
Raw Steel	70%
Engineering Capacity	over 70%
Chemical Industry	"By far the greater part"

10. Transport difficulties seemed to indicate that little could be gained from Russia.
11. The I.I.C. thought stocks plus domestic production would extend to 4½–5½ months of war.
12. The F.C.I. (AT) had grasped in 1936 that refineries were not nearly as important as synthetic plants.
13. The words were actually those of the C-in-C Bomber Command.

Chapter 1
1. Bomber Command Appreciation on the Ruhr Plan, 27 January 1940. In the case of 14 December, the S.A.S.O., Bomber Command attributed the losses to causes other than enemy fighter action.

Chapter 2
1. It is impossible to compare in actual figures British estimates and German statistics of stocks owing to various definitions of the word 'stock'.
2. Calculated from German figures.
3. This Mr. Dewdney thought was 'conservative' for a 500lb. bomb.
4. The bombs were assumed to be of 500lb. each.
5. His estimates for the more important individual plants were:

Scholven	58% undamaged.
Gelsenkirchen	68% undamaged.
Homberg	50% undamaged.
Leuna	86% undamaged.
Magdeburg	72% undamaged.
Poelitz	80% undamaged

Chapter 3
1. For instance, a private individual writing from Surrey in August 1941 advised the Air Ministry that the "total destruction of Cologne Cathedral would, if carried out at the psychological moment, compass the final breakdown of the German's morale". He based this belief upon the existence in Germany of a legend to the effect that the destruction of the Cathedral would presage the downfall of Germany. To clinch matters Germany should be flooded with leaflets celebrating the awful event in verse which was to begin: "Cöln (sic) Cathedral has been destroyed; Calamity now you can't avoid." At the Air Ministry the Director of Bomber Operations was officially advised that the author of this suggestion showed "an accurate sense of values". The D.B. Ops. himself thought the idea worth keeping in mind. Subsequent papers do not, however, explain the eventual collapse of Germany when Cologne Cathedral was the only remaining landmark in the stricken city.
2. Or so it was supposed.
3. Initial Equipment Aircraft.
4. This was, however, no argument, since it reflected on the difficulty of target finding, not on the tactics of incendiarism.

Chapter 4
1. *The War in the Air*, op.cit. Vol. VI. Appendices p.19. Extract from a paper by the Minister of Munitions, Mr. Winston Churchill, 21 Oct. 1917. Compare this, however, with the following extract from a memorandum addressed

by Mr. Churchill to the War Cabinet on 5 March 1918. "Again, if either side possessed the power to drop not five tons but five hundred tons of bombs each night on the cities and manufacturing establishments of its opponent, the result would be decisive." See *The World Crisis*, op.cit., Vol. II., p.1268.
2. The report also stated that these photographs (actually 633 but given as 650, presumably a round figure) which purported to show the target area, were taken on "over 500 different sorties". This presumably means that either the word "sortie" was misused, or that some of the aircraft had taken more than one picture of the "purported" target area. This curious statement was not explained in the report and aroused no comment, even by those who were critical of the report.
3. The broad principles of the working of this famous radar aid to navigation have been given much publicity since the end of the war. There is a good account in the R.A.F. Narrative, *The R.A.F. in the Bomber Offensive against Germany*, Vol. IV. It should therefore suffice to say here that the navigator of an aircraft flying within range of the transmitters (300 miles) was enabled to translate precise time measurements made by pulses registered on his set into longitude and latitude by means of a latticed chart. The ground positions which were thus obtained were of extraordinary accuracy. Normally, and especially when the lattice lines offered an acute cut, an aircraft could be more accurately pinpointed when flying at height than would have been possible by picking up land marks even in broad daylight. Even when the Germans had devised effective methods of jamming the reception of the pulses by aircraft which were actually over Germany, the navigator still had the opportunity of making very accurate wind calculations while he was still over the North Sea and these were frequently the basis of a successful flight even if the meteorological forecasts proved to be incorrect.
4. This comment was written in pencil on the appropriate page of the Butt report and it was not signed or initialled. A careful comparison of the hand with specimens of Sir Richard Peirse's handwriting reveal it to be in his, beyond all possible doubt.
5. Note by S.A.S.O. on Butt Report. 21 Aug. 1941. The general impression is, however, that they gave them to the crews in which they had the most confidence. See Sir Arthur Harris' Despatch.
6. One set had already been lost over Germany.

Chapter 5
1. The C.A.S. instructed the D.C.A.S. verbally to prepare a paper on bombing policy on 2 January 1942.
2. The Washington War Conference.
3. *The White House Papers of Henry L. Hopkins*, Robert E. Sherwood (Eyre & Spottiswood, 1949), Vol II., p.495.

4. ibid, p.506. Mr. Sherwood does not disclose the source of this quotation.
5. *The Goebbels Diaries*, translated and edited by Louis P. Lochner (Hamish Hamilton, 1948), p.63ff.
6. ibid, p.57.
7. The Cabinet had already approved the policy of the February Directive.
8. General Reconnaissance.
9. Memorandum by the First Lord of the Admiralty on Bombing Policy, 14 February 1942.
10. Prof. Blackett has subsequently proved to his own satisfaction that the strategic bombing offensive had practically no influence on the outcome of the war. See his *Military and Political Consequences of Atomic Energy*, Turnstile Press, 1948.
11. This excluded 6,000 heavy bombers which were to be built in the United States of America.
12. *War Room Manual of Bomber Command Operations 1942*, Part VI.
13. For instance, the average number of operational aircraft on which the C-in-C could count per raid in March 1942 was 421, in September only 331, and in December 419.
14. This principle was accepted in an agreement between General Arnold, Admiral Towers and Air Chief Marshal Portal in Washington on June 1942.
15. Heavy bombers include Stirlings, Halifaxes, Manchesters and Lancasters. In other words, they were bombers which had, or ought to have had, (note the case of the Manchester) four engines. Medium bombers included Wellingtons, Hampdens, Whitleys. Light bombers included Blenheims and Mosquitoes.
16. In March 1942 there were an average of 7 Lancasters available for each operation. By December this number had increased to 145.
17. *War Room Manual of Bomber Command Operations 1942*, Part VI, p.4. Bomber Command dropped 45,501 tons of bombs in 1942 as against 31,646 tons in 1941. In 1942 Bomber Command flew 29,929 bombing sorties, as against 30,508 in 1941. The total number of Bomber Command sorties in 1942 did, however, exceed those flown in 1941 (36,426 as compared with 32,262). This was due to the increased mining and reconnaissance activity in 1942.
18. The whole story of the development, production and use of Gee is intensely interesting and well documented. The subject of radar and its effects upon the bombing offensive is worthy of separate treatment. It is only possible to allude to the question in this volume.
19. Sir Arthur Harris has handsomely acknowledged this in his *Bomber Offensive*.
20. Paper on the Role and Work of Bomber Command by Sir Arthur Harris, dated 28 June 1942.
21. It is unfortunately impossible to digress further and analyse these operations in greater detail. Apart from their significance already shown

they are mainly of importance for the tactical lessons which they indicated, for these were in time to exert the most powerful influences upon bombing policy.
22. The first raid by more than 100 bombers on Italy was delivered at Genoa on the night of 22 October.
23. Though this did not mean that the Prime Minister had been entirely convinced by all Sir Arthur Harris' claims.
24. Though they did not say so it seemed likely that the Chiefs of Staff had in mind the bloody engagement at Dieppe earlier in the year.
25. This was a significant reversal of the policy at the beginning of the year.
26. There were frequent reports on the German oil position put before the Cabinet in 1942. Mr. Oliver Stanley, for instance, submitted a report to the Chiefs of Staff on 13 April. He concluded that an oil offensive should be undertaken as soon as Ploesti could be attacked.
27. Interest in ball bearings had been growing ever since February 1942.

Chapter 6
1. Notably by the United States Strategic Bombing Survey and the British Bombing Survey Unit.
2. B.B.S.U. *Effects of Strategic Air Attacks on German Towns*, p.13. This figure was calculated from photographic reconnaissance in preference to German records which are self-contradictory.
3. Secret Report from the Reichpropaganda Amt, Schwerin, to Hitler, Goebbels etc. 29 April 1942. According to his diary, it is apparent that Goebbels did receive this report which he says came from Gauleiter Hildebrandt. See *Goebbels Diaries*, 30 April 1942, p.146.
4. The index of German armaments production in 1942 was: Jan. 103; Feb. 97; Mar. 129; Apr. 133; May 135; June 144; July 153; Aug. 153; Sept. 155; Oct. 154; Nov. 165; Dec. 181.
5. *Fuehrer Directives 1939–1941*, p.57: Hitler to Brauchitsch, Raeder, Göring and Keitel, 9 October 1939.
6. A decrease in ammunition production was ordered after the fall of France and a general decrease in arms production after the initial Russian success.
7. For instance, the speed with which the Heinkel works at Rostock recovered from the effects of the damage inflicted by Bomber Command was one of the few things upon which Göring was able to congratulate the aircraft industry in 1942.
8. There was a steady increase in the size of the German night fighter force deployed in the West. Its strength rose from 207 in January 1942 to 255 in April, 273 in July, 352 in October and 382 in January 1943. German night fighters were "borrowed" bombers and other types adapted to the purpose.
9. Göring's address to aircraft industry, 13 September 1942.
10. All the same he did so at length.

11. Average monthly production in 1941 (all types)   952
    Average monthly production in 1942 (all types)   1,274
    Average monthly production in 1943 (all types)   2,091
    Average monthly production in 1944 (all types)   3,343 (Jan–Oct./Nov. only)
    According to figures derived from Planungsamt/Hauptabt. Planstatistik/Statistische Leitstelle and arranged in a table, presumably by the Institüt für Wirtschaftsforschung.
12. The extent to which the offensive arm of the Luftwaffe was beginning to show signs of eclipse is shown by the following figures of aircraft production. In 1941 the average monthly production of combat fighters was 244 and that of combat bombers 336. In the first six months of 1942 the figures were 391 and 329 respectively. As the Luftwaffe began to expand the tendency for fighter production to outstrip bomber production became more marked.

Chapter 7
1. A target system is a number of targets all related to a single object.
2. Assuming that Ploesti could be bombed by some other force.
3. The Combined Chiefs of Staff arranged at Casablanca that the British C.A.S., acting as their agent, should be responsible for the strategic operation of the R.A.F. and U.S. Bomber Commands in the U.K. The Commanders of the two forces were, however, left with the power to decide upon feasibility and method.
4. It is interesting to notice that this passage of the Directive is heavily marked with emphasising lines on the Bomber Command copy, and that this same passage was similarly marked on the Bomber Command copy of the Casablanca Directive.
5. The Casablanca Directive.
6. The conference was held on 9 June 1943.
7. *Global Missions*, General of the Air Force H.H. Arnold (Harper and Brothers, New York, 1949), p.178.
8. *Window* was the code name for thin metallised strips of paper dropped by the bombers to confuse the German radar defences.
9. For an illuminating account of tactical developments and technical methods at this time, see *Bomber Offensive*, op.cit., Chapter VIII.
10. By which he really meant the Luftwaffe.
11. A dispute which eventually ended with a message from General Arnold to Sir Charles Portal: "The Spitfires you sent me by ship have landed at London after crossing the Atlantic under their own steam", *Global Mission*, op.cit., p.496.
12. By which of course he meant his own and not the American plan.
13. A protest against the build-up of the Fifteenth Air Force in Italy at the expense of the Eighth in the United Kingdom.

14. In other words, the A.C.A.S.(I) believed that the tactics of evasion, that is, the methods of the "guerre de course", were capable of defeating Germany. In this assumption he overlooked the fact, already suspected by the D.C.A.S., that the area bombing offensive was not proving decisive. He also overlooked the fact that these tactics of evasion were exhausting themselves. Evasion of the enemy air force would obviously allow it to grow stronger and five months later Sir Arthur Harris himself pointed out "that the strength of German defences would in time reach a point at which night bombing attacks by existing methods and types of heavy bomber would involve percentage casualty rates which could not in the long run be sustained". He added that, "tactical innovations which have so far postponed it are now practically exhausted. Remedial action", he continued, "is therefore an urgent operational matter which cannot be deferred without grave risk". The "remedial action", which Sir Arthur Harris called for, was the "provision of night fighter support on a substantial scale". When his Command later turned to daylight operations, Sir Arthur Harris made "impassioned" appeals for long range fighter escorts. Thus, there were times when it appeared that the C-in-C Bomber Command recognised that destruction of the German Air Force was, as the Americans knew and the majority of the British Air Staff had agreed, the essential preliminary to a successful bombing offensive.
15. *The Times*, "Bombers Over Europe", 4 January 1944.
16. War Room Monthly Summary of Bomber Command Operations, 1944.
17. U.S. Eighth Bomber Command Diary of Operations.

Chapter 8
1. In the early R.A.F. daylight flights of 1939–40, in the Battle of Britain and in the early American attacks on Germany.
2. Interrogation of Albert Speer, report No.26, 13 August 1945.
3. *The Goebbels Diaries*, 29 July 1943.
4. *The Goebbels Diaries*, 9 March 1943.
5. U.S.S.B.S., "A Detailed Study of the Effects of Area Bombing on Hamburg, Germany". See also *The Bomber's Baedeker* (1944), Part I pp.303–328.
6. This, and what follows, is based upon a Secret Report by the Police President of Hamburg issued in translation by the Home Office, Civil Defence Department, Intelligence Branch, January 1946.
7. Speech by Speer to Gauleiters at Posen, 6 October 1943.
8. Speech by Speer at Sonthofen, 28 July 1944.
9. The possibility that these figures were 'doctored' does exist, but at least it is obvious the fighter force did not "cease to exist" and that, on the contrary, it did expand enormously in size.
10. Interrogation of Albert Speer, 6th Session, 30 May 1945.
11. The Casablanca Directive.

12. By which is meant a group of targets upon whose functioning all aspects of war making depend, e.g. oil supplies and production, transport, ball bearings, power, or indeed, if it can be assailed, morale.

Chapter 9
1. Plan for the completion of the Combined Bomber Offensive, 5 March 1944. This plan was submitted by Spaatz to Eisenhower and Portal.
2. The Prime Minister presently "ruled" that "there can be no question of handing over" R.A.F. Bomber Command to the Supreme Commander.
3. See *Enemy Coast Ahead* (Michael Joseph Ltd, 1946) by W/C Gibson, V.C., who led the attack.
4. *Bomber Offensive*, op.cit., p.266. "I myself did not anticipate", Sir Arthur Harris writes, "that we should be able to bomb the French railways with anything like the precision that was achieved."
5. The attacks on flying bomb sites, first used by the Germans in June, were a measure of defence for the United Kingdom, in the same sense as the R.A.F. attacks on the German aircraft industry in 1940, but they were also part of the invasion plan because the flying bombs might have been used against the bases and communications of the Allied armies.
6. B.B.S.U. *Strategic Air War*, op.cit. p.41. Of these 3,645 (Fortresses and Liberators) belonged to the Eighth and Fifteenth Air Forces and 1,601 to Bomber Command.
7. General Marshall, did suggest, after he had heard the British proposals, that there should be a physical division, and that part of the bomber force should be assigned to the Supreme Commander.
8. Memorandum by Tedder on "Air Policy to be adopted with a view to (the) rapid defeat of Germany", 25 October 1944.
9. Special Operations Executive.
10. A breathing tube which enabled submarines to remain under water for much longer periods than hitherto.
11. The area bombing offensive absorbed the following (British) tonnages in 1945: January, 11,931; February, 21,888; and March, 30,278.

Chapter 10
1. In this attack, carried out on 30/31 March 1944, 95 R.A.F. bombers were shot down over Germany from a total of 795 dispatched.
2. Address by Speer to a conference of building organisers concerned with the repair of oil plants, 2 June 1944.
3. The attack of 547 tons was against Poelitz on 29 May, and this stopped production completely at the plant for a short time.
4. On 3 August he claimed that, in July, 3,115 new fighters and "destroyers" (Zerstörer) were produced and 935 damaged machines repaired. If, however, this total of 4,050 aircraft was really delivered to the Luftwaffe, it

is to be wondered what happened to them. Speer later claimed that most of them were "destroyed on the ground or else smashed up in some other way".
5. Nevertheless, Hitler ruled in November that the flak programme should enjoy first priority, i.e. a higher priority than aircraft production.
6. Speer to Guderian, for Hitler, 15 December 1945 (copy). After the war Speer expressed it as his opinion that the loss of the peripheral territories in the land campaign would ultimately have caused a food crisis in Germany, but that, industrially, she could have held out until 1946, if it had not been for the air raids.
7. For example, 15.5% of the total electric plant capacity of Germany was knocked out by bombing in December 1944.
8. Report by Speer to his close collaborators, 27 January 1945. The loss of territory did, of course, contribute to this.
9. For instance, Speer reported to Hitler in April 1944 that the position of the building industry had been becoming increasingly strained ever since the summer of 1943. By April 1944, 320,000 men, or some 30% of the industry's whole labour force, was employed upon the repair of air raid damage. The need to repair houses did in some cases interfere with the repair of damaged factories.
10. This was due to the flak programme for defence against bombing; 30% of the total German production of guns in 1944 was devoted to the flak programme.

Appendix I
1. The hazards of this type of calculation had already been demonstrated by the fantastic calculations of the effect bombing would have which were worked out on the multiplication system before the war, using results in the 1914–1918 war as the basis.
2. See for instance leading and special articles in *The Times* Newspaper, "The Use of Statistics" and "Measuring Production: The Pitfalls and Problems of Statistical Comparison", 19 January 1950.

ANOTHER OFFICIAL HISTORY AVAILABLE
www.pen-and-sword.co.uk

STALAG LUFT III
An Official History of the 'Great Escape' PoW Camp

Opened in the spring of 1942 to house captured Allied airmen, Stalag Luft III at Sagan was planned and built to make escape particularly difficult, especially tunnelling. This, though, did not deter the prisoners. Numerous escape attempts followed, involving prisoners trying to go over, through or under the wire fences. In some cases they succeeded.

It is for two of the successful escapes that Stalag Luft III is best known – both of which went on to be depicted in films. The so-called Wooden Horse escape in October 1943 resulted in the three prisoners involved all making a 'home run'. Three further 'home runs' resulted from the mass escape which occurred the night of 24/25 March 1944 – the so-called 'Great Escape'.

Drawn from the information and testimonies of those who were held in Stalag Luft III, this official history of the camp was prepared for the War Office at the end of the Second World War but was never released to the general public.

ISBN: 978-1-47388-305-5

ANOTHER OFFICIAL HISTORY AVAILABLE
www.pen-and-sword.co.uk

HITLER'S V-WEAPONS
The Battle Against the V-1 and V-2 in WWII

At 04.08 hours on the morning of 13 June 1944, two members of the Royal Observer Corps were on duty at their post on the top of a Martello tower on the seafront at Dymchurch in Kent. At that moment they spotted the approach of an object spurting red flames from its rear and making a noise like 'a Model-T-Ford going up a hill'.

It was a development that they, and many others throughout the UK, had been anticipating for months. The first V1 flying bomb, an example of what Hitler had called his *Vergeltungswaffen* or Vengeance Weapons, to be released against Britain was rattling towards them. The two spotters on top of the tower may well have been aware that a new Battle of Britain had just begun.

From August 1943, every effort was undertaken by the RAF and the USAAF Eighth Air Force to destroy every site lined to the V-weapons – including those of the V2 rocket. This book, written by the Air Ministry's Air Historical Branch, is the official account of the measures undertaken by the Air Defence of Great Britain, Fighter Command, Anti-Aircraft Command, Bomber Command and even the Balloon Command to defend the UK from what was potentially the greatest threat it had ever encountered.

ISBN: 978-1-52677-005-9

ANOTHER OFFICIAL HISTORY AVAILABLE
www.pen-and-sword.co.uk

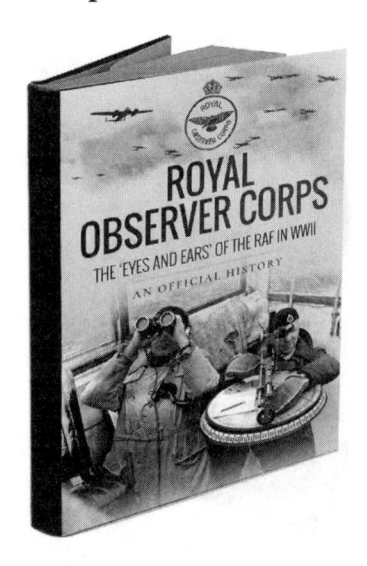

ROYAL OBSERVER CORPS
The 'Eyes and Ears' of the RAF in WWII

The key roles played by the Royal Observer Corps in the Second World War have, all too often, been overshadowed by more glamorous arms of the defence forces. Between the radar stations, detecting the German aircraft approaching over the Channel, and the Sector Controls were the little sand-bagged posts of the Observer Corps that provided over-land tracking of the enemy formations. The Royal Observer Corps (the 'Royal' prefix being approved in 1941) proved a vital link in the communication chain in the defence of the UK, particularly in the Battle of Britain, as it provided the only means of tracking enemy aircraft once they had crossed the coastline. The highly-skilled Observers were also able to identify and count the enemy aircraft, turning blips on a screen into actual types and numbers of German machines.

In this official history of the ROC written shortly after the war, the corps' operations throughout the conflict are set out in great detail. This includes a section on the last flight of Rudolf Hess, as well as one detailing the work of those who were selected for employment as Seaborne Observers on ships during the D-Day landings, where their specialist identification skills were used to prevent the all-too prevalent instances of 'friendly fire'.

ISBN: 978-1-52675-291-8

ANOTHER OFFICIAL HISTORY AVAILABLE
www.pen-and-sword.co.uk

STALAG LUFT I
An Official Account of the PoW Camp for Air Force Personnel 1940–1945

Located by the Baltic near the town of Barth in Western Pomerania, Germany, Stalag Luft I was one of a number of Stammlager Luftwaffe, these being permanent camps established and administered by the Luftwaffe, which were used to house Allied air force prisoners of war.

Originally built for RAF personnel, by the time the camp was liberated by the Russians in May 1945, the camp contained approximately 7,500 American and 1,300 British and Commonwealth prisoners. The camp had expanded from the original single RAF compound, to a total of three. On 30 April 1945, the prisoners were ordered to evacuate the camp in the face of the advancing Soviet Red Army but refused. After discussions between the senior American and British officers and the Kommandant, it was agreed that to avoid unnecessary bloodshed the guards would depart, leaving the prisoners behind. The next day, the first Soviet troops arrived.

This official history of Stalag Luft I was prepared for the War Office just after the war, but was never released to the general public. It explores all aspects of the camp, from its administration, to the supply of the food and conditions the prisoners endured. Inevitably the author also investigates the subject of escapes, as well as the reprisals that followed.

ISBN: 978-1-52670-879-3